BLOODSTOCK

Bloodstock

*Breeding Winners
in Europe
and America*

James Gill

ARCO PUBLISHING COMPANY, INC.
New York

Copyright © 1977 Carter Nash Cameron Limited

Published by Arco Publishing Company, Inc.
219 Park Avenue South, New York, NY 10019

Library of Congress Cataloging in Publication Data
Gill, James.
  Bloodstock.
  Includes index.
  1. Horse breeding   2. Race horses   I. Title.
SF291.G4   1977   636.1'2   77-8671
ISBN 0-668-04139-0

Produced by Carter Nash Cameron Limited
25 Lloyd Baker Street, London WC1X 9AT

Designed and edited by Tom Carter
Picture research by Victoria Burgess

Set by SX Composing Ltd, 61 Oakwood Avenue,
Leigh-on-Sea, Essex
Printed by Page Bros (Norwich) Ltd, Mile
Cross Lane, Norwich, Norfolk NOR 45N

Contents

Preface

The studs featured in this book combine historical importance with the promise of an influential future and are located in the ancient horse centres of Normandy, Kildare, Kentucky and Newmarket, which is taken to include Sandringham. The book is thus concerned to commemorate the successes of an elite minority and to examine the ideas and the techniques of stud management on which historic achievements have been based. It is not an attempt at a comprehensive survey of the thoroughbred industry, neither does it set out to be historically fair, insofar as many studs with glorious pasts no longer have much of a role to play, and references even to the great days of Lord Derby, for example, are no more than passing. However, if all the studs dealt with here are old-established and successful, they are otherwise violently different in any number of ways. Some are commercial outfits run by entrepreneurs, some are the private province of rich horse-lovers, often with theories to test, and no interest in the yearling sales. Some stud owners, notably Marcel Boussac, have achieved miracles through inbreeding, others, like Maxwell Gluck, disdain such practices.

Commercial breeders, on the whole, are not, or cannot afford to be, great theorists, but many of the odder ideas on which faith has sometimes been pinned crop up from time to time in this survey – dosages theories, for instance, which, it is fair to say, most regard as poppycock. Indeed, it is often alleged that horses finishing last in sellers are as likely to have the correct dosages as classic winners, but, then, the late Aga Khan was a believer, and he didn't do so badly.

The position of Newmarket as England's racing headquarters is attributed to James I, who, from 1605, did most of his hunting in the area, while the suitability of Normandy for horse-breeding was recognised by Louis XIV, when he established the royal stud at Le Pin, now the French National Stud, and of no consequence in the thoroughbred world. Outlines of the historical background to the horse industries of Kentucky and County Kildare are provided at the beginning of the appropriate sections.

None of the studs examined in this book quite predates the thoroughbred, although the influence of the English Royal Studs on its evolution through a large number of early importations is indicated in the Sandringham chapter.

By and large, the people on whose views this book has been based are practical men, who think that Mendelism is all very well if one is growing beans. No blueprint for the production of good racehorses, of course, emerges, and there seems to be no approach which hasn't had its successes and its failures. If one is to believe what they say, thoroughbred breeders believe in luck to a superstitious degree. What this survey does seem to confirm, however, is that a man who knows his pedigrees, concentrates on good stock and takes trouble to complement idiosyncrasies of temperament and conformation, will, unless his luck is lousy, produce good horses from time to time. Thanks are due to all the stud owners and managers quoted herein. In addition, I should like to record my appreciation of help received from the following:

America
Mrs Amelia King Buckley, Messrs Ed Bowen, Humphrey and John Finney, Jim Peden, Andy Skapura, and Bob Stokhaug.

France
Mr David Powell and Mme Guite Powell, M Jean Romanet.

Ireland
Captain Sean Berry.

England
Col Robin Hastings, Sir Noel Murless, Messrs Sam Sheppard and Julian Wilson.

In the American section, asterisks are used to indicate an imported horse. Some distinguished European horses sent across the Atlantic have had the same names as earlier, American-bred stock, so that Blenheim, for instance, emerges in that section as *Blenheim II.

Although it is still conventional in England and Ireland for a horse's earnings to be computed on the basis of win money only, some stallion owners have taken to following the Americans and the French in the not unreasonable practice of including place money. In this book the conventions of each country have been followed in the appropriate sections.

SANDRINGHAM AND NEWMARKET

The Royal Studs

'Of such outlandish horsses as are dailie brought over unto us, I speake not, as the genet of Spaine, the courser of Naples, the hobbie of Ireland, the Flemish roile, the Scotish nag, bicause that further speech of them commeth not within the compasse of this treatise, and for whose breed and maintenance (especiallie of the greatest sort) King Henrie the eight erected a noble studderie, and for a time had very good success with them, till the officers waxing wearie, procured a mixed brood of bastard races, whereby his good purpose came to little effect.'

Thus William Harrison in *The Description of England*, incorporated in the edition of Holinshed's Chronicles published in 1586, by which time, in fact, Queen Elizabeth, assisted by her Master of the Horse, Robert Dudley, Earl of Leicester, had done a great deal to restore the prestige enjoyed by the royal studs in her father's day, having commissioned an Italian expert, Prospero d'Osma, to compile a report on them in 1576. It is not clear when the studs, at Tutbury in Staffordshire and Malmesbury in Wiltshire, had been established, but it is a fair bet that they were started when Henry VIII's stock grew too numerous to be accommodated at Hampton Court and at the Eltham Stud, which dated from the reign of King John.

That royal tradition of horse-breeding which was to contribute much to the evolution of the thoroughbred, and which has continued, more or less uninterrupted, to the present day, effectively began with Henry, although earlier sovereigns had imported oriental stock, principally for hunting and military purposes, with racing an inevitable concomitant. There are various traditions linking mediaeval kings with racing, and Richard II, when Prince of Wales, for instance, is supposed to have been beaten in a match with the Earl of Arundel, while an ancient ballad, quoted by Lord Suffolk in the Racing Volume of the *Badminton Library*, purports to describe horseracing in Richard I's camp:

'Two steedes fowned King Richard,
That Von Fazell, that other Syard,
Yn this worlde they hadde no pere;
Dromedary, neither destrere.
Stede, rabyte, ne cammele,
Goeth none so swift without fayle,
For a thousand pounde of golde
Ne shoulde the one be solde.'

Top: *King Henry VIII*. Above left: *Francesco Gonzaga*. Above right: *The Earl of Essex*.

Henry, though, was the first real racing monarch, a large-scale importer and a systematic breeder and legislator. He enacted a number of laws designed to improve and increase the horse population, so that dukes and archbishops were required to keep seven entire horse of at least 14 hands, while every clergyman with a £100 benefice and every layman whose wife 'should wear a

French hood or bonnet of velvet' had to have one. Broodmares were to be at least 14 hands, and no entire horse more than two years old measuring less than 15 hands was to be turned into 'any forest, chase, moor, heath, common or waste' where mares and fillies were kept. There was a flourishing trade at this time in barbs bred at the Marmolata Stud on the Lake of the Mincio, and Francesco Gonzaga, Marquis of Mantua, made Henry a present of some mares and stallions in 1514. The next year the king received some Spanish horses from Ferdinand of Aragon, and there were frequent importations for the rest of his reign, with the Dukes of Urbino and Ferrara among the eminent foreign breeders who supplied him. Royal agents were regularly dispatched in search of good stock, and Hore's *Annals of the Turf* records that in 1520 Sir Gregory de Cassalis acquired the best horse in Italy on Henry's behalf. Further gifts from Mantua and Charles V of Spain followed.

The king kept his racers at Greenwich in the charge of Thomas Ogle, Master of the Horse. Leonard, Launcelot and Christopher were the names of three of the stable's four jockeys, while Privy Purse accounts also include a reference to 'polle that keepeth the barbary horse'. Elizabeth maintained the Greenwich stable, as well as the studs at Tutbury and Malmesbury, although d'Osma, who notes in the introduction to his report that he was seeking 'fitting remedies for past shortcomings', was of the opinion that the Wiltshire establishment should be scrapped: 'You already know the site of

17th century Italian horse.

Malmesbury, and into how many sections it has been divided because it is small; and that because it is located in a damp, clayey valley, the fodder produced there is greatly injurious to a mare with foal, since the foal in its womb does not receive proper nourishment. . . . I may say in Tutbury there are the means necessary for the welfare of the mares and colts and for their food, since the soil is very dry, and there are many valleys.' This advice was not taken, and in 1596 there were 54 horses at a rather tumble-down Malmesbury, according to an inventory ordered by Richard Devereux, Earl of Essex, who had been appointed Master of the Horse on Leicester's death in 1588. The last surviving account of the stock there was prepared shortly after the assassination in 1628 of George Villiers, Duke of Buckingham and Lord High Admiral of England, who had been appointed Master of the Horse by James I in 1616.

Queen Elizabeth, whose best stock was descended from her father's importations, does seem, on matters of breeding policy, to have accepted d'Osma's arguments, however: 'There is another breed got by crossing, as we have said, a large mare with a small stallion, and vice versa, which have been hybridised and are therefore called bastard horses. Among these you will not find one that has the back, speed, appearance, health and beauty that is found in ordinary breeds. . . . The animals should be set apart and proper order maintained.' Tesio, who suggests in his book that the Royal Mares mentioned in Volume One of the General Stud Book were descended from Elizabeth's horses, observes: 'This means that the writers who up to now have believed that the thoroughbred is the result of a mixture of native and oriental blood are mistaken, and their conclusions are therefore incorrect.

George Villiers, first Duke of Buckingham, and Elizabeth I hawking. Right: *Charles II at Datchet by J Barlow.*

The great classic winners of all countries are descended almost exclusively from Oriental stock.' Although James I was a hunting man with little interest in racing, his reign saw some momentous developments and Newmarket's position as a horse centre is traditionally regarded as being down to him. Buckingham ensured that English stock was dramatically improved through the best foreign blood, furnishing not only the royal studs, but also his own. In 1620 he married Lady Katherine Manners, only daughter of the sixth Earl of Rutland and heiress to the Helmsley estate, and it is likely that some of his Moroccan and Spanish horses would have been sent there and crossed with the native stock. James I had, in 1605, received a present of 'a dozen gallant mares all with foal, four horses and eleven stallions, all coursers of Naples', which were sent to Greenwich, but it was on Buckingham's appointment that the trade in horseflesh really picked up. The Markham Arabian was bought for the king in 1616, when Sir Thomas Edmonds also brought over 'half a dozen Barbary horses', which went to the royal paddocks at Newmarket. The next year, George Digby, brother of John, English Ambassador to Madrid, was sent to Italy to buy more. Thereafter Buckingham frequently had Andalusian stock sent over by his friends at the Court of Madrid, while Hore records that, on August 1, 1621, 'there passed through Exon six horses and mares, which the Marquis of Buckingham had sent for into Barbary'. Around this time, the king wrote to Buckingham: 'God thanke the maister of the horse for provyding me such a number of faire usefull horses, fitte for my hande: in a word, I never was maister of such horses.' The breakdown of negotiations for the marriage of the Prince of Wales to the Infanta of Spain in 1623 had some beneficial effects on English stock, too, and Buckingham, who had accompanied the prince on his mission, was presented with some horses from the royal stud at Cordova for his own and for the king's use. A number of barbs found their way into the country

during the reign of Charles I, but the royal studs were dispersed under the Commonwealth, without, however, any loss of enthusiasm for eastern stock. A pure Arab, then a rarity in England, was purchased for Cromwell in 1657, and strenuous efforts, possibly successful, were made to obtain more.

Barely a week after his return from exile, Charles II appointed James D'arcy Master of the Royal Stud with a view to the re-establishment of Tutbury, the preamble to a Command signed by Sir Charles Harbord, Surveyor General, on September 10, 1660, reading: 'Forasmuch as His Majesty hath determined to restore his Race and Breed of Horses as in the time of his Royall Father of ever blessed memory, and hath appointed you to be Stoodmaster and Keeper of the same.' D'arcy, who had married Isabel, daughter of Sir Marmaduke Wyvill and thus acquired the Sedbury estate, where a famous stud was long maintained, and royal mares accommodated, reported that Tutbury was beyond repair. On July 2, 1663, Charles issued a commission, which began: 'We have been informed that divers goods and chattells, horses, mares and geldings sometyme in the possession of our late deere Father, King Charles the First, or in our possession in the Castle of Tutbury, and race, there, have been imbezeld and taken away and deteyned from us by persons who have not right or title thereunto.' Shortly afterwards, Charles made an unsuccessful attempt to sell the Tutbury land, which was never again employed as a breeding farm.

The early stud books, under the heading 'Royal Mares', stated that 'King Charles the Second sent abroad the Master of the Horse to procure a number of foreign horses and mares for breeding, and the mares brought over by him (as also many of their produce) have since been called Royal Mares'. C. M. Prior, in his *The Royal Studs of the 16th and 17th Centuries*, denies this yarn and scorns the footnote, added in the 1891 stud book: 'Charles I had at Tutbury, Staffordshire, in 1643, a number of mares and stallions, described as racehorses, which, from the records, included three Morocco mares.' There were, Prior points out, citing Hore's *Annals of the Turf*, no fewer than 140 horses at Tutbury when an inventory was compiled on July 27, 1649, and there is no evidence that Charles II sent abroad to augment the already considerable stocks of eastern horses in the country at the time of his accession.

The present lay-out of several of the paddocks at Hampton Court dates from the reign of Queen Anne, when the stud, reopened in the time of William and Mary, was expanded. Although 'Butcher' Cumberland is credited with breeding both Eclipse and Herod, his father George II, cared no more for the turf than had George I, and the next real enthusiast to occupy the throne was George IV, winner, as Prince of Wales, of the 1788 Derby with Sir Thomas, by Pontiac, three years before the Escape scandal occasioned his temporary retirement from the turf. Sir Thomas was not home-bred, and the first Derby winner to be produced by the royal stud was Moses, a son of either Whalebone or Seymour, who was successful in 1822 in the colours of the Duke of York, inventor of the silly drinking game 'Cardinal Puff'. Moses, who stood at Hampton Court before being sold to

'Prinny' en route to Ascot.

the Duke of Richmond, was a disappointment at stud. King William IV maintained the Hampton Court Stud, which, by 1834, housed 23 mares and four stallions and was divided into 43 paddocks of three to five acres each, but it was dispersed on his death. The revival came, at the instigation of the Prince Consort, in 1850.

Although Queen Victoria did not race the produce of the royal stud in her own colours, she bred on a large scale and generally had around 50 brood-mares, twice as many as the present queen. The stud comprised about 200 acres of paddocks and more than 80 boxes, with an annual auction of yearlings conducted by Tattersalls within a circle of the prospective buyers' carriages. Thus, at the 1890 sale, Lord Marcus Beresford stood on top of a coach to bid for La Flèche on behalf of Baron Hirsch, who was sitting on the box with the Prince of Wales, and who was accorded three cheers when the filly was knocked down for the then record price of 5,500 guineas. La Flèche (St Simon – Quiver, by Toxopholite) was well worth it, and her 16 victories included the 1,000 Guineas, Oaks and St Leger. In the St Leger she beat Sir Hugo, to whom she had run three parts of a length second in the Derby, a race she would assuredly have won had her jockey, George Barrett, not had one of his turns and elected to lie a long way out of his ground, shaking his fists and screaming abuse at his rivals. La Flèche's tremendous late run that day took a lot out of her, and she only just scraped home in the Oaks from The Slew, who had finished down the field in the Guineas. For some reason Barrett, who subsequently went totally mad, was given the Oaks ride on La Flèche.

La Flèche's granddaughter Cinna won the 1,000 Guineas in 1920 and went on to breed Beau Père and Mr Standfast, both of whom earned con-siderable antipodean distinction. Cinna's sire was Polymelus (by Cyllene

B

17

Above: *La Flèche*. Below: *Sainfoin*.

out of La Flèche's half-sister by Hampton Maid Marian), winner of £16,725 on the track and five times champion sire. Queen Victoria had also bred a full sister to La Flèche in Memoir, winner of the Oaks and St Leger for the Duke of Portland in 1890, when the Derby also went to a Hampton Court-bred, Sir James Miller's Sainfoin (Springfield – Sanda, by Wenlock), who became sire of Rock Sand, but was otherwise nothing special at stud. Sainfoin's sire was also bred at Hampton Court, where he retired to stud at a fee of 100 guineas, after winning 16 races, including the Champion Stakes. Springfield, foaled in 1873, was by the Hampton Court stallion and 1860 St Leger winner, St Albans, and out of Viridis, by Marsyas. Other royal stallions of the era included Orlando, who was awarded the 1844 Derby after Lord George Bentinck had exposed Running Rein as a ringer, and the 1872 2,000 Guineas winner, Prince Charles. Among the notable horses bred in the early part of Hampton Court's Victorian period were The Earl (St James's Palace Stakes), Temple (New Stakes) and Sir Amyas (July Stakes).

The studs at Sandringham and Wolferton, on the royal estate in Norfolk, now house all the Queen's breeding stock, although, until 1976, some of her young horses were kept at Hampton Court, which is still used to rest the Queen Mother's jumpers during the summer. Sandringham and Wolferton studs were established by the Prince of Wales in the 1880s and, under the managership of Lord Marcus Beresford, they took over the mantle from Hampton Court, dispersed in 1894. The produce ran in the colours of the Prince of Wales, who thus soared into the empyrean with Florizel II, Persimmon and Diamond Jubilee, all by St Simon out of Perdita II, by Hampton. Perdita II started her racing career as a selling plater but improved to win seven races before one A. Falconer accepted what he thought the generous offer of £900 made on behalf of the Prince. Florizel II (1891) won the St James's Palace Stakes, the Gold Vase at Royal Ascot, the Goodwood Cup, the Manchester Cup and the Jockey Club Cup, Persimmon (1893) the Derby, St Leger, Eclipse, Ascot Gold Cup and the Jockey Club Stakes, and Diamond Jubilee (1897) the Triple Crown, the Eclipse and the New-market Stakes. All three stood at the royal stud for a fee of 300 guineas. Florizel II sired Volodyovski, while Persimmon not only got Sceptre in his first crop, but also sired two Oaks winners, Keystone II and Perola, success-ful in 1906 and 1909 respectively, and the winners of the St Leger in 1908 (Your Majesty) and 1911 (Prince Palatine). Diamond Jubilee, who, both on the racecourse and at stud, was a bit of a handful, was sold in 1906 to South America, where he did very well. Persimmon, four times leading sire, died of a fractured pelvis in 1908, a year before the king won the Derby with Minoru (Cyllene – Mother Siegel, by Friar's Balsam), leased from her breeder, Colonel Hall-Walker.

The first top-class horse bred at the royal stud in King George V's time was Friar Marcus (by Cyllene's son Cicero out of Persimmon's daughter Prim Nun), foaled in 1912, a top sprinter, unbeaten at two, winner of £9,435 and sire of Friar's Daughter, dam of the Aga Khan's Bahram and

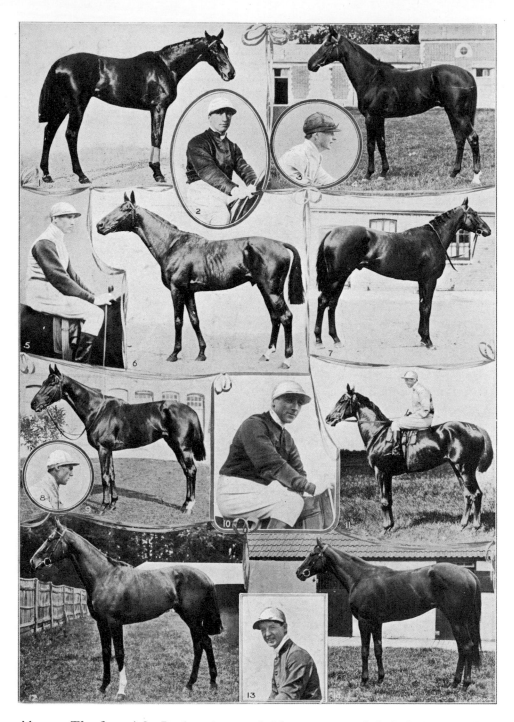

Above: *The first eight Derby winners of this century, and their jockeys.* Left to right from the top: *Diamond Jubilee, Volodyoski, Ard Patrick, Rock Sand, St Amant, Cicero, Spearmint and Orby. Inset are their jockeys H. Jones, L. Reiff, J. H. Martin, R. Cannon, D. Maher, who rode Rock Sand, Cicero and Spearmint, and J. Reiff.* Right: *Persimmon in 1895, and Cyllene.*

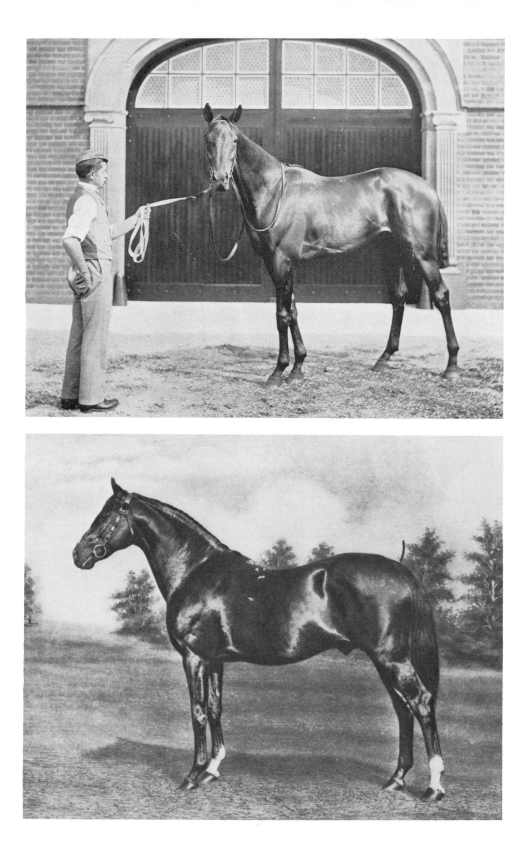

Dastur. The king's home-bred Scuttle (Captain Cuttle – Stained Glass, by Tracery) won five races, including the 1928 1,000 Guineas and £11,800, while the last of the good horses produced by the royal stud to run in the colours of George V was Limelight (Pharos – Vervaine, by Louviers), foaled in 1929, who numbered the Newbury Spring Cup and the Hardwicke Stakes among his eight wins, worth £8,899. Limelight's pedigree was not the kind of thing that Captain Sir Cecil Boyd-Rochfort and Captain Charles Moore, appointed trainer and manager respectively by George VI, would have approved of, and they were at some pains to keep the royal string free from the taint of that middle-distance handicapper, Phalaris. The legacy of this policy is that the Queen's present stud manager, Michael Oswald, can look to Phalaris as an outcross at a time when most breeders are desperately searching for stallions of a different line, and current advertisements for Condorcet even contain the bewildering claim that he is 'completely free of Phalaris blood for four generations'.

Of the families currently represented at the royal stud the oldest-established is that of Feola (Friar Marcus – Aloe, by Son-in-Law), second in the 1936 1,000 Guineas and third in the Oaks for Lord Derby. Her produce at Sandringham included Hypericum (by Hyperion), winner of the Dewhurst and the 1946 1,000 Guineas, dam of Restoration and second dam of Ben Marshall, Foretaste, grandam of Lassalle, Knight's Daughter (by Sir Cosmo), dam of Round Table, Angelola (by Donatello), dam of Aureole, and Above Board (by Straight Deal), dam of Doutelle. Above Board, winner of the Yorkshire Oaks and the Cesarewitch in 1950, also produced Above Suspicion (1959 St James's Palace and Gordon Stakes), and the minor winners Credence and Arbitrate. Arbitrate, a daughter of Arbar, is now at the royal stud, and is dam of the modest successes Autograph (by Auriban), Crown Court (by Kauai King), Wide of the Mark and Valuation (both by

Left: *Highclere and her 1977 foal by Busted.* Above: *Strip The Willow (ex Near Miss, by Nearco) at Sandringham, with her colt foal by Bustino.*

Gulf Pearl). She visited Upper Case in both 1975 and 1976. Wide of the Mark was foaled in 1972 and was due to produce her first foal, by Zeddaan, in 1977. The record stakes-winning filly trained in the British Isles, Highclere, dropped a Mill Reef foal in 1976 and was due to Busted in 1977. By Queen's Hussar out of Highlight (Borealis – Hypericum), Highclere won the 1,000 Guineas and the Prix de Diane in 1974, and earned a total of £129,724 in win money. She was the result of the first mating between Highlight and Queen's Hussar, which took place when Brigadier Gerard was two, and Lord Carnarvon's stallion still rather unfashionable. Light Duty, a full sister to Highclere, foaled in 1972, produced a Mill Reef foal in 1977, while Highlight returned to Queen's Hussar in 1975, when she was barren, 1976 and 1977. Highlight is also dam of Gloss, winner of five races, Leading Silk, by Counsel, and Tammuz, by Tamerlane, who took the Schweppes Gold Trophy at Newbury in 1975.

Aureole, champion sire of 1960 and 1961, who stood at Wolferton for 20 years, has one daughter, Dismantle, among the Sandringham broodmare band. Dismantle is a half-sister to the Queen's Joking Apart (by Jimmy Reppin) out of Strip the Willow, by Native Dancer. Second in the 1953 Derby, Aureole went on to establish himself, at four, as the best horse in Europe, with victories in the Coronation Cup, the Hardwicke Stakes and the King George VI and Queen Elizabeth Stakes. His progeny won well over £1 million, and included St Crespin III, winner of the Prix de l'Arc de Triomphe and the Eclipse in 1959, St Paddy, and Aurelius and Provoke, St

Leger victors of 1961 and 1965 respectively. His son Vienna became sire of Vaguely Noble.

At the October Sales in 1961, the Queen bought a yearling filly by the 1958 John Porter Stakes and Ormonde Stakes winner Doutelle, a sire who was to survive only four seasons at stud, but who still made a considerable mark with Pretendre, Fighting Ship and Canisbay. The filly, out of Amy Leigh, by Bobsleigh, and called Amicable, won the Nell Gwyn and the Lingfield Oaks Trial, and has since proved quite a success as a broodmare with the 1970 Lancashire Oaks winner Amphora (by Ragusa) and the 1971 Park Hill Stakes winner Example (by Exbury) the best of her offspring. Her daughter, the minor winner Firework Party (by Roan Rocket) was due to drop her first foal, by Blakeney, in 1977. The 1965 Eclipse winner Canisbay, now doing well as a sire in Italy, is represented at Sandringham by his daughter Mey (ex Almeria), winner of a couple of small races and now dam of Zetland (1975), by Zeddaan, and a Connaught yearling filly. Mey was due to Ribero in 1977. Almeria was the leading staying filly of her generation, winning the Ribblesdale Stakes, Yorkshire Oaks and Park Hill Stakes, and, as a four year old, running second to Ballymoss in the 1958 King George VI and Queen Elizabeth Stakes. Inbred 2 × 3 to Hyperion – as also is Highlight – Almeria was by Alycidon out of Avila, and dam of Albany (by Pall Mall), winner of the Sandleford Priory Stakes and Prix de Psyche in 1971, who has herself now produced a winner in Card Player (by Crepello). Albany's half-brother Magna Carta won the Ascot Stakes and the Doncaster Cup in 1970, and a total of eight races. Avila, winner of the Coronation Stakes and

Left: *Albany and her Connaught foal.*
Above: *Escorial with her foal by Luthier.*

two other races, is also represented at Sandringham by her daughter Alesia (by Alycidon) and her great granddaughter Escorial (Royal Palace – Asturia, by The Phoenix). Alesia has bred eight individual winners in Zaloba (by Zarathustra), Altruist (by Above Suspicion), Home Park (by Pardal), Quick Match (by Match III), County Palatine (by Charlottesville), Pantomime (by Silly Season), Carlton House (by Pall Mall) and Formula (by Reform). Escorial won the Green Shield Stakes at Ascot in 1973 and the Musidora Stakes at York in 1974, and produced a grey colt by Zeddaan in 1976 and then visited Luthier. Joking Apart and Dismantle belong to the third of the principal Sandringham families, founded by their fourth dam, Young Entry, a daughter of Foxhunter out of Fair Venus, by Fairway. Blenheim's dam Malva also has a granddaughter at the royal stud in Mulberry Harbour, whose daughter by Exbury, Export, is in the band, too. Mulberry Harbour has produced the winners Crest of the Wave (by Crepello), Combined Operation (by Persian Gulf), Palm Beach (by Pall Mall), Export, Close Harmony (by Tudor Melody), Rekindle (by Relko) and Maroon (by

Roan Rocket). There is another link with the glories of yesteryear at Sandringham through Cross Purpose, by Crepello, who is out of Menai, a half-sister to Canisbay, by Abernant. Another half sister to Canisbay, Strathcoma (by St Paddy) was sold at the 1976 Newmarket December Sales for 7,400 guineas in foal to Town Crier.

Almost all the royal mares are pattern race winners, or daughters, half sisters or dams of pattern race winners, and the Queen's stud manager, Michael Oswald, will have no truck with the theory that good race fillies do not make good broodmares. Fresh blood introduced to the stud in recent years has brought the families of both Grundy and Bruni to Sandringham. Guinea Sparrow (Grey Sovereign – Parakeet, by Colombo) purchased as a seven year old at the December Sales in 1967 has, as second dam, Lundy

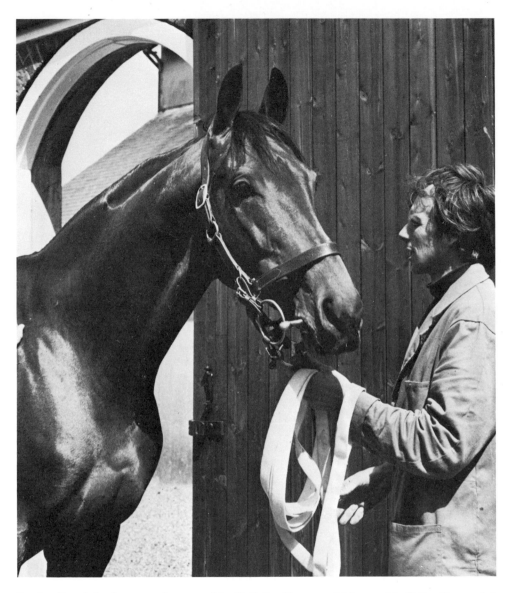

Left: *Sandringham stud groom Mr F. C. Scallan, and his son Mr J. Scallan, with Persimmon's statue in the background.* Above: *Bustino at Her Majesty's Wolferton Stud.*

Parrot, whose daughter Lundy Princess produced Word from Lundy, while the second dam of Heathfield (1966), bought in the 1969 December Sales, is Whimbrel, third dam of Bruni. Guinea Sparrow, who won four races, is best known as dam of Gilding, by Kauai King, winner of the Ascot 1,000 Guineas Trial in 1976, her only other winner being Sir Ivor's daughter Golden Ivy. Heathfield (Hethersett – Court Caprice, by Court Martial) is dam of the winner Ascot Heath (by Sovereign Path) and Crofting (by Crepello).

Joe Mercer brings Bustino, right, *to win the 1975 Coronation Cup from Ashmore (Yves St Martin) and Mil's Bomb (Geoff Lewis).*

Her Majesty won the Lancashire Oaks in the first year of her reign with Stream of Light, since when more than 50 more pattern races have fallen to horses bred by her. The first English classic to be won by a horse owned and bred by the Queen was the 1958 2,000 Guineas, which went to Pall Mall (Palestine – Malapert, by Portlaw). The reputation she enjoys for a close knowledge of pedigrees and a deep understanding of breeding is, by all accounts, well justified, and she is involved in all decisions of consequence.

There are generally two stallions on the royal estate, but Ribero was dispatched from Sandringham at the end of the 1976 season, and there is, as yet, no news of a replacement. Bustino, who stands at Wolferton, though, seems much more likely to prove a success at stud. A son of Busted (by Crepello), Bustino is out of Ship Yard, by Doutelle, and thus a half-brother to the good stayer, Oarsman (by Aureole) second in the 1971 French St Leger. The royal yearlings are kept at the Polhampton Stud near Kingsclere, next door to one of the Queen's trainers, Ian Balding, and only a few miles away from the other, Major Dick Hern at West Ilsley.

The National Stud

Since the National Stud moved to its present location, it has operated as a stallion station for the benefit of the indigenous breeding industry, with a brief to prevent the export of successful stallions and of great racehorses with stud potential. Originally designed to accommodate six stallions, it could, if necessary, handle a couple more, especially if they were not all up to a normal book, as is nowadays the case, in fact, with Tudor Melody (1956), who is restricted to 11 mares a season. One or two changes in the stallion line-up are in any case imminent, with Dr Carlo Vittadini's Habat due to transfer to Beech House for 1978 and the future of Star Appeal, whose owner, Waldemar Zeitelhack, sent him here on a two year agreement in December 1975, still in doubt. Blakeney, Mill Reef and Grundy, who made up the 1977 quota, however, are permanent fixtures, and, of course, in their prime.

There is, in the tan floor of the covering yard, a small, hollowed-out area, where Tudor Melody's mares often stand to make things easier for the old

Never Say Die at the National Stud in Newmarket shortly before it was officially opened by the Queen.

horse, these days right down on his fetlocks. He returned 100 per cent fertility in 1976, while the overall National Stud figure was 91.04 per cent, with Mill Reef getting 39 out of 42 in foal, Blakeney 37 out of 44, Habat 42 out of 46, Grundy 32 out of 33 and Star Appeal 22 out of 25. The fitness of the stallions is guaranteed for the breeding season with half-an-hour's lunging and a four-and-a-half mile walk every morning, although Tudor Melody, sweet-natured, but a loner by nature anyway, is excused this regime, being turned out into a paddock while the other stallions remain in their boxes. The stallions are got up in preparation for the season at the beginning of November, and continue daily exercise until the end of June.

Most of the land on which the National Stud now stands was an arable farm, enclosed by the July, Beacon and Town Plate courses, until it was acquired on a 999-year lease from the Jockey Club in 1964. Never Say Die and Tudor Melody took up their duties in Newmarket three years later, by which time a six-stall stallion complex, three circular yards, 12 foaling boxes, and two mare and foal units, with covered exercise areas in the rear, had been built. The Old Heath Stud, forming a spur abutting on the Cambridge Road, had also been incorporated. Since 1971 two stalls used for fodder storage have been added to either side of the stallion unit, three more groups of 20 boxes have been built and new yards erected near the Stud entrance to accommodate maiden mares and foreign mares. This last building carries the inscription 'DG 1974', placed there in recognition of the services of the Stud's former Director, Colonel Douglas Gray, after he had retired in July 1975.

The Horserace Betting Levy Board had relieved the Ministry of Agriculture of responsibility for the National Stud one year before the lease was taken on the Newmarket land. The decision to move the National Stud to headquarters was linked with a significant change of policy, long sought by independent English breeders, and all the mares were sold out of its previous home, the 400-acre Sandley Stud at Gillingham in Dorset. By this time, the National Stud had bred some notable horses, the first, and most influential, being Blandford, sire of the Derby winners Trigo, Blenheim, Windsor Lad and Bahram. Blandford was foaled in 1919 at Tully, in Kildare where the British National Stud had been established four years earlier with livestock donated to the nation by Colonel 'Willie' Hall Walker. The stud itself was purchased at the Government's own valuation of £47,625 from Hall Walker, whose fortune derived from his family's brewery in Liverpool, and who was duly created Lord Wavertree. His gift consisted of six stallions, 43 broodmares, 10 two-year-olds, 19 yearlings and 300 head of cattle. Blandford, a son of Swynford out of White Eagle's daughter Blanche, almost died of pneumonia as a foal, and the case looked so hopeless that Captain Henry Greer, the first Director of the Stud, even offered to give him to the veterinary surgeon in attendance. No such generosity was necessary, however, and Blandford survived to fetch 720 guineas as a yearling at the Newmarket December Sales. He suffered from bad legs and ran only four times, but he won three races,

Lord Wavertree (top left), *Captain Sir Henry Greer and Blandford.*

earned £3,839 and was, according to his trainer, R. C. Dawson, a better
horse than Captain Cuttle, the Derby winner of his year. Blandford got the
2,000 Guineas winners Bahram and Pasch, the 1,000 Guineas winner Cam-
panula, was champion sire in 1934 and 1935 and was altogether responsible
for the winners of 308 races worth £327,840 in Britain, figures which do no
justice to his tremendous world-wide influence on the breed.

Top: *Bahram arrives at Epsom for the 1935 Derby*. Above: *Pasch wins the 2,000 Guineas in 1938*.

In the days when the National Stud was breeding its own horses, its best products were generally leased to the sovereign, although, between the wars, a number of them ran in the colours of Lord Lonsdale, who thus took the 1922 St Leger with Royal Lancer (Spearmint – Royal Favour, by White Eagle). When King George VI won four of the classics in 1942, it was with

National Stud-bred horses. The 2,000 Guineas fell to Big Game, a son of Bahram out of Tetratema's daughter Myrobella, herself bred at Tully and the winner of £16,143 from 11 victories, while Sun Chariot (Hyperion – Clarence, by Diligence) took the fillies' Triple Crown. Sun Chariot went on to distinguish herself as a broodmare, producing Blue Train, Gigantic, Landau and Pinza's son Pindari, who won four races, including the Craven Stakes at Newmarket, the King Edward VII Stakes at Royal Ascot and the Great Voltigeur at York. He also ran third in the 1959 St Leger in Her Majesty's colours. Carrozza (Dante – Calash, by Hyperion) won the 1957 Oaks for the Queen, who also raced the last of the high-class horses bred by the National Stud, Hopeful Venture, winner of seven races worth £83,000, second in the St Leger of 1967 and now at stud in Australia. The best of the other horses bred at the National were probably Chamossaire, winner of the St Leger in 1945 for Squadron Leader S. Joel and leading sire of 1964, Annetta (1944 Irish 1,000 Guineas) and Challenger, America's champion sire of 1939. Captain Greer, knighted in 1925, retired as Director of the National Stud in 1933, to be succeeded by Noble Johnson, whose assistant, Peter Burrell, took over four years later, remaining in charge for the next 34 years. One of the yards at the National Stud is now named after Burrell, and Wavertree and Rosebery are similarly commemorated, while the mare and

Big Game.

Top left: *Carrozza*. Top right: *Lord Rosebery (then Lord Dalmeny) in 1912.*
Above: *Papyrus arrives back from America, October 1923.* Right: *Never Say Die.*

foal units are called Astley and Bentinck, the circular yards Beacon, Bunbury and Rous.

The Tully land was sold to the Irish Government in 1943, when the stock was moved to Gillingham. In 1949 the Stud expanded its operation by leasing J. P. Hornung's 600-acre West Grinstead Stud, where Burrell, whose family's estate was alongside, had worked before joining the National. It was here that Papyrus (Tracery – Miss Matty, by Marcovil) had stood after a racing career in the colours of Benjamin Irish, which had brought victory in the Derby of 1923, second place in the St Leger and total earnings of £17,863. He was sent to Belmont Park in the October of his three-year-old campaign for a match with the American Horse of the Year, Kentucky Derby and Belmont Stakes winner Zev (The Finn – Miss Kearney, by *Planudes), but was well beaten. At stud he got the winners of 282 races worth £112,149 without siring anything special. National Stud stallions during the Gillingham and West Grinstead era were Jock Scot, Tenerani, Elopement, Pindari, Sammy Davis, Alcide and Never Say Die.

Never Say Die, Nasrullah's best son to race in Europe, completed two seasons at the Woodland Stud, before Robert Sterling Clark made a present of him to the National, with the proviso that he should cover 10 Irish mares a year. He died in the autumn of 1975, and was buried at the National Stud, having headed the sires' list once, thanks largely to Larkspur's fluke Derby win, in 1962. His other classic winner was Never Too Late, who took the 1,000 Guineas and the Oaks in 1960. Tudor Melody (Tudor Minstrel – Matelda, by Dante) was ranked top of the Free Handicap after running six times as a two-year-old and winning five, his victories including the Zetland

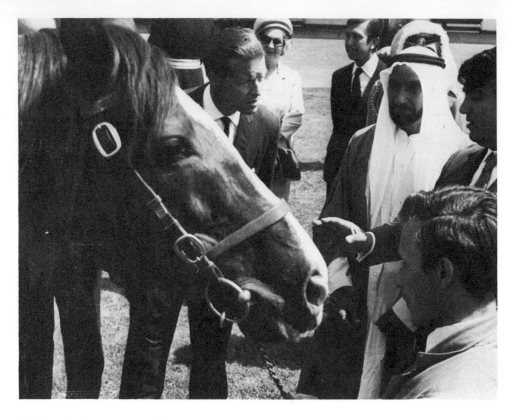

Michael Oswald, now manager of the Royal Studs, but then at Egerton, intro-duces Tudor Melody to Sheik Zaid. Right: *Blakeney wins the 1969 Derby.*

Stakes and the Prince of Wales's Stakes at York and the Chesham Stakes at Ascot. He earned £5,988 that season, and was then sent to America, where he won two races in two seasons for modest pickings of $7,800, before taking up stud duties at Mount Coote in County Limerick. In 1966 the National Stud bought ten shares in him at a cost of £52,000 to prevent the Americans getting their hands on him again after he had made a promising start at stud. His first three crops, in fact, produced the winners of 88 races worth £205,101, and he was champion sire of juveniles in 1968 and 1970. By the end of 1976 he was responsible for the winners of 353 races and £600,487, his best son being Welsh Pageant, out of Picture Light, by Court Martial, winner of 11 races and £53,527 and now standing at Woodditton. Third in the 1969 2,000 Guineas to Right Tack and Tower Walk, Welsh Pageant won the Totalisator Free Handicap at Newmarket, the St James's Stakes at Epsom and the Northern Goldsmiths' Handicap at Newcastle as a three-year-old. He went on to win the Lockinge Stakes at Newbury twice, the Queen Anne Stakes at Royal Ascot, the Queen Elizabeth II Stakes at Ascot and the Hungerford Stakes at Newbury. The best of Tudor Melody's progeny otherwise are Kashmir II, winner of the Prix Robert Papin and the 1966 2,000 Guineas and a successful sire in France, Tudor Music, Owen Dudley,

Magic Flute, Tudor Rhythm, Tudenham, Taros, Harmony Hall. Tudor Harmony and Golden Horus.

Towards the end of its first year in business at Newmarket, the National Stud acquired the American horse Stupendous (Bold Ruler – Magneto, by *Ambiorix), who had won 11 times from 35 starts and earned $251,113. He ran second to Kauai King in the Preakness of 1966, when he won the $50,000 Gotham Stakes, and, the next year, took the Whitney Stakes, in record time, and the Arlington Handicap, both these races being worth the same as the Gotham. Stupendous was in one respect aptly named, and frequent calls were made on the breeding roll, an apparatus seldom employed on English studs, but he proved no great shakes as a sire, and was banished to Japan in 1972. His smartest son in England is Dakota (Right Royal V – Ardneasken), whose best season was 1975 when he won the Ebor Handicap at York and the St Simon Stakes at Newbury, and a total of £23,869.60. The next year, although he failed to win a race, he performed most creditably to finish fourth in the King George VI and Queen Elizabeth II Stakes. Stupendous's son Gloss, out of Highlight, by Borealis, made something of a mark, too, while Kronenkranich has done well in Europe.

When Blakeney arrived at the National Stud in 1971, the first mare he covered was Worden II's daughter Set Free. The result was Juliette Marny, winner of the English and Irish Oaks and a career total of £74,460. Misoptimist, Willie Ormond, True Word, Sergeant Bibot and Norfolk Light are among his other good runners so far. Blakeney (Hethersett – Windmill Girl, by Hornbeam), who was bred, owned and trained by Arthur Budgett, won once in each of the three seasons he raced, taking the Houghton Stakes at

Newmarket, the Derby and the Ormonde Stakes at Chester. He was also second in the Ascot Gold Cup, to Precipice Wood, and in the King George VI and Queen Elizabeth Stakes to Nijinsky. Blakeney, in whom the National Stud own 11 out of 44 shares, is half-brother to Budgett's other Derby winner, Morston, victorious in 1973.

Mill Reef, who broke a foreleg on the Kingsclere gallops in 1972 while preparing for an attempt to repeat his Prix de l'Arc de Triomphe win of the previous year, is unhampered by the injury in his current line of work.

Bred at Paul Mellon's Rokeby Stud, Virginia, he is a product of the Nasrullah/Princequillo nick, being by Never Bend out of Milan Mill. Never Bend's dam, Lalun, was the epitome of the E. R. Bradley/Olin Gentry maxim that an inbred mare could be put to a stallion inbred to another great line of horses. Her dam was Be Faithful, her sire Djeddah, winner of six good races in France and the 1949 Eclipse and Champion Stakes, whose pedigree shows crosses of both Teddy and Banshee (Irish Lad – Frizette) at the third and four removes. Lalun won $112,000, racing at two and three years old, and took the Beldame Handicap, the Kentucky Oaks and the Pageant Stakes. She is also dam of Bold Reason. Mill Reef's second dam was by Count Fleet, his third by Hyperion, and, altogether, several of the best strains of modern times have been yoked into his pedigree. It all came out pretty well, and Mill Reef earned £172,259 from ten wins in England, and 1,891,050 francs from two wins in France. His only defeats came in the Prix Robert Papin, when, from a bad draw, he ran second to My Swallow, and in the 2,000 Guineas, when he was three lengths behind Brigadier Gerard, with My Swallow a further $\frac{3}{4}$ length adrift. At two he won the Salisbury, Coventry, Gimcrack, Imperial and Dewhurst Stakes, at three the Greenham, Derby, Eclipse and King George VI and Queen Elizabeth Stakes and the Prix de l'Arc de Triomphe, and at four the Coronation Cup and the Prix Ganay. Mill Reef's first crop, of which only ten were in training, included the 1976 winners Miller's Lass, Millionaire, Silver Shoals (USA), Sunfish and Teddington Park. They picked up a total of £6,791 for seven victories.

Grundy (Great Nephew – Word From Lundy, by Worden II) was bred by the Overbury Stud and sold to Dr Carlo Vittadini as a yearling. He was

Grundy wins the Derby in 1975

Greville Starkey has time to look over his shoulder as he brings Star Appeal home in the 1975 Eclipse Stakes. Right: *Stallion boxes at the National Stud.*

syndicated in 1975 and retired to stud for the 1976 season after winning £326,421 from eight victories. Undefeated at two years old, he won the Granville Stakes at Ascot, the Sirenia Plate at Kempton Park, the Champagne Stakes at Doncaster and the Dewhurst. He started seven times at three and won four races – the Irish 2,000 Guineas, the Derby, the Irish Derby and the King George VI and Queen Elizabeth Stakes in record time after the famous tussle with Bustino. The National Stud bought three quarters of Grundy, who had also run second in the 2,000 Guineas to Carlo d'Alessio's Bolkonski, after his Epsom win .

The two privately-owned stallions at the National Stud stand there on the understanding that they will be available to British-based breeders with mares permanently in this country, to whom Zeitelhack is contracted to offer 15 of the 44 nominations to Star Appeal, bred by the Gestüt Röttgen and winner of £261,806 from eleven wins, which included the 1975 Eclipse, Prix de l'Arc de Triomphe and Gran Premio di Milano. Star Appeal is a son of Appiani Il out of Sterna by Neckar. The vast majority of Habat's 46 mares in 1977 were British anyway. A son of Habitat out of Sunny Boy's daughter Atrevida, Habat showed good enough form as a two-year-old to be the top English horse in the Free Handicap, rated on the same mark as the American-bred Cellini, whose compatriots, Apalachee and Mississippian, however, were respectively assessed as six pounds and one pound superior. Habat won the 1974 Ascot 2,000 Guineas Trial, but then faded from the scene, possibly more affected by the virus than anyone thought at the time, Michael Bramwell, National Stud Director, suggests. He was bred by John Sumner at the Marston Stud in Oxfordshire.

The pasture, grazed alternately by horses at the National Stud and cattle belonging to a local farmer, who leases the rights, retains a more or less pristine condition. Visiting mares arrive one month before foaling, and are boarded at one of the circular yards on the periphery of the Stud until their time. Altogether, there are enough boxes to accommodate 190 boarding mares during the season, but, with a significant number of Newmarket mares returning to base after covering, the facilities are unlikely to be stretched so long as there are no more than six stallions on the place. The foaling unit itself, manned 24 hours a day, of course, is at the centre of the outfit, next to the stud groom's house and some 300 yards from the stallion complex. There is a veterinary surgeon, Donald Simpson, resident at, though not in the permanent employ of, the National Stud. The stallions will, if necessary, cover a maximum of three mares in one day, with sessions in mid-morning, mid-afternoon and around 7.00 p.m. For covering, mares are fitted with canvas boots to minimise the effect of a kick – a rarity anyway – and a neck protector against bites. They are not hobbled, and, indeed, this device, much used in America, is generally frowned on in England in case a failure of the release catch should cause the mare to come down, and, say, break her neck or the stallion's legs.

Colonel Gray retired as Director of the National Stud in July 1975, and took up the post of consultant at Beech House. He was succeeded by his former assistant, Michael Bramwell, then aged 32, who had joined the National Stud in 1971 from Cliveden, where he had been Racing and Stud Manager.

The disposal of nominations owned by the National Stud is arranged by ballot, although Bramwell has the right to veto mares of insufficient class or suspect health, and the procedure can be dispensed with in the case of an outstanding mare or one belonging to the Queen. An advisory committee considers which stallions should stand at the National, and whether it is necessary, or desirable, to intervene to keep a particular horse in the country. Before the National Stud was taken over by the Levy Board, it could call on the Ministry of Agriculture for the odd subvention, but it is these days at the mercy of market forces, and may therefore be able to play only a limited role as the country's guardian of the best lines. A real world-beater retiring at four, for instance, would now be syndicated for something like £4 million, which in turn would mean a nomination fee of £50,000, enough to make many a British breeder blanch and to give the Advisory Committee pause.

Perhaps the last person one might expect to favour any relaxation of the prohibition on artificial insemination is the Director of the National Stud, but Bramwell would not be against it in the case of a mare, unable through injury to be covered in the normal way, provided it was carried out on the premises where the stallion normally stands. To go further than this, he says, would entail too great a security risk, and the Jockey Club is extremely unlikely anyway to modify the rules, but he does not feel that the quality of the foal can be affected by the method of impregnation. The great Tesio, of course, took a different view, and in his book *Breeding The Racehorse* propounded the agreeably romantic theory that the transmission of nervous energy is bound up with the 'pleasurable spasm'.

Banstead Manor Stud

In the early 1920s Henry Morriss, grandfather of the present owner of Banstead Manor Stud, was returning on the Transiberian Express to China, where he spent most of his life. Catching sight of some unusual horses, he made enquiries, discovered they were the result of crossing Mongolian ponies with a fleeter breed and promptly entrained several with a view to engineering some coups at the Shanghai racemeeting. The ruse worked – the China pony being, by all accounts, strongly reminiscent of molasses in January – until, in the last race, Morriss brought out the largest of his importations and was tumbled. Duly warned off, he turned his attention to the English turf, and, starting in 1921, gave Fred Darling an annual commission to procure on his behalf the best yearling going. He struck gold the second year, and thus carried off the 1925 2,000 Guineas and Derby with Manna.

Hugo Morriss's father, as a boy, leading in Henry Morriss at Shanghai Races.

Needing a place to stand him, Morriss purchased Banstead Manor and also installed Artist's Proof and a number of mares. By 1927 the establishment was functioning as a public stud, and the new owner had a film made of his stock and staff. The one reel which survives at Banstead Manor includes footage of some Swynford foals. Manna (Phalaris – Waffles, by Buckwheat) did pretty well as a sire for Morriss, getting one classic winner in Colombo, out of Lady Nairne, first in the 1934 2,000 Guineas and third in the Derby. Altogether, Colombo earned £26,228 for Lord Glanely from nine wins in 11 starts, before retiring to stud, his get including Happy Knight, 2,000 Guineas winner of 1946, and Dancing Times, who took the 1,000 Guineas in 1941. Manna's daughter Pasca out of Soubriquet (Lemberg – Silver Fowl, by Wildfowler) produced the 1938 2,000 Guineas and Eclipse winner Pasch (by Blandford), the 1941 St Leger runner-up Château Larose (by Château Bouscaut) and Pasqua, dam of Pinza, Sir Gordon Richards's only successful mount in the Epsom Derby, who won the race in 1953. Pasch, who died after one year at stud, and Chateau Larose, who was sent to the Argentine, both ran in the Morriss colours, but Pinza, having been sold *in utero* to Fred Darling's representative at the Newmarket December sales, was purchased as a yearling for 1,500 guineas by Sir Victor Sassoon. Pinza's sire, the French-bred Chanteur II, a son of Château Bouscaut, stood at Banstead Manor after winning 3,156,150 francs in seven successes at home and £9,019 for his three victories in England. He was twice second in the Ascot Gold Cup,

Top left: *Henry Morriss's ponies being loaded on the Transiberian Express en route to Shanghai.* Left: *Manna with Steve Donoghue up.* Above: *Fifinella.*

and was champion sire in 1953, when Pinza also won the King George VI and Queen Elizabeth Stakes at Ascot. Soubriquet's other principal contribution to the fortunes of Banstead Manor was to produce Tai Yang (by Solario), unbeaten winner of £4,611, and sire of the winners of more than 100 races. The family of Soubriquet, a half-sister to the 1916 Derby and Oaks winner and fine producer, Fifinella, has not been represented at Banstead Manor since the death, in 1958, of her disappointing daughter, Little Mary.

Henry Morriss, who was proprietor of *The China News* and had a number of other business interests in Shanghai, died out East two years before it transpired that, when his wife sold Pasqua, the mare was carrying a Derby winner. He would, however, most certainly not have appreciated the irony of Fred Darling's involvement after the affair of Pont l'Evêque's Derby. The Banstead Manor-bred Pont l'Evêque won at Epsom for Darling, who had bought him as a two-year-old when Morriss, subsequently imprisoned by the Japanese, was somewhat preoccupied with the threat to his interests in China. Pont l'Evêque's form as a juvenile was not, in any case, much to write home about, and he failed to reach a place in either of his outings. As a three-year-old, however, he showed marked improvement, and it was agreed that, in the event of his winning his Derby trial, the Newmarket Stakes, Morriss should buy back a half share. When, after a poor run at headquarters, Pont l'Evêque managed the dramatic reversal of form he needed at Epsom, Morriss transferred his string to the Hon George Lambton, then 80 years old.

Pont l'Evêque, a son of Barneveldt and therefore a tail-male descendant of Son-in-Law, took up stud duties at Lordship, but was banished to Argentina after a couple of years. His dam, the French-bred Ponteba, a daughter of the 1925 Prix du Jockey-Club winner Belfonds, was carrying him when Morriss bought her, aged six. The year Pont l'Evêque won the Derby his grey half-sister by Mahmoud, Pontoon, was foaled at Banstead Manor. After winning three races, including the Rutland Handicap at Newmarket, and a total of £1,407, Pontoon became the foundation of one of the four most important families in the development of the stud, producing the winners Seaplane II, whose five victories were worth £1,763, Westminster Bridge (dam of Ahoy, who earned $209,665 in America, and other winners across the Atlantic), Rumbling Bridge, John Peters, who netted £2,018 in six wins, My Poppet, Twist One, Rainbow Bridge and Lady Alice, dam of winners in Japan. Her daughter Sea Spray, not herself successful on the racecourse, is second dam of Sea Hawk II, winner of the Grand Prix de Saint-Cloud in 1966, while Pontoon's non-winning daughters Geifang Gem, Bridge and Forth Bridge also produced winners. My Poppet, by My Babu, is now a 26-year-old pensioner at Banstead Manor. Her daughter by Major Portion, Boule de Suif, foaled in 1969, produced a bay filly by Upper Case in 1976. The winner of the Willerby Plate at Beverley as a two-year-old, and the Thurlow Handicap at Newmarket in 1972, Boule de Suif is half-sister to Intervener, by Supreme Court, Tune Time, by Tudor Minstrel, Popocatepetl, by Acropolis, Pamplemousse, by Mossborough, Ninon, by Never Say Die, and Grey Moss, by Ballymoss, who stood at Banstead Manor from 1959 to 1967. Intervener won the Solario Stakes at Sandown, ran second in the Dewhurst and earned $126,772 in America, where he was successful in the Meadowland Handicap, the Equipoise Mile and the Princeton Handicap. Popocatepetl, winner of the Princess Stakes at Newmarket, is dam of the twice-successful Ballycano; Pamplemousse took the Fitzwilliam Stakes at York, while Grey Moss was first in the 1966 Dee Stakes at Chester.

Another mare to have started an important Banstead Manor family was

Lady Woolverton and the Hon George and Mrs Lambton.

Foxtrot, foaled in 1943, winner of the Zetland Nursery, the 1946 Ebor Handicap and a total of five races worth £4,108. A daughter of Foxhunter out of the Phalaris mare Première Danseuse, she was dam of the winners Fe Shaing, Square Dance, Final Swing, Time and Chance, Nautch Dance, Geifang Belle and Welsh Fox. Nautch Dance and Time and Chance produced winners themselves, the latter's most distinguished son being Random Shot, who earned £20,315 in six wins and took the Ascot Gold Cup in 1971, while both Final Swing and Square Dance won over timber, as well as on the flat. Square Dance, winner of the 1956 Triumph Hurdle, had run second in the Horris Hill Stakes at Newbury. The last time this family put Banstead Manor in the limelight was in 1972, when Pentland Firth, whose second dam was Geifang Belle, ran third to Roberto and Rheingold in the Derby. Pentland Firth, a son of Crepello, now at stud in South Africa, was out of Free For All by Fair Trial. His full-brother Crepello Gift was a winner, too, while Free For All also produced Free Boy (by Sica Boy), winner of three races and £1,995, Lay About (by Aggressor), who won Kempton's Coventry Stakes and one other flat race for a total of £2,066 and Dalroy (by Fidalgo) whose flat race earnings of £1,362 came from three victories, including the Bunbury Stakes at Epsom. Lay About and Dalroy both scored over hurdles too. Free For All, a half-sister to the winners All Mine, Games Court, Belle of the Ball, Chester Belle and Dinner Gong, was destroyed, aged 17, at

Tommy Price and Hugo Morriss outside Isinglass's box at Banstead Manor.
Right: *Wollow*

Banstead Manor in March 1973, the last of the Foxtrot family on the place.
Her last foal was Trop Chère (1971) by Never Say Die.

Hugo Morriss has been running Banstead Manor Stud since the death,
in 1963, of his father, whose greatest success as a breeder was probably
Alcaeus, by Court Martial, second in both the English and Irish Derbys of
1960, winner of the Dee Stakes at Chester the same year, and of the Ormonde
Stakes there in 1961. He ended up at stud in Italy. Sold as a yearling, Alcaeus
was a son of the third of the Banstead Manor foundation mares, Marteline
(1948), a daughter of Court Martial out of Meraline by Mieuxcé. Chateau
Bouscaut appears in Marteline's pedigree too, as sire of the second dam,
Merina. Winner of the Cherry Hinton Stakes and runner-up in the Solario

Stakes, Marteline, also produced the winners Neanderthal, Parthian Shot and Near The Line. Near The Line is dam of Sapper (by Aggressor), winner of Salisbury's Champagne Stakes and Newbury's Donnington Castle Stakes, and of Ombra del Sol, by Ballymoss, a nice winner in Italy. Marteline's daughter Deianira is also the dam of winners, including Soleiman, successful in France and Italy, and Vleuten, who scored in France.

A mare for which Banstead Manor has high hopes is Abernant's daughter Bas Bleu, foaled in 1969. Her first foal was Baccalaureate (1975) by Crowned Prince, a stallion in which Hugo Morriss has a stake. She produced a colt to Brigadier Gerard the next year, was barren to Grundy in 1977 and was then sent to Habitat, who seems to do well with Abernant mares, the best-known result of this cross thus far being Steel Heart, out of A.1., winner of four races and £60,287. Bas Bleu belongs to the family of Blue Star II, that mare having been bought in France by Hugo Morriss's grandfather after she had won several races in two seasons, including the Prix de la Forêt, the Prix Isonomy and the Criterium de Maisons Lafitte. Top filly in the French Free Handicap of 1937, she was by Blandford's French-bred son Blue Skies, who was also sire of Chanteur II's dam, La Diva. Her daughter Lusignan won three races and then produced Dinkie Melody, a winner, dam of winners and grandam of Swift Harmony – whose four races, worth £3,264, included the Chesham Stakes at Ascot – and Golden Love, winner of the Joe Coral Newbury Autumn Cup, the Commonwealth Handicap at Sandown Park, and a total of £11,873 from seven wins. Lusignan was also dam of Portofino, who won £4,730 on the track, taking the Somerville Tattersall Stakes at Newmarket and the Brighton Derby Trial, Blue Book (£3,119) first in the Wokingham Stakes at Ascot and second in the Stewards' Cup at Goodwood, Geifang Star and My Blue Heaven, dam of Halloween and other National Hunt winners. Blue Star II's daughter by Court Martial, Blue Stain, dam of the speedy Ink Spot, also produced Blue Shadow (by Crepello), dam of Primerello (by Primera), Bas Bleu and Upanishad (by Amber Rama). Primerello won £5,686 and four races – the Sandwich Stakes at Ascot, the Kenneth Robertson Handicap at Newbury, the Doonside Cup at Ayr and the Yorkshire Stakes at Doncaster, as well as two races in Belgium. Bas Bleu won £3,606 in her four victories from as many starts at three years old – the Oulton Stakes at Yarmouth, the Powderhall Plate at Nottingham, the Standish Stakes at Haydock and the William Hill Silver Vase Handicap at Newmarket – and the next year won one race and ran into a place in the Ayr Gold Cup. Upanishad registered her first win in 1976.

Bas Bleu and her dam are owned in partnership with Hascombe Stud, but Boule de Suif and the rest of the broodmare band belong outright to Hugo Morriss. At the moment he has on the stud the American mare Angel Falls (Sir Gaylord – Cascade II), Ribot's full-sister Rossellina, Bas Bleu's half-sister Lapis Lazuli, by Zeddaan, Io (Tenerani – Fatimite, by Mahmoud),

Left: *Upper Case.*

49

D

Refifi, Scala di Seta and Sealing Wax. In 1976 Angel Falls, Blue Shadow and Scala di Seta produced Upper Case colts, Boule de Suif and Lapis Lazuli fillies by the same stallion, and Sealing Wax a Moulton colt. Rossellina, dam of the 1967 Italian Derby winner, Ruysdael, had the Averof filly she was carrying when Morriss purchased her. Io (1957) won two races, worth £1,032, and ran fourth in Never Too Late's Oaks. She is dam of Shai, by Shantung, winner of the Andy Capp Handicap at Redcar in 1965, second in the Rowley Stakes and third in the Horris Hill, and a full brother to the useful performer Soie. The minor winners Paros (by Pardao) and Iotude (by Gratitude) are also sons of Io.

Shantung is the old man of Banstead Manor's current trio of stallions. Bred in France by Baron Guy de Rothschild, and foaled in 1956, he won his only race as a two-year-old, the Prix Mousko at Saint-Cloud, and the next year won the Prix Edgard de la Charme at Saint-Cloud and the Prix de la Rochette at Longchamp for career earnings of 3,026,650 francs. After one year at stud in France, he came to Banstead Manor, where, by the end of 1976, he was the sire of the winners of 114 races worth £197,291. In 1976 he had four winners – the best being Tierra Fuego – of a total of £7,492.

Shantung is pre-eminently a sire of fillies, and his most successful runners have been his classic-winning daughters Ginevra (1972 Oaks), Full Dress II

Shantung and (right): *Wollow.*

(1969 1,000 Guineas) and Lacquer (1967 Irish 1,000 Guineas), winners of £41,624, £24,446 and £16,240 respectively. Lacquer was sold at the end of her racing career to John Hay Whitney, and produced, for Greentree, a couple of runners familiar to English racegoers in Brilliantine, by Stage Door Johnny, and Bright Finish, by Nijinsky. She went to Grundy in 1977, having dropped a good-looking Nijinsky colt at the British National Stud. The best of Shantung's progeny otherwise have been Attalus (£6,902), Gay Garland (£6,874), Dutch Delight (£6,525), Humberside (£5,669), Pinchow (£4,691), who has also won over timber, Shai (£4,578), Moire (£4,173), Setsu (£3,936), Shanghai (£3,777) and Alangia (£3,663). He has also got a large number of good winners abroad.

The classic American nick of modern times – 'the nearest you can get to the Hereford/Angus cross with an inbred animal like the racehorse', as Morriss puts it – is also represented at Banstead Manor in the shape of Upper Case (Round Table – Bold Experience, by Bold Ruler), who won six races, including the Florida Derby and the Wood Memorial, and retired at the end of his three-year-old campaign in 1972 with total winnings of $241,310. His dam, foaled in 1962, was the winner of $91,477 in ten starts, her biggest success being in the 1964 $50,000 Sorority Stakes. Although Upper Case's first crop did include six individual winners abroad, four of them came late in the season, and did not have sufficient impact to create a rush for his services in 1977, although he has hitherto always filled quickly.

Banstead Manor's new stallion, Wollow, was syndicated for £1,250,000 before he ran a disappointing fifth to Empery in the 1976 Derby. Although his racing career also finished on a disappointing note – in the ruck to Vitiges in a Champion Stakes more affected than normal by the draw – such a late-season reverse could hardly detract from an illustrious career. Unbeaten as a two-year-old in four races (Trumpington Maiden Stakes, Fitzroy House Stakes and William Hill Dewhurst Stakes, all at Newmarket, and the Laurent Perrier Champagne Stakes at Doncaster) he went on to add five more victories in 1976 and bring his career winnings to £200,806. His 2,000 Guineas victory from Vitiges prevented a French clean sweep of the English classic races, and he also won the Clerical Medical Greenham Stakes at Newbury, the Sussex Stakes at Goodwood, the Benson and Hedges Gold Cup at York and the Joe Coral Eclipse at Sandown on the disqualification of Trepan. Restricted by syndicate agreement to 36 mares in 1977, with 46 in 1978, Wollow, Morriss thinks, might well make an effective cross with Habitat.

That Banstead Manor is a very pretty place is in a large measure due, as Hugo Morriss happily points out, to its impractical lay-out, which dates from his grandfather's time. A few buildings have been added in recent years without affecting what Morriss terms the 'inside out' design of the place,

Top left: *Cover Girl and her Upper Case foal.* Bottom left: *In-foal mares on the way to the Banstead Manor foaling unit.* Below: *Isinglass.*

with small groups of boxes cropping up at odd places on the periphery of the stud's 360 acres. Still, successful breeding does not necessarily require the efficient appearance of a custom-built stud, and Banstead Manor is doing quite well financially at the moment. Perhaps this helps Morriss to take a philosophical view of the plight of British breeders and he is disinclined to argue for tax concessions to put us on an equal footing with our competitors at a time when other British industries are having a hard time, too. He generally keeps back one or two of his horses to race, and currently has Harry Wragg and Sir Mark Prescott training for him.

In the heyday of Colonel Harry McCalmont towards the end of the 19th century, Banstead Manor was part of the master of Cheveley Park's estates. Lord Randolph Churchill was then in the habit of spending the Newmarket season as tenant of Banstead Manor House, a Queen Anne building pulled down in the 1920s by Henry Morriss, who, his grandson explains, was 'a bit of a vandal'. The great Isinglass was foaled here in 1890, and the shed where he was dropped still stands. At the time of the Domesday Book Cheveley consisted of two royal manors, one of them, Broad Green, being occupied in the Middle Ages by the Benstede family – hence the name of the Morriss stud.

Banstead Manor yard where visiting mares are kept.

Beech House Stud

Martin Benson, fastidious owner of Beech House, had three air raid shelters
built when war broke out – one for himself, one for his great stallion Nearco,
who had just completed his first year at stud, and one for the servants.
Nearco, at the time, was the most expensive horse ever, having changed
hands for £60,000 immediately after his Grand Prix de Paris win in 1938,
his fourteenth victory from as many starts at distances ranging from five
furlongs to $1\frac{3}{4}$ miles. The deal was handled by Edward Coussel of the British
Bloodstock Agency, whose approach to Tesio's representatives at Longchamp elicited the response that no such trifling figure as the £50,000

Nearco.

Above: *Martin Benson, and the Maharaja of Rajpipla leading in Windsor Lad after his Derby win.* Right: *Windsor Lad with Charlie Smirke up.*

Benson had given the Maharaja of Rajpipla for Windsor Lad between his Derby and St Leger victories of 1934 would be considered. So great was the demand for Nearco's services as a stallion that Benson abandoned his original plan to race the horse and arranged his syndication, retaining five shares for himself. By the end of July he was in residence at Newmarket.

Windsor Lad, meanwhile, was pretty well finished as a stallion, being withdrawn after the 1938 season, only his third at stud, to be operated on for what Colonel Douglas Gray, now at Beech House, describes as a brain tumour, although Sir Charles Leicester's book says the trouble was with the horse's sinus. It was not until Windsor Lad was 12, however, that he was put down: some unsentimental insurance interests, having refused to countenance humane destruction, made an appropriate disbursement and stood him as the 'property of a syndicate of Lloyds underwriters'. Windsor Lad, whose best son was the 1942 Irish Triple Crown winner, Windsor Slipper, was an admirably poor foal-getter for the *Caveat Emptor* men. Benson, a bookie by trade – he was the celebrated 'Duggie' who never owed – caused some amazement in Newmarket by, so they say, changing his shirt three times a day. Local gossip also suggests that it was as the result of a card game that Windsor Lad changed hands, a suggestion scornfully repudiated by the Maharaja's son, now working as a racing journalist in Paris. 'I'm the gambler in our family,' he says. 'My father would never have played for that sort of sum, and racing for him was really only a social thing. In any case, do you really think he would have had to get rid of a horse to meet that kind of obligation? The truth is he was sold impetuously after being beaten in the Eclipse, when Charlie Smirke had an off day.' At all events, Benson retired Windsor Lad at four, by which time he had won £35,257 from 10 wins in 13 starts, and the Beech House Stud had been acquired from Charles Heckford to accommodate him. Heckford stayed on as manager until 1958, when the place was sold to Sir Victor Sassoon, living at the adjoining Newlands Stud, which, when the price was right, he had also allowed to be absorbed into the Benson demesne.

If there is no doubt that Nearco (Pharos – Nogara, by Havresac) had as great an impact on the international racing and breeding scene as almost any stallion in the history of the thoroughbred, opinions do seem to vary as to how many times he topped the English sires' list. Both Sir Charles Leicester and the American *Thoroughbred Record* say three, the latter authority specifying 1947, 1948 and 1949. *Ruff's Guide,* however, has him champion in 1947 with £42,554 and 1949 with £52,545 13s, but gives the palm in 1948 to Big Game (Bahram – Myrobella, by Tetratema) with £40,690. *Pedigrees of Leading Winners, 1912–1959,* published by the Thoroughbred Breeders' Association has yet a different tale to tell, agreeing that Nearco was champion in 1947 but varying slightly on the total won by his progeny, which it sets at £45,087 5s. Although, for 1948, there is no serious dispute about the amount won by Big Game – the TBA reckons

£40,891 15s – Nearco, on this table, comes out in front with £41,541 15s. The amounts by Nearco's name for 1949 tally in both *Ruff's* and *Pedigrees of Leading Winners* but, of course, the TBA has him second to Bois Roussel (Vatout – Plucky Liège, by Spearmint), whose progeny is down as winning £57,161 10s. Nearco was, by general consent, champion broodmare sire in 1952, 1955 and 1956, while the names of Nasrullah, Dante, Royal Charger, Nimbus and Mossborough, for example, are ample reminders of his status as a sire of sires. His English classic winners were Nimbus (1949 2,000 Guineas and Derby), Dante (1945 Derby), Masaka (1948 Oaks), Neasham Belle (1951 Oaks) and Sayajirao (1947 St Leger). Nearco died at Beech House in June 1957.

Throughout its history Beech House has functioned mainly as a public stud, with neither enough resident mares nor sufficient continuity of ownership for powerful dynasties to be connected with the place. Its most fruitful period followed its acquisition by Noel Murless on behalf of Sir Victor Sassoon, for whom he had trained since 1952, assuming responsibility for the breeding side three years later. The greatest Sassoon broodmare of the era was certainly Crepuscule, a chestnut daughter of Mieuxcé out of Red Sunset, by Solario, foaled in 1948. Her produce included Honeylight, by Fairway's son Honeyway, winner of £14,899 5s and five races, including the 1,000 Guineas and Free Handicap of 1956, Crepello, by Donatello (by Blenheim), foaled in 1954, winner of the Dewhurst, 2,000 Guineas and Derby for a total of £34,201 5s, and Twilight Alley (1959) by Alycidon, Ascot Gold Cup winner of 1963. Crepuscule also produced Crepina (by

Sir Victor Sassoon's Pinza being led in after his Derby win. Below right: *Alycidon, ridden by D. Smith, comes home an easy winner of the 1949 Ascot Gold Cup with Black Tarquin (E. Britt) second.* Right: *Alycidon.*

Pinza), dam of Rangong, winner of the Geoffrey Freer Stakes and the St Simon Stakes in 1969 and the Yorkshire Cup in 1970. He is now at stud in New Zealand. The 1960 Derby and St Leger winner St Paddy, a son of Aureole, was also bred by Sassoon's Eve Stud, being out of Bois Roussel's daughter Edie Kelly, who, now 27, lives in retirement at Murless's Woodditton Stud, along with Pinza. Twilight Alley stood for a while at Beech House, but couldn't live the Gold Cup down and was sold. Crepello, put down at Beech House at the age of 20, is sire of the winners of some £100,000, his best known being Busted, Mysterious, Caergwrle, Candy Cane, Celina, Cranberry Sauce, Crepellana, Great Wall, Linden Tree, Lucyrowe, Pentland Firth, Soderini, The Creditor, Vervain and Yelda. The Creditor, who won the Jersey Stakes, the Queen Elizabeth II Stakes and the Lockinge, as well as running third in the Champion, produced both Abwah, by Abernant, and Owen Dudley, by Tudor Melody, to add to Crepello's considerable reputation as a sire of broodmares. Abwah, who now stands at the Grimstone Stud, Melton Mowbray, is still half-owned by Beech House. Crepello also sired Bleu Azur, dam of Altesse Royale (1971 1,000 Guineas, Oaks and Irish Oaks) and Zest, dam of Ginevra (1972 Oaks). Imperial Prince, exported to Australia as a stallion after the 1975 season, was also a half-brother, by Sir Ivor, to Altesse Royale.

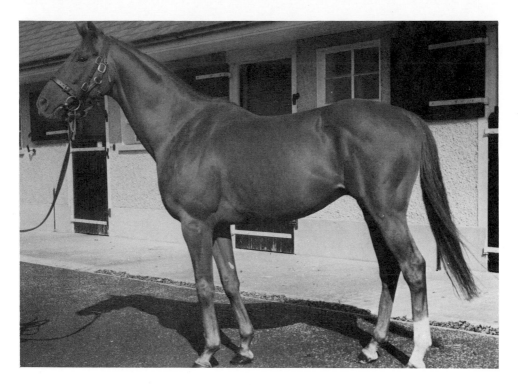

Top left: *Beech House stud groom Michael McFarling with St Paddy*. Bottom left: *Connaught (Sandy Barclay) wins the 1970 Prince of Wales Stakes at Royal Ascot*. Above: *Parnell*.

Although St Paddy, as gentle a stallion as one could wish to meet, has his detractors as a sire, he has so far got the winners of more than 200 races worth in excess of £400,000. Easily his best son is Connaught, out of Nagaika, by Goyama, in the opinion of Noel Murless a peerless horse at a mile and a quarter. Murless, certainly, would have loved the chance to take on Mill Reef and Brigadier Gerard at that distance. Connaught, winner of seven races and £69,212, was undefeated in his last season's racing, as a five-year-old in 1970, when he won the Prince of Wales's Stakes from Hotfoot, breaking his own track record, and took a scintillating Eclipse by $2\frac{1}{2}$ lengths from Karabas. He has made a fairly propitious start at Woodditton Stud with 50 races worth more than £83,000 won by his progeny at the end of 1976. That season 24 races worth £55,557.82 went to his 13 individual winners, who included Sir Montagu, Miss Pinkie, Lady Constance and Paddington. St Paddy, who carries his years extraordinarily well and still serves some 40 mares a year, is also sire of Parnell, Sucaryl, Maina, Calpurnius, St Chad, St Pauli Girl and Paddy Me. Of his more recent runners, the most impressive has been Patch, winner of £16,533, who took the Lingfield Derby Trial, by ten lengths from Anne's Pretender, and the Great Voltigeur in 1975, when he was also a head second to Val de l'Orne in the Prix du Jockey-Club. Patch, who took up his duties at the Raffin Stud, County

Palatch with her filly foal by Grundy.   **Right**: *Lester Piggott and Rheingold after their victory in the 1973 Prix de l'Arc de Triomphe.*

Meath, in 1977, is out of Match III's daughter Palatch, winner of the 1967 Yorkshire Oaks and the Musidora Stakes, and the dam of Grundy's first foal, a bay filly dropped at Beech House on January 31, 1977. Palatch is one of a handful of mares kept at Beech House by Dr Carlo Vittadini, who bought the place from Louis Freedman in 1975. The best of the other mares currently in residence are Crowning Mercy, by Supreme Court, dam of No Mercy, Forever, by Never Say Die, dam of Hobnob (Fr) and Orange Triumph, by Molvedo, dam of Orange Bay. In 1977 Crowning Mercy and Forever were due to produce Habat foals, Orange Triumph an Ortis foal. The best of the foals produced at Beech House from now on will probably be kept in England, although Vittadini has never been one to keep a large broodmare band and there are unlikely to be many home-breds running in his colours on English tracks.

Freedman had taken over Beech House in August 1971 from Lady Sassoon, formerly Evelyn Barnes, from Dallas, Texas, and nurse to Sir Victor, whom she had married in 1959. Sir Victor died, aged 79, in the Bahamas a year after St Paddy had brought him the fourth of his Derby wins, which came in the space of eight years. The Sir Oliver Lambart-bred Hard Ridden, who had won for him in 1958 to follow in the footsteps of Pinza and Crepello, was a son of the sprinter Hard Sauce, who stood at Sassoon's Thornton Stud, near Thirsk, out of Toute Belle II, by Admiral Drake. He cost Sassoon 270 guineas as a yearling. Sassoon, who also bred horses at the

Killeen Castle Stud in Dunsany, County Meath, from 1952 to 1968, kept large numbers of mares – too many, said Murless, as he set about trimming the band to 25 after his death. The best of the foals were picked out and sent to Yorkshire each year – generally to Murless's Cliff Stud at Helmsley, where the limestone subsoil makes for ideal conditions, and where a number of notable horses have thus come to be reared in recent years, among them St Paddy, Twilight Alley, Sweet Moss, Sucaryl, Attica Meli, Owen Dudley, Milly Moss and Mil's Bomb. Crepello's daughter Mil's Bomb was out of Bally's Mil, a half-sister to Sweet Angel, dam of the 1965 Royal Lodge Stakes winner, Soft Angels, also by Crepello. Soft Angels was also a half-sister to Sweet Moss and Sucaryl. George Pope's 1973 1,000 Guineas and Oaks winner, Mysterious (Crepello – Hill Shade, by Hillary) was foaled at Beech House, and she too was reared by Murless in Yorkshire.

Among Sir Victor Sassoon's best known horses on the track was the fine sprinter Princely Gift, one of Nasrullah's last crop before he went to America. Bred by Alfred Allnatt at the Aston Rowant Stud, Princely Gift, who was out of Blue Peter's daughter, Blue Gem, cost 5,000 guineas at the Newmarket July Sales as a yearling. Murless sent him out to win nine races, worth £6,673, in the course of three seasons' racing, during which he was only twice out of the first four in 23 starts. Probably his best performance was his last, when he won the Portland Handicap with 9st 4lb. He was syndicated and sent to the Old Connell Stud, Newbridge, County Kildare, where he remained until he was put down at the age of 22. His last crop were three-year-olds at the time of his death, by which time he was responsible for the winners of 383 races, and £431,668. Known pre-eminently as a sire of sires, Princely Gift has several sons at stud in the British Isles, including Sun Prince, So Blessed, and Realm. His best-known grandson, Rheingold, did

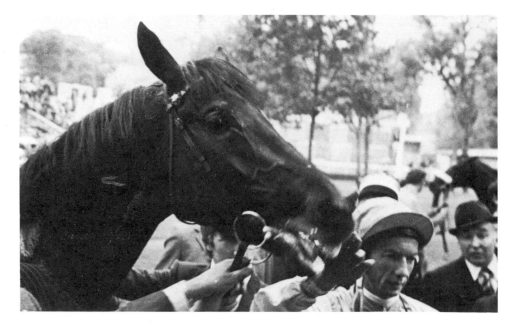

not demonstrate his class until his sire, Fabergé II, who was second in the 1964 2,000 Guineas, had been exported to Japan, where other Princely Gift stallions, exported after spells at English studs, include his biggest stakes winner, Frankincense, Tesco Boy, Floribunda and Tribal Chief. Frankincense (ex Amethea, by Hyperion) had six wins and earned £18,596, his principal victories coming in the William Hill Gold Cup at Redcar in 1967 and the Lincoln Handicap and the Cecil Frail Stakes the next year. Another good stakes winner by Princely Gift now standing in Japan is Berber, out of Desert Girl, by Straight Deal, whose three wins brought £10,001 in prize money and included the St James's Stakes and the Richmond Stakes.

Princely Gift's other principal money earners on the track were Sun Prince (ex Costa Sola, by Worden II), So Blessed (ex Lavant, by Le Lavandou) and Realm (ex Quita by Lavandin), who won £17,840, £13,888 and £13,596 respectively. The best runners out of Princely Gift mares seen on British tracks have probably been Prominent (High Hat – Picture Palace), Lombardo (Ragusa – Midnight Chimes), and Bitty Girl (Habitat – Garvey Girl).

The 1968 St Leger and Irish Derby winner Ribero (Ribot – Libra, by Hyperion), bred in Kentucky by Mrs Julian Rogers, transferred to Beech House from Sandringham after the 1976 season, having failed to set the world alight since he retired from the track in 1969. A full brother to the 1967 St Leger winner Ribocco, Ribero has sired Riboson, Romper and Riboreen.

Below: *Ribero*.   Top right: *Sir Noel Murless*. Bottom right: *Isonomy*.

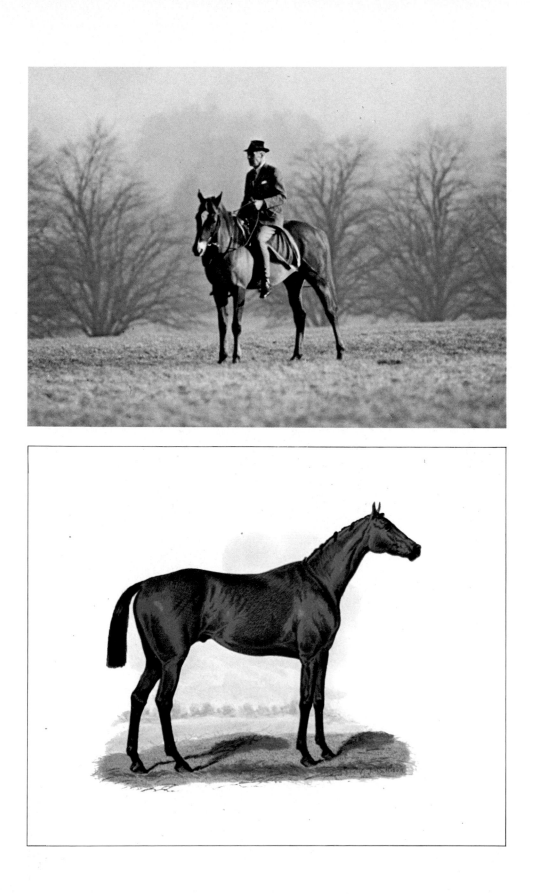

Brook Stud

Few breeders in recent years have been so closely associated as Sir Kenneth Butt, owner of the Brook Stud at Cheveley, with that most beguiling of creatures, the flying two-year-old filly, whose dazzling displays of precocious speed so often augur punter's gloom on 1,000 Guineas day. The first three foals of the doughty Brook Stud mare, Pristina, dropped in consecutive years, were Mange Tout, Hecla and Rose Dubarry, the last named running third in the Guineas of 1972, the same year as Lady Butt's Jacinth made her electrifying debut. Mange Tout (by Gallivanter) won the 1969 Windsor Castle Stakes at Ascot and the Molecomb Stakes at Goodwood, as well as

Left: *Rose Dubarry, Tony Murray up, after winning the Lowther Stakes.*
Below: *Jacinth and her colt foal by Habitat.*

E

Sir Kenneth Butt and stud groom L.S. Aldous with the great Brook Stud mare Pristina and her tenth foal, her first colt.

earning top rating for a filly in the French Free Handicap after taking the Prix d'Arenberg and running Tower Walk to three quarters of a length in the Prix de l'Abbaye. Hecla (by Henry The Seventh) was the eight-lengths winner of the Cherry Hinton Stakes, while Klairon's daughter, Rose Dubarry, bought as a yearling for 30,000 guineas by H. J. Joel, was awarded top weight for a filly in the Free Handicap and remained unbeaten at two, climaxing her campaign by coming round Deep Diver, Mansingh, Maximilian and Flintham to win the Norfolk Stakes at Doncaster after appearing hopelessly boxed in. In the Lowther Stakes at York she easily accounted for Waterloo, who went on to win the 1,000 Guineas. Although Red God's daughter Jacinth is not a home-bred, both her dam (Jaffa, by Right Royal V) and her grandam (Mistress Gwynne, by Chanteur II) were products of the Brook Stud. Jacinth won both her two-year-old races, the George Lambton Stakes and the Cheveley Park Stakes, and then ran second in the Guineas before capturing the Coronation Stakes, the Falmouth Stakes and the Goodwood Mile. She was also second to Thatch in the Sussex Stakes, beaten on merit, says Butt, who thinks different riding tactics would have won her the Guineas. Retired to the Brook Stud, she dropped a dead Blakeney foal in 1975, was rested the next year, but produced a bay Habitat colt on February 24, 1977.

66

The fourth of Pristina's ten foals, Princess Tina, by Sovereign Path, won a couple of small races before retiring to the Brook Stud and producing a bay colt by Thatch, which fetched 42,000 guineas at the 1976 Houghton Sales. The Brook Stud draft then also included Princess Tina's half-sister by Mill Reef, knocked down for 5,000 guineas less. In 1977 Pristina visited Dancer's Image, after dropping, on March 24, her tenth foal, and her first colt, by Amber Rama.

Pristina's sire, Petition, bred at the Brook Stud, was by Fair Trial, out of Art Paper, by Artist's Proof. The theatrical entrepreneur, Sir Alfred Butt, father of Sir Kenneth, paid 250 guineas for the dam as a yearling in Dublin the same year as he bought the stud, 1934. Petition won the New Stakes at Royal Ascot, the Richmond Stakes at Goodwood, the Gimcrack Stakes at York and the Champagne Stakes at Doncaster as a juvenile, and his preparatory race as a three-year-old before being injured at the start of the 2,000 Guineas. 'He sat on his backside,' says Sir Kenneth, 'and didn't eat a thing for six weeks.' He came back the next year to win the Victoria Cup and the Eclipse Stakes and £18,023, before retiring to stud for the 1949 season. He met with consistent success, was champion sire in 1959, leading sire of two-year-olds in 1961, and achieved immortality by getting Petite Etoile. Sir Alfred also bred and owned the 1946 Oaks winner Steady Aim (Felstead – Quick Arrow, by Casterari), who went on to produce seven individual winners herself, and Solario's daughter, Solar Flower, winner of four races worth £10,241 15s and third in the 1,000 Guineas and the Oaks of 1938. When much of the Brook Stud pasture was ploughed up in the war, both Solar Flower and her dam, Serena, by Winalot, were sold in Ireland to Joseph McGrath, for whom she produced two Champion Stakes winners in Solar Slipper and Peter Flower, as well as Arctic Sun.

Before Sir Alfred Butt bought the Brook Stud, it had been occupied by Sir Richard Garton, who leased it from Archie Falcon's widow. Falcon, originally a newspaper correspondent and subsequently a professional gambler, never looked back after having his shirt on Spearmint for the 1906 Derby. He became an owner and breeder, and stood his stallion Tremola (by Tredennis) at the Bungalow Stud, Woodditton, purchased from the trainer Martin Gurry, who, after winning the 1890 Derby with Sir J. Miller's Sainfoin, proposed to present the St Agnes Church in Newmarket with a communion plate inscribed 'From Gurry to God'. In 1925, the Woodditton stud was sold to Sir Victor Sassoon, who rechristened it 'Eve', the name under which he raced in India, and Falcon bought the Brook Stud, which did not, however, really function as a thoroughbred nursery until Butt took over.

Sir Alfred Butt's principal reason for buying the stud was that he needed a place to stand Orpen, a bay son of Solario out of Harpy, by Swynford, purchased for 65,000 guineas at the sale, on 2,000 Guineas day in 1932, of the recently-deceased Sir John Rutherford's horses in training. Orpen, who had won the Union Jack Stakes and the St George Stakes at Liverpool and the Hardwicke Stakes at Ascot, had also run second in the Derby and

Petition (right in the leading group), ridden by Kenny Gethin, wins the Eclipse Stakes from Sayajirao (Charlie Smirke) and Noor (W. Johnstone)

St Leger and third in the 2,000 Guineas of 1931. For Butt he won the Churchill Stakes at Ascot and, at five, the Yorkshire Cup. He was second in Foxhunter's Ascot Gold Cup before retiring to stud, where his only progeny of much merit was the 1938 Irish Oaks winner, Conversation Piece. In 1933 Butt paid 370 guineas for Serena, in foal to Tremola's son Stingo, while Quick Arrow cost 700 guineas as a five-year-old at the Newmarket Sales in January 1942, and produced Steady Aim from her first mating.

That Pristina should have produced such speedy daughters is not all that surprising in the light of her pedigree, which is very much along the same lines as Petite Etoile's. Pristina's dam, Tina II, is a daughter of Tulyar, a grandson of Bois Roussel, who was sire of Petite Etoile's dam, Star of Iran. Mumtaz Mahal is fourth dam of both Tina II and Petite Etoile, whose second dams, Bibibeg and Mah Iran respectively, are both by Bahram. Tina II, who did not race, cost Butt 7,300 guineas as a three-year-old at the

Newmarket December Sales of 1960. She was bred by the Aga Khan and Prince Aly Khan, as was Petite Etoile, winner of £56,641 10s and eight races, including the 1959 1,000 Guineas and Oaks, the Sussex Stakes and the Champion Stakes, and indubitably one of the finest fillies who ever graced the English turf. Tina II is also dam of Ovaltine, by Match III, winner of the 1967 Ebor and the 1968 Goodwood Cup.

The best price ever paid for a Brook Stud yearling was the 63,000 guineas for which a Welsh Pageant colt out of Galicia changed hands at the Houghton Sales in 1976. This was the first foal of Galicia, who won only a couple of small races, but is half-sister to My Heart, a successful stallion in Australia, and to Ardneasken, dam of Warpath and Dakota. Galicia, by Great Nephew, is out of Alice Delysia, by Alycidon, dam of half a dozen winners and one of two half-sisters, out of Daring Miss, who played a prominent part in the development of the stud a few years ago. The other was Mistress Gwynne, whose son Corinto (by Grey Sovereign) won the Britannia Stakes and the William Hill Gold Cup before becoming a successful sire in Australia too. Daring Miss, purchased as a fourteen-year-old in 1953, also produced Eliza Doolittle, who was exported and became dam of Julie Andrews, winner of the South Africa 1,000 Guineas and Oaks. At the time of her purchase, for 7,800 guineas, Daring Miss was in foal to Rockefella, producing Misbehave, an own sister to Gay Time, Elopement and Cash and Courage, who was consigned to the yearling sales and went on to win the Alington Stakes at Newmarket as a three-year-old.

In 1964, the year of Petition's death, the American stallion Royal Record II stood his first season at Brook Stud, having been imported and syndicated by Butt and bloodstock agent Keith Freeman. Royal Record II came with a deeply impressive Kentucky pedigree – he is a son of Nasrullah out of the prolific producer of winners Belle Histoire (Blue Larkspur – La Troienne) – and a racing record which spanned four seasons with twelve wins at distances ranging from six furlongs to a mile and five, and earnings of $140,000. After only four years, however, he was exported to Japan, having, as Butt cryptically puts it, been 'killed by someone'. His greatest achievement at stud here was probably to sire the Princess Royal Stakes winner Seventh Bride (ex Little Miss Muffet, by Tourment), dam of Polygamy (by Reform), 1974 Oaks winner, and her full-sister, One Over Parr, who took the Lancashire Oaks and the Cheshire Oaks the next season. Their half-sister by Crepello, Bedfellow, failed to live up to expectations in 1976, her only victory being a walk-over, and by that time there was only the occasional ripple to remind racegoers of the American stallion's spell in this country, with Shuwaiman, a three-year-old Alcide colt out of his daughter Kentucky Blues, achieving the one real 1976 win in which he had a hand, a maiden event at Sandown in the autumn.

Currently standing at Brook Stud is the syndicated Amber Rama, who was bought for 210,000 francs at the 1968 Deauville Yearling Sales by F. Mathet on behalf of M. Arpad Plesch. Amber Rama was at his most effective at sprint distances, a peculiarity presumably attributable to the ether in America, where he was bred by Mrs P. A. B. Widener II, since his pedigree suggests a mile should have been well within his compass:

Jaipur	Nasrullah	Nearco	Pharos Nogara
		Mumtaz Begum	Blenheim Mumtaz Mahal
	Rare Perfume	Eight Thirty	Pilate Dinner Time
		Fragrance	Sir Gallahad III Rosebloom
Pink Silk	Spy Song	Balladier	Black Toney Blue Warbler
		Mata Hari	Peter Hastings War Woman
	Bayrose	Sir Gallahad III	Teddy Plucky Liège
		Artistic Rose	Challenger II Dogana

A son therefore of the 1962 Belmont Stakes winner, and half-brother to the Poule d'Essai des Poulains winner Blue Tom, and the Prix du Jockey-Club runner-up Timmy My Boy, Amber Rama never won beyond six furlongs, the distance of the Prix Morny, for two-year-olds, in which he easily beat Breton, who just as comfortably reversed the form in the furlong-longer Prix de la Salamandre the same year. Earlier, he had won the Prix de la Reine Blanche at Chantilly and the Prix Robert Papin at Maisons-Lafitte from Irish Word, Belmino and Caro. The next season he took fourth place in Nijinsky's 2,000 Guineas before reverting to his proper trip and beating the course record in the King's Stand Stakes at Royal Ascot, with Hunter-combe, Balidar, Prince Tenderfoot, Raffingora and Tribal Chief behind him.

By the end of 1976 Amber Rama had sired the winners of 29 races at home, but probably his most impressive runners so far have been the French-based colts, Earth Spirit and Comeram, both from his first crop. Earth Spirit, out of Eagle Eye, by Victory Morn, won three times as a two-year-old in France in 1975, when he also ran second, at a head, to Take Your Place in the Observer Gold Cup. He reappeared to take the 1976 Prix Jean Prat at Chantilly, before being placed second in the St James's Palace Stakes on the disqualification of Patris, who had dead-heated with Radetzky, and running sixth of nine $6\frac{1}{2}$ lengths behind Wollow in the Sussex Stakes. Comeram, who is now in America, was a short-head second to Northern

Amber Rama.

Treasure in the Irish 2,000 Guineas. A son of Comely, by Boran, Comeram won three races in France as a two-year-old, and was placed second to Manado in the Grand Criterium. At three he was the all-the-way winner of the Prix de Pontarme at Chantilly. Pristina, who in 1977 visited Dancer's Image, has a year-younger, and much less distinguished, full sister at Brook Stud in Petitpoint. Of the other mares on the place, the most gifted racer was Shebeen, by Saint Crespin III out of the Nearco mare Bacchanalia. Shebeen, winner of the Houghton Stakes on her only appearance as a two-year-old, was kept off the course by the virus until the August of her three-year-old season, but still managed to win the Cumberland Lodge Stakes and the Princess Royal Stakes. The latter triumph was repeated in the course of a four-year-old campaign which also brought victory in the 1975 Jockey Club Stakes, her last season before preparing for an assignation with Reform. Her dam, put down at Brook Stud in 1976, was a stayer, and produced the 1964 Northumberland Plate winner, Peter Piper (by Faubourg II), as well as two other winners at two miles in Rustalia (by Rustam) and Carlburg (by Crepello). She was also the dam of Lady Bingo (by Match III), a winner in Italy, where she ran fourth in the Oaks, and of the good miler Revellarie (by Romulus).

Mares and foals being brought in at the Brook Stud.

The Brook Stud is run as a commercial operation, and almost everything is sold except the fillies needed to perpetuate the successful families. 'We sell the lousy ones as foals,' Butt remarks, but most of the stock is nowadays offered at the Houghton Sales, where the Brook Stud draft of seven aggregated 175,100 guineas in 1976. The previous year the Brook yearlings averaged 8,860 guineas, compared with 11,716 guineas in 1972, their first year at the Houghton. Before that Brook Stud yearlings had a consistently successful record at the October Sales. 'I should say that Jim Philipps and I are about the only breeders in the Newmarket area making a profit at the moment,' says Butt. 'In those circumstances there must be a very strong case for breeders' prizes to be introduced in this country too.'

Dalham Hall Stud

The Hon James Perrott Philipps, Managing Director of Dalham Stud Farms Ltd., has a sharper eye than most for the opportunities offered by the Kentucky-based stallions, and he took an interest in both Youth and Empery, when they retired to stud at Gainesway for the 1977 season. To Empery he sent Stogumber and I've-a-Bee; to Youth Lalibela. Skyjinni, a mare in which Dalham owns a half-interest, also visited the 1976 French Derby and Washington D.C. International winner. Both I've-a-Bee (Sir Ivor – Honey Portion, by Major Portion) and Skyjinni (Nijinsky – Swift Lady, by Sailor) are themselves American-bred, while Stogumber is by Habitat, a product of the Nuckols Brothers' Hurstland Farm in the Blue Grass, out of Another Daughter, by Crepello. Lalibela (Honeyway – Blue Mark, by Blue Train) is dam of Million (by Mill Reef), the colt for which Lady Beaverbrook paid the record British price of 202,000 guineas at the Houghton Sales in 1975, when the Dalham Hall draft of seven fetched 369,000 guineas, comfortably the best-ever average and aggregate achieved by a vendor on this side of the Atlantic, despite the fact that Etienne Gerard was kept back. That year Dalham Hall also finished in the top twenty on the breeders' list with winners of close on £40,000.

'Jim' Philipps's father, Sir Laurence (later Lord Milford) founded Dalham Hall Stud at Gazeley in 1928, the name being transferred to the present farm, previously known as Derisley, in 1970, when Patrick McCalmont bought the original spread. The stud was established to stand Flamingo, winner of the 2,000 Guineas and second in the Derby in 1928, the first horse Sir Laurence owned, bought at the Doncaster Yearling Sales on his behalf by Jack Jarvis. Jarvis, who had been given the commission to buy when he happened to meet Sir Laurence to seek permission to course hares at Six Mile Bottom, remained the Philipps trainer for many years. Flamingo, by Tracery's son Flamboyant, out of White Eagle's daughter, Lady Peregrine, had the successful jumps sire Flamenco in his first crop, and also got the 1939 Ascot Gold Cup winner, Flyon, out of Acquit, by Hurry On, but was generally a disappointment at stud. Flamingo's half-brother Horus (by Papyrus), also bought as a yearling, ran fourth in the 1929 St Leger for Sir Laurence before retiring to stand at the newly-acquired Derisley, one of five farms to have been carved out of Sir Alex Black's enormous stud when he died. The present Someries, Hadrian, Dunchurch Wood and Derisley Wood studs were also fragments of this property, which lay between the

Above: *Flamingo, C. Elliott up, 2,000 Guineas winner of 1928*. Right: *The Hon J. P. Philipps and stud groom Alec Notman with Great Nephew*.

Newmarket Railway Station and the Cheveley/Stetchworth Road. Sir Laurence purchased Lady Peregrine, a half sister to the 1917 Kentucky Derby winner, Omar Khayyam, on the death of her owner, Sir John Robinson, and bred, in 1931, a full sister to Horus, Honey Buzzard, who in turn dropped the great Dalham Hall stallion Honeyway in 1941. Honeyway, who numbered the July Cup, the Victoria Cup, the Cork and Orrery Stakes and the Champion Stakes among his 16 victories, sired the winners of 744 races. His son, the current Dalham Hall stallion, Great Nephew (ex Sybil's Niece, by Admiral's Walk) is a grandson of the Philipps foundation mare Sybil's Sister (Nearco – Sister Sarah), bought as a three-year-old at the 1946 December Sales. Sybil's Niece, whose three victories included the Queen Mary Stakes at Royal Ascot, is half-sister to the winners Sybil's Nephew, Welsh Nephew, Rich Relation, Sybil's Boy, Sweet Delphine and Saint Sybil. There are two daughters of Sybil's Niece in the Dalham Hall broodmare band at present – Another Daughter, who has produced the minor winners Stogumber and Another Princess (by King Emperor), and whose son by Habitat fetched 53,000 guineas at the 1976 Houghton Sales, and Aunty Mabel (by Sir Ivor) whose son Our Brigadier by Brigadier Gerard, was among the foals of 1975 retained by Philipps and who is now in training with Bruce Hobbs. Aunty Mabel was the result of a nomination given to

Philipps by his friend, Raymond Guest, who was also responsible for introducing him to Vincent O'Brien.

I've-a-Bee's dam is one of three granddaughters of Honey Buzzard at Dalham Hall, half sisters out of Run Honey, by Hyperion. The eldest of them, foaled in 1957, is Running Blue who was rested in 1975 and mated for the last time in 1976, when she visited Mill Reef, and few things would give Philipps greater pleasure than to see her foal, due on June 2, bring a final distinction to the career of one of his favourite mares. 'She should have won the Oaks,' he says, 'but Jarvis scratched her without telling me. He must have got out of the wrong side of bed that morning, and decided she wouldn't stay. Anyway, she was still in the Lingfield Trial, so we ran her there in heavy going, and she couldn't have won more easily. Poor old Jack was very upset about it afterwards, and, of course, he never won the Oaks. He died before Sleeping Partner ran in the race, so she was sent to Doug Smith.' Running Blue, who had already won the Free Handicap, and run third in the 1,000 Guineas, never won again, although she did finish second in the Coronation Stakes and fourth in the Princess of Wales's Stakes before retiring to the stud, where she has produced seven individual winners in Dominion Day (by Charlottesville), Saintly Blue (by St Paddy), Relkarunner (by Relko), Northern Tavern (by Charlottesville) Sir Penfro (by Sir Ivor), Burleigh (by Charlottown) and Padroug (by Sir Ivor). Another of the 1975 foals retained by Philipps, Ivor's Honey (by Sir Ivor), now in training with Vincent O'Brien, is out of Honey Portion, and half-sister to some useful

75

winners in Honeyville (by Charlottesville), Praefectus (by Primera), Cider Honey (by Alcide), Honey Crepe (by Crepello) and I've-a-Bee. Honey Portion produced a Mill Reef colt in 1976, and was due to Grundy before visiting Habitat in 1977, while her half-sister Honey Match (by Match III), dropped a Rheingold filly in January 1977 before visiting Home Guard. Her son by Thatch fetched 48,000 guineas at the Houghton Sales in 1976, while, the year before, 17,000 guineas was paid for her daughter by King Emperor, Miellita, winner of Goodwood's 1976 Selsey Stakes first time out. Honey Match's second foal, Honey Sea (1973), by Sea Hawk II, is a winner in Germany.

At the 1976 Houghton Sales the last foal of Welsh Way, a daughter of Abernant out of Honeyway's own sister Winning Ways, was sold for 6,000 guineas. Winner of the Acorn Stakes at Epsom in 1956, and twice successful in Newmarket handicaps as a three-year-old, Welsh Way bred the winners Welsh Dee (by Alcide), Picton (by Ballymoss) and Welsh Saint (by St Paddy), who won six times, earned £8,538 and is now a successful stallion at the Collinstown Stud, County Kildare.

Both Honeyway and Great Nephew were rigs during their racing careers, and the last Philipps heard of the latter's son, Full of Hope, who was still running as a seven-year-old in France during 1977, his condition remained a fine advertisement for the proposition that monorchism is hereditable. Honeyway's deficiency was the reason for the provision, in the syndication agreement made after his victory in the 1946 Champion Stakes, that all monies should be refunded in the event of his proving infertile, as, indeed, he did. Returning to the track, Honeyway notched three further wins to bring his career earnings to £10,919 14s 6d before Jarvis was able to ring Lord Milford and gleefully announce:'That ball's come down.' Great Nephew, after three seasons' racing, blossomed at just the right time, and returned an 89 per cent fertility record in his first crop, foaled in 1969. He continued in fine fettle, and in 1974 got all his mares in foal, a fact which Philipps now regrets publicising, since breeders then sent him their oldest and most difficult mares, barren, in some case, for several seasons. Still, the mares he got in foal in 1976 included Crystal Palace (Solar Slipper – Queen of Light, by Borealis), foaled in 1956 and dam of Royal Palace, and the 1957 daughter of Vimy, out of Martial Loan, by Court Martial, Sans Le Sou, dam of Busted. Great Nephew was Honeyway's highest stakes winner, with earnings, including place money, of £12,376 in England and 735,955 francs in France. At two, although Jarvis held no very high opinion of him, he won the Norfolk Stakes at Newmarket, where he also participated in a race started from stalls, then being phased in by the Jockey Club, to the disgust of many conservative elements. The splendid Jarvis was naturally one of them, but Philipps, as a Jockey Club member, decided to take a lead, and so Great Nephew reported for the rehearsal which in those days was compulsory before stalls races. He was ridden by the stable's second jockey, Stan Smith, who claimed acquaintance from India with the new contraption, and accompanied by a pony to

Two great trainers : Sir Jack Jarvis (left) *and Etienne Pollet.*

show him the way. The pony, of course, dug in and refused to enter, while Great Nephew submitted like a lamb. He went on to run second in the 1966 2,000 Guineas, ridden by Bill Rickaby, specially brought out of retirement for the race. Rickaby followed the trainer's instructions – to ride him like Honeyway – to the letter, and had him well dropped out at the Bushes, but found that he did not quite have the foot to catch Jimmy Lindley on Kashmir II, who beat him a short head. More misfortune followed in the Lockinge, when Paul Cook pulled up on Great Nephew too soon, and was mortified to discover the photograph had gone against him. Since the horse was not entered for any more good races, Philipps suggested to Jarvis that they might go to France, but the old trainer's view of that country and its denizens was decidedly dim, and he would have no truck with the scheme. Jacqueline O'Brien suggested that Great Nephew be sent to Etienne Pollet, and she put Philipps in telephone contact with the French trainer, whom he did not then know. Pollet's considerable international reputation owed nothing to a willingness to accommodate more horses than his yard could comfortably take, but his initial reluctance evaporated when he learned the identity of his proposed new charge, whose Guineas run he had seen, noting on his race-card that Great Nephew, who had slipped up in his trial at Kempton and was effectively without a race that year, looked the pick of the field but unfit. Great Nephew, he observed to Philipps on the telephone, was the only horse in the world he would consider taking on at that time, and although the Gallic exaggeration of the compliment would doubtless have made Jarvis scowl, the move proved entirely beneficial, with victory that year in the Prix Michel Houyvet at Deauville, and 1967 wins in the Prix de Paques at

Le Tremblay, the Prix Dollar at Longchamp and the Prix de Moulin de Longchamp. He also ran second to Busted in the Eclipse. Great Nephew, thanks largely to Grundy, was champion sire in 1975, with £291,048.70 won by his progeny in England, while his 16 individual winners at home in 1976 captured 32 races worth £38,189.20. All in, he had 42·1976 winners, who earned £272,860 from their 112 victories.

Full of Hope, trained by G. Delloye, in 1976 beat Trepan three lengths in the Prix Edmond Blanc at St Cloud, won the Prix du Chemin de Fer du Nord from Gravelines at Chantilly, and beat Ivanjica, by 2½ lengths in the Prix d'Ispahan at Longchamp. He is a son of the enormous Alpine Bloom (Chamossaire – Fragrant View, by Panorama), herself the winner of four races worth £4,895, and third in the 1958 1,000 Guineas. He was such a size as a yearling that the Dalham Hall grooms regarded him as unsellable, until Pollet turned up and gave 14,000 guineas.

Fragrant View produced in 1959 a full sister to Alpine Bloom in Alpine Scent, who dead-heated for the Hyperion Stakes and won two other races. Her daughter of 1966, Fragrant Morn (by Mourne), bred by Monsieur E. Coupey, was at the Dalham Stud until November 30, 1976, when, together with Piccadilly Lil and Victorian Era, she was weeded out of the broodmare team and sent to the Newmarket Sales. Fragrant Morn, whose first foal, Alpine Nephew, won £14,107 and ran third in the Observer Gold Cup of 1973, was knocked down for 9,400 guineas. She was in foal to Great Nephew, as was Victorian Era (High Hat – Palmy Days, by Epigram), who fetched 5,000 guineas. Piccadilly Lil, winner of the Blue Seal Stakes at Ascot in 1969, was bred by the Middleton Park Stud. By Pall Mall out of Northern Beauty, by Borealis, and half-sister to 12 other winners, she was in foal to Welsh Pageant at the time of her sale. A few weeks previously her Upper Case filly had fetched 3,000 guineas there, the cheapest of the 1976 Dalham Hall draft. The most recent addition to the band is Pilgrim Soul (Tudor Melody – The Nun, by Saint Crespin III), a two-year-old winner at Salisbury in 1974, bought from the Hon J. J. Astor at the 1975 December Sales for 6,200 guineas. She produced her first foal, an Upper Case filly, on February 26, 1977, and then visited Star Appeal.

The distaff side at Dalham Hall provides ample confirmation of the Philipps faith in the best American bloodlines. Two of the mares, bred at Darby Dan Farm, were bought privately, for 20,000 guineas each, after they had been led out unsold from the Newmarket ring in December, 1970. Neither Oh So Fair (Graustark – Chamdelle, by Swaps) nor Little Firefly (Bold Ruler – Indian Nurse, by Mahmoud) had achieved more than minor victories when racing in Ireland, and Vincent O'Brien advised John Galbreath that they were not worth keeping. Oh So Fair, whose second dam, Malindi, was own sister to Nasrullah, has made a great start at stud. Her first foal, Roussalka (1972), by Habitat, won the Cherry Hinton Stakes, the Coronation Stakes, the Nassau Stakes twice and a total of seven races worth £49,675. Oh So Fair's second foal was the useful winner My Fair Niece (by

Great Nephew), her third Etienne Gerard, his sire's first winner, who took two races in 1976 worth £3,528.50, and the Jersey Stakes at Royal Ascot in 1977. Philipps now has Oh So Fair's 1975 son by Mill Reef, Palm Island, in training with Vincent O' Brien. Barren to Charlottown in 1976, having been covered only once, Oh So Fair dropped a full-sister to Roussalka on February 1, 1977, and then visited Busted. The relatively disappointing Little Firefly's foals thus far are Great Firefly (1972), by Great Nephew, who was once placed second, Heavenly Spark (1974), by Habitat, who changed hands at the Houghton Sales for 30,000 guineas and then joined Scobie Breasley in France, a Run the Gantlet colt, sold for 5,000 guineas in 1976 and a Busted filly, foaled in 1976. All three fillies bred by Dalham Hall that year were kept back, the others being by Thatch out of Piccadilly Lil and by Great Nephew out of Grey Shoes. Great Firefly is now back at Dalham, having already produced her first foal, by Star Appeal. She was sent to Run the Gantlet in 1977. The Raymond Guest-bred Goosie, bought at the Saratoga Yearling Sales in 1970, won three times in Ireland and once at Ascot, before retiring to the stud. Her first foal, unraced as a two-year-old, was Goosie Gantlet, by Run the Gantlet, and she went on to produce a King Emperor colt in 1975, and a Rheingold colt in 1976. She produced a Brigadier Gerard foal in 1977, when she was sent to Grundy. Goosie, a daughter of Sea Bird II, was first foal of the unraced Tom Fool mare, Belle Foulee, and cost Philipps $200,000.

Goosie and her foal by Brigadier Gerard.

Mares and foals being brought in from the paddocks to their boxes.

Oulanova, who joined the Dalham Hall broodmare band only a couple of months before Pilgrim Soul, was bred in France, but her pedigree is purely American. A daughter of Nijinsky out of the Johns Joy mare Our Model, she was a winner at Saint Cloud in 1975 before being consigned to the Deauville Sales by her breeder, the Comtesse de Chambure. She was mated in 1976 with Great Nephew, and in 1977 she visited Brigadier Gerard.

Before the War Philipps indulged his first love, and avoided competing with his father, by keeping mares to breed steeplechasers at Stoke Mandeville and at Stondon Massey. At the 1938 Newmarket December Sales he managed to get Lord Derby's Sweet Lavender, twice barren to Pharos, for 30 guineas. He sent her to Horus, who immediately did the trick, but both the mare and her filly foal, Hyssop, were put down on Lord Milford's orders while Philipps was away serving with the Leicestershire (Prince Albert's Own) Yeomanry. When he returned in 1946, the responsibility for the Gazeley stud devolved on him, and the jumpers were gradually dropped, although, as he ruefully recalls, the 1963 Grand National winner, Ayala, was bred here. 'We sent the mare to the 1950 Ascot Gold Cup winner, Supertello, but everyone said the foal was no good, so we got rid of him very cheaply,' he says. 'It was naturally particularly galling that he should have won at Aintree from Carrickbeg, who was owned by my nephew Gay Kindersley, and ridden by John.'

After the War the Tesio-bred stallions Naucide, Nicolaus and Nakamuro each spent a few seasons at the stud, and then Philipps stood the late Frank Measures's Grey Sovereign, who retired at the time the Gazeley property was sold. He died, aged 28, at Keith Freeman's stud in January 1976. As a racehorse Grey Sovereign (Nasrullah – Kong, by Baytown) displayed much of his sire's temperament, and was particularly difficult at the starting gate. Nevertheless, in three seasons' racing, he won eight races, worth £8,162, before embarking on a stud career, which produced the winners of 503 races worth £400,000. Grey Sovereign has continued to exert considerable influence in recent years, principally through his son Sovereign Path, who stands at the Burgage Stud, County Carlow, Ireland, and whose progeny includes Wolver Hollow, Humble Duty, Spanish Express, Warpath, Petite Path, Supreme Sovereign, Town Crier, Royal Match, Miss Paris, Estaminet, Sovereign Eagle, Alaska Highway, Everything Nice and Damastown. 'We never got a good Grey Sovereign for ourselves, though,' Philipps says. 'The only one on the place now was bought by Vincent O'Brien as a yearling.' This is Grey Shoes (ex Evening Shoe, by Panaslipper), bred by Commander N. J. W. Barttelo and foaled in 1970, a winner at two in Ireland and at Yarmouth the next season. In 1977 she visited Grundy.

Philipps took over the Derisley Stud, in Duchess Drive, Newmarket, in 1957, and later stood Charles Engelhard's Romulus, Indiana and Tin King there as well as Honeyway, who remained active at stud until his son was ready to take over. When the old Dalham Hall Stud was sold to McCalmont, who was required to rename the place 'Gazeley', Philipps appointed Alec Notman, who had been second man at Lord Derby's Woodland Stud for 15 years, as his manager. Notman remembers Ribot from his season at Woodland as by no means the firebrand he was subsequently supposed to have become, although he did have one or two idiosyncrasies not incompatible with some form of Italian maltreatment.

Dalham Hall was formed into a limited company to avoid the ravages of estate duty, but Philipps now regrets the move in the light of subsequent changes in fiscal law, and sells all his yearlings one year in every three to meet the authorities' requirement that he show a profit at least that often. In 1977 all seven yearling colts at Dalham were destined for the sales ring. That year Ivor's Honey was one of three fillies in Philipps's eight-strong racing string, the others, also two-year-olds, being Running Ballerina (Nijinsky – Running Blue), in training with Bruce Hobbs, and Liebfraumilch (Rheingold – Lalibela), who was with Michael Stoute.

Philipps is not entirely convinced now that it was a good idea to sell the Gazeley property, since the 158 acres of the new Dalham Hall Stud sometimes seem a little cramped and he would not nowadays stand a second stallion unless it was necessary to ensure the transfer to England of one or other of the American-based stallions which he thinks rightfully belong there. He took the opportunity of mentioning to Nelson Bunker Hunt at the 1976 Washington D.C. International that it would make more sense to stand Empery in England, while it also seemed obvious that the services of Vaguely Noble would be more appreciated by European breeders than by the Americans.

Barring some such dramatic move – and John Gaines must be unlikely to endorse the Philipps view – there are no plans to take shares in any more stallions. Philipps, at the moment, has three in Great Nephew and one each in Brigadier Gerard, Habitat, Mill Reef, Run the Gantlet, Relko, St Paddy, Upper Case, Welsh Pageant and Welsh Saint, while, of course, nominations are annually bought to others.

A new covering yard, built at Dalham Hall in 1975, doubles as a covered exercise area in early-season bad weather, the trying board swivelling back against the wall. There are two American-style barns on the farm, one with 12 boxes, one with 20, while the main yard can take 30 mares. There is an isolation unit at Philipps's home nearby, and mares returning from abroad are always turned out in the paddocks there. The Dalham Hall paddocks are harrowed and rolled in the spring, and dressed every third year with calcified seaweed. Droppings are mechanically collected and the pasture is grazed in the summer by Charollais/Jersey cross cattle bred by Mrs Philipps.

Brigadier Gerard wins the 1972 King George VI and Queen Elizabeth Stakes at Ascot from Parnell and Riverman. Bottom: *Word From Lundy at Dalham Hall with her colt foal by Habitat.*

Plantation Stud

It is ironic that the highest stakes winner to have come from the Senior Steward's blue-blooded stock so far should have been a jumper, yet Lanzarote had earned that distinction by the time he was killed in 1977 trying to become the first former champion hurdler to take the Cheltenham Gold Cup. Lanzarote, who earned £61,215 over jumps and also won a 15-furlong Edinburgh maiden race as a three-year-old in 1971, was by Milesian out of Slag, by Mossborough, and a year younger own brother to Rio Tinto, who was *in utero* when Lord Howard de Walden bought the dam. In 1966 Slag, who had only one ovary, had dropped Scoria, by Kalydon, winner of the 1970 Cesarewitch. Slag was sold in 1971 carrying Tudor Flame, by Sing Sing, who won a moderate event at Salisbury as a two-year-old. Her last foal in Lord Howard's ownership, Remodel, by Abernant or Reform, made up into a nice filly and won three races at three years old before fracturing her femur on the way to Newbury races and being put down.

Ken White brings Comedy of Errors over the last in the 1974 Cheltenham Trial Hurdle, with Lanzarote (Richard Pitman) in second place. They finished in that order.

Top left: *Hyperion at Newmarket in 1933*. Top right: *Lord Derby's Sansovino, with T. Weston up, after winning the 1924 Derby*. Bottom left: *Lord Derby's Fair Copy at Epsom in 1937*. Bottom right: *Epsom Races, 1925. Lord Derby with his son Lord Stanley* (left) *and the Hon George Lambton* (centre).

Hyperion, Fair Copy, Sansovino, Borealis and Nepenthe all held court at Plantation when it was owned by the Earl of Derby, who sold the place to Lord Howard in July 1958. Lord Howard brought all his mares over from

Cheveley Park and, three years later, purchased the Templeton Stud in Berkshire, where he now sends all his young stock in the autumn. Lord Howard is the outright owner of So Blessed, who stands at his Thornton Stud, near Thirsk, which was acquired from Lady Sassoon in 1967 and which used to belong to the Earl of Derby too. Established by Commander Clare-Vyner and taken over by the 17th Earl in 1918, the stud was eventually relinquished by the 18th Earl to R. C. Colling, who, a year later, sold out to Sir Victor Sassoon.

Of the horses which went with the Thornton Stud when Lord Howard bought it, the most notable was Parmelia, a half-sister to St Paddy by Bally-moss, who won the Ribblesdale Stakes at Ascot and the Park Hill Stakes at Doncaster in 1970, as well as being placed in all her other races that year – the Musidora Stakes, the Irish Guinness Oaks, the Princess Royal Stakes, the Prix Vermeille and the Golden Hind Stakes. Her first two foals were winners, Rebec, by Tudor Melody, taking the Cecil Frail Stakes at Haydock and the Compton Stakes at Newbury as a three-year-old in 1975, Ormeley, by Crepello, recording his one victory the same year, as a juvenile, in the Sancton

Borealis.

Stakes at York. Rebec was sold at Newmarket in September 1976, for 3,400 guineas; Ormeley fetched 26,000 guineas there in December as a stallion prospect for Australia. Lord Howard also bought the Sassoon mares Soft Angels, Collyria, Amorella, Golden Dusk, Lotus Blue and Queen's Keys at the time of the Thornton Stud purchase.

Dark Ronald.

Lord Howard's original plan for 1977 was to send no fewer than five of his mares to So Blessed, but in the event Doubly Sure visited the Gestüt Schlenderhan's Priamos, leaving Benita, Collyria, Fortune's Darling and Soft Angels to travel to the Thornton Stud – still, by the standards of most breeders, quite a few eggs to have in one basket. The German stallion is a tail-male descendant of Dark Ronald, purchased from England for £25,000, who stood at the Hauptgestüt Graditz and was champion sire from 1918 to 1922 inclusive. A dominant influence on German thoroughbred stock, Dark Ronald sired Prunus, sire of the Gestüt Schlenderhan's Oleander, one of the greatest racehorses to have been bred in that country. Priamos's sire Birkhahn won the German Derby in 1958 and was leading stallion in 1965, 1967, 1968 and 1970. Priamos himself raced for four seasons – although injury prevented his running more than once at three – and scored in 14 races to earn £66,000, his victories including the Prix Dollar at Longchamp, the Prix Jacques le Marois at Deauville, the Grosser Preis von Dortmund, the Grosser Preis von Gelsenkirchen and the Zukunfts-Rennen at Baden-Baden. A foal of 1964, he is out of the Dante mare Palazzo.

Doubly Sure (by Reliance II), dam of Kris (1976) by Sharpen Up, and an Amber Rama filly dropped on March 26 the next year, had her finest moment on the track when running second in the Bedale Plate at Thirsk as a three-year-old in 1974. The unfortunate stud record of her dam, Soft Angels (Crepello – Sweet Angel, by Honeyway), however, suggests that she might have a crucial role to play in perpetuating the family at Plantation. Soft Angels' first, and best, foal was the Tudor Melody filly Dulcet, dropped in 1968, who won the Findon Stakes at Goodwood and the Bridget Handicap at Epsom, but died before being covered. In 1969 Soft Angels produced the Romulus filly Wolfling, whose racing career was hampered by a broken pelvis, but since then Doubly Sure has been her only live foal. Wolfling was sent to the Newmarket December Sales in 1975, when she was knocked down for 2,000 guineas, along with Lord Howard's Electric Blue, who fetched 100 guineas more. Electric Blue was bred in the hope that she might combine the blinding pace of her sire, Sing Sing, with the toughness and gameness which characterised the four-year racing career of her dam, Blue Over, by Democratic. It didn't quite work out like that, though, and Electric Blue recorded just one small success at two years old, and two at three. At Plantation she produced Grill Room (1973), by Connaught, Eltham (1974), by Royal Palace, and Fused, by Busted. The family has now disappeared from the stud.

When Lord Howard bought Amorella, by Crepello, she was carrying Calzado, by Saint Crespin III, winner of two flat races, nine hurdles and two steeplechases, but probably best known as Lanzarote's pacemaker. Amorella also produced Flirtigig, by Silly Season, for Lord Howard, a winner once in 1971 and once in 1972 and now dam of the winner Miss Pert, by Roan Rocket. Lotus Blue, by Charlottesville, is another of the former Sassoon mares to have a daughter on the Plantation Stud – Jujube, by Ribero, winner of five races from six attempts as a three-year-old in 1975 and now dam of a High Top colt. Queen's Keys, by Right Royal V, a half-sister to Paddington and to Abbie West, is still on the Plantation Stud, but Golden Dusk, by Aureole, has been sold on. Her son by So Blessed, Beatic, is now a stallion at the Vine House Stud, near Preston.

Altogether Lord Howard has had to suffer more than his fair share of disappointments with potential breeding stock in recent years. In 1975 his Guipure, by Crepello, was developing into a useful two-year-old before she had to be shot at Lingfield. A half-sister to seven winners, including Entanglement and Magic Flute, now a Plantation broodmare, Guipure was out of Filigrana (Niccolo – Gamble in Gold, by Big Game), who was purchased by Lord Howard in 1956. Another grievous blow was the loss of Almiranta, who had to be put down in 1972 after producing just one foal to live, which was destroyed as a yearling anyway. The winner of the Princess Elizabeth Stakes and the Park Hill Stakes, Almiranta was out of the talented but ungenuine Rosario, a full sister to Amerigo (Nearco – Sanlinea, by Precipitation). Lord Howard bought Sanlinea as a yearling in 1948 for £8,100. Winner of the 1,000 Guineas Trial at Kempton and third in the St Leger to Scratch II, she produced seven winners for Lord Howard, easily the best being Amerigo, who ran in England only as a two-year-old, winning the Coventry Stakes by

Left to right: *Boarding mares Honeygail and Photo Flash, with her Mill Reef colt; Lord Howard de Walden's Major Barbara, with her Busted colt, and his Pot Pourri with a filly by Welsh Pageant; Palmintin (boarder) with her Saritamer filly.*

six lengths but achieving little else of note, In America, however, he was magically transformed, winning 12 races and $419,171. He went on to become a successful sire, particularly of broodmares. Of Rosario's six foals, five were winners. Her daughter Antalya, successful in the Lord Orford Stakes at Newmarket, became dam of Attalus (Washington Singer Stakes, Newbury, Doonside Cup and Scarborough Stakes, Doncaster) as well as a couple of decent winners in South Africa. Another daughter, Pot Pourri, by Busted, after winning four races worth £3,139.70 as a three-year-old in 1973, returned to Plantation and was mated initially with Roan Rocket, the resulting colt being named Potshot. In 1976 she produced a Brigadier Gerard filly, and in 1977 a Welsh Pageant filly.

Lord Howard's other important foundation mare, Silvery Moon (Solario – Silver Fox II, by Foxhunter) was also bought in 1948 when, in foal to Watling Street, she cost £6,800. Her six winners included two fillies who were to become in turn successful broodmares, Malcomia, by Sayani, and Argentina, by Nearco. Malcomia, who numbered the Ebbisham Stakes at Epsom among her three victories, produced Oncidium, by Alcide, in 1961.

The winner of the Coronation Cup at Epsom, the Lingfield Derby Trial, the Jockey Club Cup at Newmarket, the Royal Stakes at Sandown Park and the Cocked Hat Stakes at Goodwood for a total of £26,589, Oncidium might well have won the Ascot Gold Cup as well if he hadn't been doped. He went on to great success at stud in New Zealand. His half-sister by Hornbeam, Ostrya, won the Ribblesdale Stakes in 1963 and ran second in the Park Hill Stakes before joining the broodmare band at Plantation, where she has been consistently successful. She was visiting Habat for the third successive year in 1977, after producing a grey filly, Laelia, in 1976 and then slipping twins. The seventh of her foals to win, Catalpa, by Reform, was an impressive, surprise winner of the Ribblesdale Stakes in 1976 before retiring to visit Habitat. There were two other four-year-old debutantes on the stud in 1977, Helcia (by Habitat out of Bella Paola's half-sister Rhevona, by Rockavon), who cost Lord Howard 21,000 guineas as a yearling, and the home-bred Dame Foolish (Silly Season – Major Barbara, by Tambourine II), whose half-sister by Hard Sauce, Hardware, three times a winner at three in 1973, is also at Plantation. Helcia, who usually made the frame in her races, but never won, visited Welsh Pageant; Dame Foolish, twice a winner at two, and second in both the Cheveley Park Stakes and the Nell Gwyn Stakes, went to High Top.

Those splendid racers Falkland (by Right Royal V), Averof (by Sing Sing) and Tierra Fuego (by Shantung) are probably the best-known of the

string of good horses produced by Argentina, three times a winner herself. Unfortunately for Lord Howard he sold the mare carrying Averof.

The Plantation Stud covers 140 acres and has 51 boxes. It boards mares visiting Newmarket stallions each season with H. J. Joel and Rozza Dormello-Olgiata among its biggest and most distinguished clients. Every horse bred by Lord Howard, who currently has 18 broodmares, goes into training, Henry Cecil, Peter Walwyn and Ernie Weymes having charge of the flat racers, Fred Winter the jumpers. Perhaps his most prominent runner at the moment is Fool's Mate (Busted – Spring Fever, by Botticelli), P.T.S. Laurels Stakes winner from Royal Match in 1976. Fool's Mate, whose third dam, Social Gulf, was purchased by Lord Howard in 1951, is a half-brother to the minor winner of 1975, Simmering, by Ribero. Both are gelded, the operation on Fool's Mate having been performed on the same day as he was hobdayed. Perhaps, Plantation Stud manager Leslie Harrison observes, the breed would be sounder if this were normal practice.

Lord Howard paid a record £25,000 for a filly out of training when he bought Lost Soul's granddaughter Fortune's Darling in 1959. That year, as a three-year-old, she had won only one minor event at Stockton to supplement her two important juvenile successes in the Great Surrey Foal Stakes at Epsom and the Lowther Stakes at York, bringing her total earnings in first place money to £6,416 13s. The old mare, whose two-year-old daughter by Connaught, Cassiar, and whose three-year-old son by Ribero, the gelded Carissimo, were with Henry Cecil in 1977, dropped a Ribero filly on March 4 that year having proved barren to So Blessed in 1976. By Fair Trial out of Tinted Venus, by Tudor Minstrel, she has produced several minor winners, the best of them, Roan Rocket's daughter Benita, winning once as a two-year-old in 1970 and twice in 1971 over sprint distances. Benita's first foal, the gelded Hell Bent, by Busted, ran once in 1976 as a juvenile, down the field at the York September Meeting.

Lord Howard also splashed out a bit at the December Sales in 1971 when he paid 30,000 guineas for Pampas Flower (Pampered King – Verdura, by Court Martial), who had proved disappointing on the track, with one modest win from nine outings in two seasons' racing. She belongs, however, to a family which consistently produces winners. Of her dam's twelve surviving foals, eleven were successful on the track, Gratitude, Pharsalia, Heathen and Highest Hopes being the best of them. Gratitude and Heathen are both sires now, while Pharsalia is herself dam of eight winners, and Highest Hope's first foal is the winner Highest. Verdura (by Court Martial) was out of Bura (Bahram – Becti, by Salmon Trout), dam of Bazura, who was exported to the United States and there produced not only Bagdad, but also his full

Above left: *Maiden mares at Plantation*. Left to right: *Mrs O. Fox Pitt's Great Granddaughter and Lord Howard de Walden's Dame Foolish and Helcia*. Left: *Stud groom Pat Burstow with Hardware and her colt foal by Brigadier Gerard*.

brother Bazaar, the winner of 16 races and $71,268, who is now a sire. Bura produced five winners altogether. Pampas Flower's first foal, a Royal Palace gelding named Queluz, has won on the flat and over hurdles, while her two-year-old daughter, La Pampa, by Crepello, was with Peter Walwyn in 1977, when Pampas Flower visited Thatch after dropping a Reform filly on February 20.

In 1977 So Blessed's speedy two-year-old Edna's Choice seemed likely to add to the reputation of Lord Howard's stallion, which rests principally, so far, on the achievements of Duboff, Honeyblest and Blessed Rock. A crack sprinter by Princely Gift out of Lavant, by Le Lavandou, So Blessed, whose six victories included the 1967 Cornwallis Stakes and the 1968 Nunthorpe Stakes, earned £13,888 6s in first place money. Lord Howard also owns a third of Royal Palace in partnership with his breeder Jim Joel and Lady Macdonald-Buchanan.

It was one of Lord Howard's cheaper purchases which has probably proved his shrewdest investment to date. Looking for something to win the Brocklesby Stakes he gave 670 guineas for Vermeil, then a foal, who went on not only to oblige at Lincoln, but also to take the Albermarle Stakes at Ascot and three other races. The Senior Steward's latest acquisition is Blanche Hardy, by Ribot out of a daughter of Belladonna, who had a Sir Gaylord colt foal at foot in 1977, when she visited Bolkonski. She was bought from Rozza Dormello-Olgiata.

Pat Burstow and Leslie Harrison, with the hound Bedlam.

COUNTY KILDARE

The Curragh

The Curragh's position as Ireland's racing centre probably traces to the third century, when the Fena of Erin, exponents of the new art of horse-riding, served Finn in Kildare. Chariot racing, established at pre-Christian festivals like the Aonach Tailtean in County Meath, continued in Ireland for centuries after this, and, indeed, the Brehon laws of the 9th century laid down that every man in the country learn to drive. It is clear from the illustrations in the Book of Kells, however, that bareback riding was a conventional means of transport by A.D. 700, and ridden races remained part of the fun of the annual fair held on the Curragh.

The Curragh, which derives its name from the old Irish Cuirrech, meaning racecourse, would be the ideal environment for the breeding and running of horses were it not for the cold weather which sometimes persists throughout the Spring, and leaves the animals rather more backward than those in, say, Tipperary. In the words of the 1846 *Parliamentary Gazetteer of Ireland*, though, the Curragh is:

'a fine undulating down, rich in perpetual verdure, exceedingly soft and elastic in its sward, pleasingly variegated in its swells and irregularities of surface, and usually dotted and sprinkled all over with numerous flocks of sheep. It forms part of the great central tableau of the country, and its highest ground has an altitude of 404 feet above sea level. In its vicinity are many villas and sporting lodges built by nobility and gentry who are addicted to the pleasures of the turf. The land is the property of the Crown; an annual grant of two plates of £100 each were procured through the suggestion of Sir William Temple, with the professed design of improving the breed of Irish horses; and George IV gave great éclat to the Curragh by attending one of its meetings during his visit to Ireland. In 1234, Richard Marshall, Earl of Pembroke, and Earl Palatine of Leinster, headed a rebel army on the Curragh against the Viceroy Lord Geoffrey de Montemarisco, and was slain in battle. The plain was the scene of several other remote conflicts; and it still exhibits numerous earthen works, most of which appear to have been sepulchral.'

Sir William Temple's interest in the Irish horse was accompanied by an admirable far-sightedness, and in his *Essay upon the Advancement of Irish Trade* in 1673 he wrote: 'Horses in Ireland are a drug, but might be improved to a Commodity, not only of greater use at home, but also fit for Exportation to other countries. The soil is of a sweet and plentiful Grass which will raise

Sir William Temple, after Lely.

a large breed; and the Hills, especially near the Sea coasts, are hard and rough, and so fit to give them Shape and Breath and sound Feet.' The quality of the Irish horse had already long been recognised, and Gerald Fitzgerald, ninth Earl of Kildare, was even bold enough to match his horses against Henry VIII's stable. In 1580, Thomas Blundeville listed the 'most worthie' breeds of horses as 'the Turk, the Barbarian, the Sardinian, the Napolitain, the Jennet of Spaine, the Hungarian, the high Almaine, the Frizeland Horse, the Flanders Horse and the Irish Hobbye.'

Records remain of some of the races held on the Curragh in the 17th century. Lord Cork, for instance, backed Lord Digby's horse against one of the Earl of Ormond's there on April 1, 1634, and lost a new beaver hat to Mr Ferrers, one of the Lord Deputy's gentlemen, while, six years later, a 40 sovereign plate donated by the Duke of Leinster's trustees was run for. By 1699 John Dutton was writing in his *Conversations in Ireland* that the Curragh:

'so much noised here, is a very large plain covered in most places with heath. It is said to be five and twenty miles round. It is the Newmarket of Ireland, where the horse-races are run, and also hunting matches made, there being here great stock of hares, and moor game for hawking; all of which are carefully preserved . . . His Majesty for encouragement to breed large and serviceable horses in this Kingdom has been pleased to give £100 a year out of his Treasury here to buy a plate which they run for at the Curragh in September. The horses that run are to carry twelve stone each . . . There is another race run yearly here in March or April, for a plate of a hundred guineas, which are advanced in the subscription of several gentlemen; and the course is four measured miles.'

Cheny started listing Irish races in 1741, the first recorded being at the Curragh on April 1, when 'an annual Prize of sixty pound Value was run for, Weight ten stone, and won by the Earl of Bessborough's Dairy Maid got by Almanzer.' Ten years later a match between Sir Ralph Gore's Black and All Black (otherwise Othello by Crab) and Lord March's Bajazet was held on the Curragh. The chicanery behind Bajazet's victory – the jockey jettisoned his weights and retrieved them for the weigh-in – resulted in Gore's challenging March, later the fourth Duke of Queensberry, to a duel. At dawn the next morning March duly apologised when his opponent turned up with a coffin specially inscribed for him.

Although, in 1757, a dispute on the Curragh was referred to the Jockey Club in Newmarket, it is thought that the Irish Turf Club first met in a coffee room at Kildare around the middle of the 18th century. It was not until 1790, however, that they assumed a governing role. The first proper handicap contested in the British Isles was won at the Curragh by the top weight, F. Savage's Governor, on June 13, 1787 – four years before the Prince of Wales's Baronet won Ascot's Otlands Stakes, generally regarded as the earliest race of this type in England. At the Curragh's June meeting of 1817, the O'Darby Stakes and the Irish Oaks Stakes were run, but it was some time before a serious attempt to introduce classic races on the English pattern was made. The first Irish Derby, worth £400 to the winner, attracted three runners and went to J. Cockin's Selim in 1864. Four years later the race, over 14 furlongs, was worth £115. The surprise winner was Madeira, twice beaten the next month at Bellewstown.

The Irish National Stud

The innovative brilliance which has characterised the development of the Irish National Stud doubtless owes something to the buffer of government ownership. Since the establishment of a Stud Company under its aegis in 1946, the Ministry of Finance has pumped £2 million into the operation – £1.3 million of it for bloodstock – while the 800 acres of land, formerly the British National Stud, at Tully, are the property of the Ministry of Agriculture. However, these advantages have been capitalised on with such boldness and *élan* that the Stud has diversified into a kind of University of the Horse,

Frank Berry on Giolla Mear after his victory in the Irish St Leger.

as well as laying on a variety of services in addition to its primary function of standing stallions at a price within the reach of that 90 per cent of Irish breeders who own four mares or fewer. There is also, as a sideline, a band of 10 broodmares, and products of the Stud, like its current stallion, Giolla Mear, who failed to reach his reserve as a yearling, have in the past raced in the colours of the President of Ireland. It is quite likely that a filly or two will be kept back and leased to Mr Hillery in the near future, although, as English experience has shown, any significant development of the private stud would be unlikely to commend itself to outside breeders. As a rule, the home mares are sent to one of the Irish National Stud stallions, all of which carry a live foal concession.

If Stud Manager Michael Osborne MRCVS lacks nothing by way of modern scientific aids, new buildings and equipment, it is, perhaps, a return to nature which has proved the most startling of his successful initiatives, with Tepukei (Major Portion – Cutter, by Donatello II) being left to run with his mares. The only small variation from mating in the wild is the removal of a mare already covered, as the stallion shows a regrettable tendency towards monogamy. Results, so far, indicate a higher than normal fertility rate, despite the fact that Tepukei, who won the White Rose Stakes at Ascot and the St George's Stakes at Chester in 1973, has been given some woeful breeders – one of the mares he got in foal in 1976 had been barren for eight years. Since his first season in 1974, Tepukei has learned a great deal about the art of seduction, approaching a mare only in the latter stages of her season, and executing a couple of exploratory mounts from the side to ensure that there will be none of the kicks he suffered in his tearaway days as the paddock rapist. The free-range services of Tepukei, who covers half-bred, hunter and Irish Draught mares, as well as thoroughbreds, cost £200.

It is by no means unusual for any of the eight other Irish National Stud stallions to be wheeled out in the morning, afternoon and evening, and a couple of years ago the oldest of them, Linacre (Rockefella – True Picture, by Panorama) happily impregnated four mares in one day. The stallions are lunged immediately before morning covering, since this has apparently increased fertility at Tully, with three or four being exercised simultaneously in the same enclosure. Even Linacre, who has been known to have a go at the other stallions, is included in these sessions, albeit warily restricted to the remotest corner. The winner of the 1963 Irish 2,000 Guineas, he raced three seasons, earning £17,002 in England and Ireland, with four victories, and 129,115 French francs, with two. Bred by Lord Ennisdale and sire of Perdu, who retired to stud in England in 1975, Linacre stands at £100, half the price of the Stud's other classic winner, Swell Fellow's sire Giolla Mear (Hard Ridden – Iacobella, by Relic). When Giolla Mear took the Irish St Leger in 1968 he was ridden by his lad, Frank Berry, better known nowadays as a jumps jockey and winner of the 1972 Cheltenham Gold Cup on Glencaraig Lady. He got the mount as a replacement for jockey Powell, who was thrown against a stanchion fracturing his thigh when trying to pull the horse up

Tepukei (top) *and Linacre.*

after his victory in the Gallinule Stakes. Giolla Mear, who also won the Player's Navy Cut and the Desmond Stakes, had had, by the end of 1976, eight winners from seventeen runners.

'Bread and butter stallions', as Osborne puts it, may be the stock-in-trade

Above: *Tudor Music (foreground), Lord Gayle (left) and Sallust at a lunging session.*
Below: *Michael Osborne, Irish National Stud manager. African Sky.*

of the Irish National Stud, but there is also scope for more ambitious investment in the shapes of Sallust (Pall Mall – Bandarilla, by Matador) and African Sky (Sing Sing – Sweet Caroline, by Nimbus), standing at £2,200 and £2,000 respectively. Sallust, whose first crop included five two-year-old winners, broke the one-mile course records at Goodwood and Longchamp in winning the 1972 Sussex Stakes and Prix du Moulin. That season he also won the Diomed Stakes at Epsom, the Prix de la Porte Maillot at Longchamp and the Goodwood Mile, suffering defeat only in the 2,000 Guineas Trial at Kempton Park. At two, Sallust, who raced in the colours of his breeder, Sir Michael Sobell, had won a maiden event at Salisbury and the Richmond Stakes at Goodwood. His career earnings were £62,284. African Sky was bred by Mimie Van Cutsem and raced for Daniel Wildenstein in France, where he was beaten only once, in the Poule d'Essai des Poulains behind Kalamoun, whom he had defeated in the Prix de Fontainebleau three weeks earlier. He had two outings as a two-year-old, five at three, and won 1,065,483 francs, including 30,000 francs for his fourth in the French 2,000 Guineas. Standing their first season at Tully in 1977 were the 1975 Doncaster Cup winner Crash Course (Busted – Lucky Stream, by Persian Gulf), at a fee of £250, and the 1976 Jubilee Handicap winner Royal Match (Sovereign Path – Shortwood, by Skymaster), at £500. The stallion line-up is completed by Tudor Music (Tudor Melody – Fran II, by Acropolis), a crack sprinter, whose 1976 runners nevertheless included the two-mile Ascot Stakes winner, Tudor Crown, and Lord Gayle (Sir Gaylord – Sticky Case, by Court Martial), whose fee, at £1,250, is the third largest in the Stud. Tudor Music, who, at two, won Kempton's Imperial Stakes, the Richmond Stakes and the Gimcrack, and, at three, the Cork and Orrery, the July Cup and the Vernons Spring Cup, stands at £600. He was bred in Limerick by Audrey King. The American-bred Lord Gayle was trained in England, without racing, as a two-year-old in 1967. The next season he won a couple of races at Saratoga and then had another year off. At five he won the March Plate at Doncaster, the Thorpe Handicap at Teesside, the William Hill Gold Cup at Redcar, the Ripon Rowels Handicap, the Mitre Stakes at Ascot and the Prix Perth at Saint Cloud.

Generally speaking the Irish National Stud will not allocate nominations for mares over the age of 20, or those due to foal later than May 1. Barren maiden mares and mares barren for the two previous years, except for those sent experimentally to Tepukei, are also excluded, while the Board of Directors retain the right to veto mares they think unlikely to breed. Where a stallion is oversubscribed preference is given to Irish breeders, and those who support the Irish industry. Otherwise nominations are disposed of by ballot.

The 40-strong Tully workforce is augmented during the season by the 20 young men and women from all over the world fortunate enough to be admitted to the School of Stud Farm Management, which, according to the students there in 1977, is unrivalled in the comprehensive and expert tuition it provides in all aspects of the industry. Lectures are given on feeding, housing, grooming and control of the horse, breeding, equine diseases, worm control and business administration and accounting systems. Books, films and other educational aids are laid on, and there is a written examination in June open to all past and present students, with special awards for the top two. Certificates of merit are issued to those who pass the examination, and there are Southern Hemisphere Travel Scholarships open to successful students of Irish nationality. Entry to the course is free, as is accommodation on the Stud, and wages of £28.50 a week, plus overtime, are paid, the students rotating from one department to another on a weekly basis. This is all a far cry from the British National Stud which also takes students, but is not, as a self-supporting outfit, equipped to provide much by way of formal educational programmes, far less to subsidise them. At Newmarket British students pay £500 the season, foreigners £700.

Competition is fierce for places on the Irish course, which is open to those aged 18–25, and which has so impressed the Japanese that they once offered a deal to fill it entirely with their own trainees. For the other six months of the year there is a residential farriers' course at the Stud, which also incorporates a Racing Apprentice Education Centre for 20 lads, indentured to local trainers, who live in and undergo general, as well as horse-related, education, for two years. An Irish Horse Museum, supervised by Joe McGrath's daughter Mary, was opened at the Stud in 1977, Arkle's skeleton having been disinterred and reassembled to become the star exhibit.

One of the girls who put Arkle back together again, Sally Harrison, handles the day-to-day laboratory work at the Irish National Stud – worm dosing, blood tests, weighing of afterbirths and so on – as well as looking after orphan foals by introducing them either to foster mothers or to the Stud's heated milk machine, a modified calf-rearer, which automatically mixes its powder and water to a strength appropriate for the suckling at the polythene nipple jutting into the box next door. Sally Harrison also manages the Stud's colostrum bank, and its frozen supplies, drawn off from Tully's half-bred mares, have been thawed, heated and bottled to save the life of many a motherless foal. The Irish National Stud also operates as a contact point between the owners of orphan foals and bereaved mares.

The laboratory is in the newest of the Irish National Stud yards, where visiting mares are received. Named after Sun Chariot and completed, on the site of the old Main Yard, in 1975, it stands next to the 16-box foaling unit. Of the four other yards, three are also named after Tully horses – the Minoru, built in 1974, the Black Cherry, completed a year earlier, and the Blandford, which dates from 20 years ago, when D. D. Hyde MRCVS was Manager. The oldest yard on the place, the Kildare, is due to be replaced soon and there are also plans to build a swimming pool for hydro-therapy. In 1977 a total of 365 boarding mares were booked in at Tully, where each yard, except for the Sun Chariot, houses a teaser in a box with a three-foot square aperture some four foot from the ground looking out over a wooden barrier, set far enough out to form a corridor, padded with jute or rubber

Irish Horse Museum at Tully, with Arkle's skeleton as centrepiece.

flooring mats, for the introduction of mares. Shy mares are given the chance to show to the teaser either by being placed in boxes alongside his, or in a paddock with the caged beast as centrepiece.

The first purchase made by the directors of the Irish National Stud Company, in November 1946, was Sir Jack Jarvis's Royal Charger, by Nearco out of Nasrullah's half-sister, Sun Princess, by Solario. The best sprinter of his generation, and winner of the Ayr Gold Cup and the Queen Anne Stakes at Ascot, Royal Charger cost the Stud 50,000 guineas. He remained at Tully until 1953, when he was sold for $300,000 to Neil S. McCarthy and Louis B. Mayer and syndicated under the managership of Leslie Combs II. If this was a good deal for the Americans, they seemed to have found the Irish coalition government in lunatic mood a couple of years later, when Tulyar was let go for £10,000 less thàn the £250,000 the Fianna Fail administration had paid in 1953 to the Aga Khan, who had bred the horse at his Gilltown Stud, County Kildare. Tulyar (Tehran – Neocracy, by Nearco) won the Derby, St Leger, King George VI and Queen Elizabeth Stakes and the Eclipse Stakes in 1952, and earned what was then a record £76,417 on the track. He was bought by a syndicate, headed by 'Bull' Hancock, and installed at Claiborne after completing the 1956 season in Ireland. Just before his first season in Kentucky, however, Tulyar showed the first signs of the physical deterioration, which seemed sure to result in an early demise. By mid-April, serious diseases of the intestine, seminal

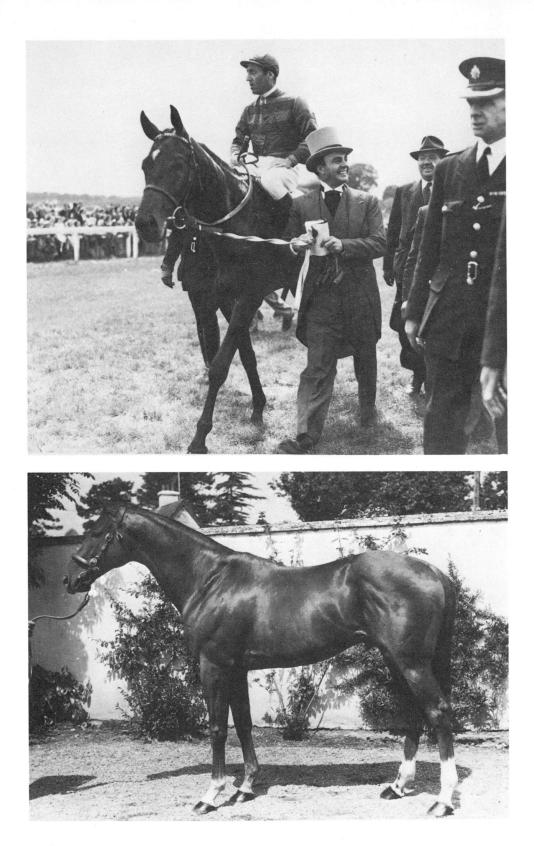

vesicle and kidney had been diagnosed, and the horse was sore, hairless and unable to stand. Miraculously, he survived, and got his first American crop in 1959.

As soon as the Tulyar deal went through, the Irish National Stud bought Vimy (Wild Risk – Mimi, by Black Devil) as a replacement, having earlier in 1955 secured Panaslipper (Solar Slipper – Panastrid, by Panorama) at a cost of £45,000 from the late Joe McGrath, who was also working hard in those days to ensure there wasn't a decent stallion left in the country. McGrath, the man who sold Nasrullah in 1949 for $372,000, had recently let the Americans have Solar Slipper and the 1951 Derby winner Arctic Prince (Prince Chevalier – Arctic Sun, by Nearco) for $900,000. Damiens, Fair Truckler, Mafoosta, Bally Donnell and Ballydam were among the other horses McGrath sold across the Atlantic, although traffic was not entirely one way, and both Great Captain and the 1952 Kentucky Derby winner Hill Gail were imported to Brownstown. Tully, meanwhile, had stopped standing great horses, and Preciptic, Miralgo, Blackrock, Whitehall, Eudaemon, Khalkis and Whistling Wind are among its more distinguished stallions of recent years.

The stallion boxes at the Irish National Stud feature lantern-type windows in the roof after the style of Colonel Hall-Walker's original stalls, six of which are still standing, and which happen to give excellent ventilation. The reason for this departure from the conventions of fenestration, however, was to force the horses to look skyward, thus intensifying the influence of the stars, which Hall-Walker believed to be of prime importance. For every new-born foal, a horoscope was charted, and only those favoured by the stars would be retained. Hall-Walker did sell Prince Palatine, winner of the St Leger in 1911, and the Ascot Gold Cup in 1912 and 1913, although it has been said in his defence that this was because he had not been available to do a horoscope on the appropriate night rather than for any unpromising configuration of heavenly bodies. Otherwise, he did remarkably well on his unusual ideas. There is still standing at Tully the covered exercise ring which he built in 1903 – probably the first in the world – and such policies inevitably added to his reputation for being eccentric, at best, until results began to vindicate him. In 1900, the first year Tully-bred horses appeared on the track, there were two winners of purses worth a total of £260. Between 1904 and 1914, however, Tully produced seven classic winners, Hall-Walker finished among the top four breeders 11 times in 15 years and was champion in 1905 and 1907. He won the Gimcrack four times in the early years of the century, and used the traditional dinner speech to canvass controversial and progressive ideas. In 1905 he advocated subsidies for breeders running their own stock, the nationalisation of racing and the introduction of pari-mutuel betting, while two years later he was deprecating the short-sightedness of

Above: Charlie Smirke on Tulyar is led in by Prince Aly Khan after winning the Epsom Derby in 1952. Left: *Panaslipper.*

Above: *Minoru.* Right: *Royal Match.*

those who were selling top-class stallions abroad. A fine amateur rider himself, with 127 winners under rules between 1877 and 1890, he was a great supporter of bumpers' events.

Hall-Walker's enthusiasm for astrology was part of an interest in oriental culture and religion he developed when serving with the British Army in India. Thus, in 1906, he brought over to Tully the Japanese gardener Eida, and his son Minoru, whose name was conferred on the foal who went on to win the 1909 Derby, leased to the King. It took the pair four years to create the Japanese gardens at Tully, which are nowadays open to the public from Easter to October, and which boast one of the finest collections of bonsai trees in Europe. The natural water supply at Tully – now no longer used – is rich in calcium and phosphorus, absorbed from the Curragh's limestone base, with the nearest overflow point, called St John's Well, just across the road from the Stud. The fine Kildare pasture also owes much to the limestone subsoil, which characterises all good horse-rearing centres, and these factors were no doubt in Hall-Walker's mind when he bought the property from James Fay. Hall-Walker's other principal service to the thoroughbred horse was to introduce the Aga Khan to breeding and racing.

The Irish National Stud's contribution to the bloodstock industry also takes in equine research, either off its own bat or by way of co-operation with outside workers investigating horse diseases, and the improvement of stud farm management through the application of up-to-the-minute farming techniques. It provides a library and information service, aims to educate visitors, especially the young, to appreciate the horse, and offers guidance for those seeking a career in the bloodstock industry. The promotion of Irish tourism is an incidental factor behind the professional landscaping of its gracious precincts and the attractive design of its yards and buildings.

Cattle are left to run side by side with horses at the Stud in the belief that they have a quietening effect as well as acting as scavengers by eating the coarser grasses and killing off parasites. The pasture is treated with organic manure in Autumn and harrowed and rolled in early Spring. Paddocks are topped in May, June, July and August. Each summer 1,500 tons of silage is conserved to feed the cattle herd of 450 head. Weather permitting, about 200 tons of hay is made and a barn drying system has been installed. The Stud is self-sufficient in oats, with 50 acres grown each year, half being the winter variety. The oats when harvested are not kiln dried but undergo an air conditioning process in tower silos. Barley for feeding to cattle and horses is also air conditioned and amounts to 30 tons. The Stud requires some 400 tons of straw, mainly the oaten kind, each year, but is able to meet only a small percentage of this from its own resources.

At the 1972 Newmarket December Sales the Irish National Stud acquired two new broodmares in Setsu (1970) and Regal Step (1972). Setsu, beautifully bred (Shantung – Twilight Hour, by Nearco) and in foal to Thatch, cost 46,000 guineas. A light-framed but impressive two-year-old, she sub-

sequently proved a slight disappointment on the racecourse. Regal Step (Ribero – Right Royal Time, by Right Royal V), a decent handicapper who won the Eglinton and Winston Memorial from Night In Town at Ayr's 1976 Western Meeting, cost 10,500 guineas. At Tully they join Engadina (Alcide – Grishuna), Mear Aille (Hard Ridden – Belle Sauvage), Eriskay (Romulus – Margaret Ann), Cat O'Mountaine (Ragusa – Marie Elizabeth), Manfilia (Mandamus – Spare Filly), Princess Ivor (Sir Ivor – Pal an Oir), Compliment (Tudor Music – Flattering) and Filigrane (Forli – Fiery Angel). There is little immediate threat of greatness in this band, perhaps, and the best racemare of recent years to retire to Tully was probably Sail Cheoil, whose performance there unfortunately seemed to support the old contention that stirring deeds on the track are often the kiss of death at stud.

Michael Osborne, whose uncle Joe bred both Brown Lad and Ten Up, was appointed General Manager of the Irish National Stud in 1970 after 13 years of general veterinary practice in England, Ireland, Scotland and America, and there could hardly be a better tribute to his talents than the efficiency with which Tully's disparate elements work. Perhaps the ancillary services of the Stud could not be provided without the relatively unambitious approach to the acquisition of stallions which official policy stipulates, but there is so much class on other Irish studs at the moment, that the industry overall hardly needs even its national showpiece to sink its funds into a flashy array of top-notch horseflesh.

Brownstown Stud

There seems little doubt that racehorses have been continuously bred at the Brownstown Stud longer than at any other thoroughbred nursery in the world, and it was already well-established by 1787, when Mr Edwards bought the Duke of Grafton's Tug, by Herod, to stand there, which he did with some distinction. An old yard, still in use at the stud, is thought to date from this period. Early in the 19th century, George Knox from County Mayo bought the place and bred there, in 1833, the great Birdcatcher, by Whalebone's son Sir Hercules out of Bob Booty's daughter Guiccioli, who, eight years later, threw Faugh a Ballagh, winner of the St Leger and the first Irish horse to succeed in an English classic. Faugh a Ballagh was also by Sir Hercules, a black horse with the tufts of white in his coat which occasionally reappear in his descendants and which are commonly known as Birdcatcher ticks.

Faugh-a-Ballagh.

Birdcatcher's greatest performance as a racehorse was probably in the $1\frac{3}{4}$ mile Peel Cup at the Curragh, which he won by more than a quarter of a mile from Freney and Normandy, highly-regarded horses both. Joseph Osborne, who apparently saw the race, wrote: 'Such a performance has rarely been seen on any racecourse. Birdcatcher, who was ridden by "English" Edwards, jumped off in front and though not a hard puller, got so excited that he ran away. After he had passed the winning post his jockey could not pull him up. Birdcatcher ran another mile down the precipitous back road to Newbridge, and was only pulled up at the turnpike close by the Cavalry barracks. He thus showed the most extraordinary speed and staying power, but the incident unquestionably affected his staying power.'

Birdcatcher ran in the colours of William Disney of Lark Lodge, which adjoins the Brownstown Stud, and where the horse stood for most of his stud career, although he held court in Newmarket in 1846, was leased to R. M. Jacques of Easby Abbey for 1848 and 1849, and also spent his last full season, 1859, in England. He is rumoured to be buried under a tree on the Brownstown Stud, and a neighbouring paddock is known by his name. He sired one Derby winner, Daniel O'Rourke, two St Leger winners, The Baron and Knight of St George, two Oaks winners, Songstress and Imperieuse, and established one of the most enduring male lines in thoroughbred history. The Baron's son Stockwell sired Bend Or, Blair Athol and Doncaster, ancestor of the Phalaris, Teddy and Panorama lines, while both the Blandford and Gallinule lines trace in tail-male to Birdcatcher's son, Oxford.

Gallinule. Top right: *Birdcatcher.* Bottom: *Stockwell.*

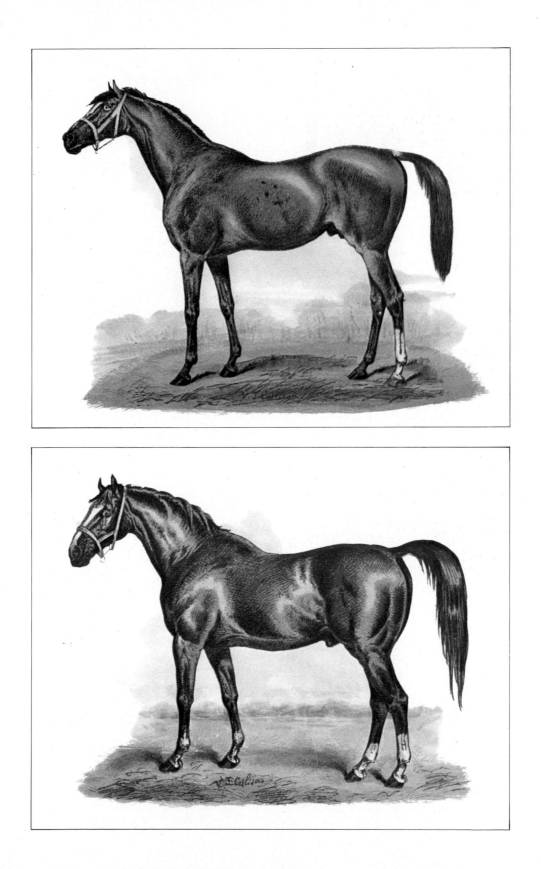

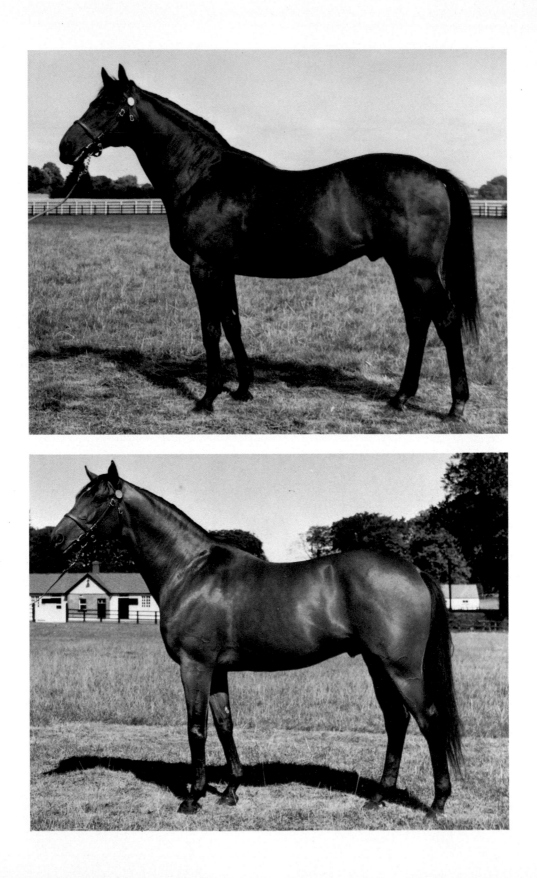

The winner of three races worth £1,985 as a two-year-old in 1886, Gallinule developed into a bleeder and had not recorded any further wins by the end of the 1889 season, when Brownstown's owner, the young Captain Henry Greer, bought him as a stallion. Gallinule, who is buried at Brownstown, is best known as sire of the great Pretty Polly, who won £37,297 from 22 wins, among them the 1,000 Guineas, the Oaks and the St Leger, and was only twice beaten, running second on each occasion. Although many of Gallinule's sons were a disappointment at stud, several of his daughters proved highly influential – Waterhen became third dam of Vatout, who sired Bois Roussel, and Hammerkop produced Spion Kop, winner of the 1920 Derby, for instance. The St Leger winners Night Hawk and Wildfowler, and the 2,000 Guineas winner Slieve Gallion were among the best racers got by Gallinule, who was also responsible for some excellent broodmare sires. Blandford's maternal grandsire, White Eagle (ex Merry Gal), was among the best of them, since he also got Dolabella, dam of Myrobella and grandam of Big Game, Lady Peregrine, dam of Flamingo, Royal Favour, dam of St Leger winner Royal Lancer, and Quick Thought, second dam of Princequillo.

When Joseph McGrath senior took over Brownstown Stud in 1940, the initial consignment of stock included a two-year-old filly by Fair Trial out of Ethereal, by Ethnarch, named Astrid. She was covered the next season by Panorama to produce Panastrid, who won the Irish 1,000 Guineas and went

Pretty Polly. Top left: *Levmoss.* Bottom: *Bog Road.*

Joseph McGrath with Lord Donaghamore and Sir Gordon Richards.

on to become dam of 1955 Irish Derby winner Panaslipper (by Solar Slipper), Chevastrid (by Prince Chevalier) and Astrid Sun (by Solar Slipper). Astrid's 1944 foal, by Bois Roussel, was Astrid Wood, dam of Feevagh (by Solar Slipper) and Kimpton Wood (by Solonaway). Yorkshire Oaks winner Feevagh produced the good handicapper, Laurence O, by Saint Crespin III, and Feemoss, by Ballymoss, dam of the Prix de l'Arc de Triomphe, Ascot Gold Cup and Prix du Cadran winner, Levmoss, by the McGrath-bred Le Levanstell. Kimpton Wood's most influential produce is Top Twig (by High Perch), useless on the racecourse but dam of the good colts Tip Moss and Twig Moss, both by Luthier. Their racetrack successes encouraged McGrath, in 1977, to send Feemoss to Condorcet (by Luthier), then embarking on his stud career at Brownstown.

Of the mares McGrath started with at Brownstown, Serena and her daughter Solar Flower proved the best producers. Solar Flower was in foal to Nearco at the time of her purchase, producing Arctic Sun, a brilliant two-year-old, who became dam of McGrath's 1951 Epsom Derby winner, Arctic Prince, by Prince Chevalier. Serena was sent to Nearco in 1941, and, although the resulting colt, Arctic Star, never raced because of a shoulder injury, he was three times champion sire of Ireland. Both Arctic Prince and Solar Flower's son by Windsor Slipper, Solar Slipper, were exported to America, but they did stand for a while at Brownstown, their legacy to Britain being principally through their daughters – Arctic Prince is maternal grandsire of Santa Claus, Park Top, Luciano and Approval, while Royal Palace is out of a Solar Slipper mare.

Godiva, by Hyperion, won the substitute 1,000 Guineas and Oaks in 1940, the year McGrath bought her half-brother, Windsor Slipper. At the next year's December Sales he gave 14,000 guineas for their dam Carpet Slipper

Condorcet.

(by Phalaris), a half-sister to the 1934 Yorkshire Oaks winner Dalmary, whose daughter Rough Shod II produced Ridan, Moccasin and Lt Stevens in America, as well as Thong, dam of Thatch, Lisadell and King Pellinore. Carpet Slipper was scarcely less influential internationally, and her 1936 daughter by Tetratema, Her Slipper, dropped Vali, dam of Val de Loir (1962 Prix du Jockey Club) and of Valoris (1966 Irish 1,000 Guineas and Epsom Oaks) and second dam of Roi Lear. For the McGraths Carpet Slipper produced Silken Slipper, by Bois Roussel, dam of Silken Glider, who won the Irish Oaks in 1957.

When Joseph McGrath senior died in March 1966, the management of his huge bloodstock empire was shared among his three sons, with Joseph handling the studs, Seamus acting as trainer and Paddy adopting an administrative role. Levmoss, of course, has been the best horse produced by the McGraths, but his performance as a stallion, though good, has been less than spectacular, with Nuthatch, Moonlight Night, Duchamp and Shantallah among his most successful runners. He transferred from Brownstown to the Manoir Saint-Georges for the 1977 season. At the same time, the McGrath-bred stallion Bog Road, by Busted was sold to Venezuela. Bog Road, winner of £38,725 on the track, is out of 1964 1,000 Guineas winner Royal Danseuse, who was also bred by McGrath.

Both Ballyciptic (Preciptic – Ballytickle, by Ballyogan) and Tarqogan (Black Tarquin – Rosyogan, by Ballyogan) have now left the Brownstown Stud to pursue careers siring jumpers, which is thought to be more their mark. In 1977, in addition to Condorcet (ex Pan American, by Pan), McGrath

Top ieft: *Furry Glen*. Top right: *Weaver's Hall*. Bottom: *Brownstown foaling unit*.

was standing three stallions bred and raced by the family – Bluerullah (Valerullah – Windsor Blue, by Windsor Slipper), Weaver's Hall (Busted – Marians, by Macherio) and Furry Glen (Wolver Hollow – Cleftess, by Hill Gail). Bluerullah won eight races, including the 1967 Lockinge Stakes, Weaver's Hall won the Irish Derby in 1973, and, the next year, Furry Glen took the Irish 2,000 Guineas. Condorcet ran 22 times, won five, was placed in 11 and earned 963,930 francs. His pedigree shows the classic Boussac cross, with Luthier tracing in tail-male to Djebel, and Pan to Astérus.

Brownstown Stud covers some 550 acres, and more than 50 McGrath mares are kept there. There are 185 boxes. In the last couple of years the McGraths have hit on a way of selling half their yearlings without giving rise to suspicions that the best are being kept at the Curragh. They consign yearlings in pairs, leaving the successful bidder to take his choice.

Kildangan Stud

For many people in the breeding business the concept of sending stallions 'down under' has taken on a starker significance since Green God and Ridan, but there seemed a fair chance, in 1977, that shareholders in the Kildangan-based Bold Lad would react favourably to a £100,000 offer for his services in Australia the next winter. In the absence of evidence that the strain of travelling or out-of-season covering was a factor in the recent antipodean deaths, Kildangan's owner, Roderic More O'Ferrall, thought the proposal not unattractive, especially since Bold Lad is now 13 years old and his stud record, though consistently good, has not quite put him in the top rank. By Bold

Bold Lad (Ire).

Ruler out of Barn Prince, a daughter of Democratic, who stood at Kildangan, Bold Lad had his most successful season on the track at two years old, when he won all four of his races – the Youngsters' Stakes at The Curragh, the Coventry Stakes at Ascot, the Champagne Stakes at Doncaster and the Middle Park Stakes at Newmarket. Coincidentally, the stallion's American-bred namesake, also by Bold Ruler, now standing at the Haras du Bois Roussel, was precocious, too, winning eight of his ten races in 1964 to be voted United States Champion Two-Year-Old. Bold Lad (USA), who is

Left: *Entrance to Kildangan's main yard, and a row of loose boxes.* Above: *Karabas.*

out of What a Pleasure's half-sister by Princequillo, Misty Morn, raced for two more seasons, and wound up with 14 wins and $516,465; Bold Lad (Ire) ran for one more year, registering his single three-year-old victory in the Tetrarch Stakes at The Curragh. His career earnings were £24,790. Bold Lad (Ire), bred by the late Beatrice, Countess of Granard, has sired the winners of more than 200 races and some £400,000, his one classic success being provided by Waterloo, winner altogether of £47,887. Otherwise, the biggest money-winners among the many good horses he has got have been Daring Display (Prix Morny, Prix du Rond-Point and Prix de la Jonchère), Boldboy (Lockinge, Greenham, Diadem and Challenge Stakes and Prix de la Porte Maillot), Brave Lad (Palace House Stakes) and Pert Lassie (Molecomb Stakes).

In 1977 More O'Ferrall, who has thus far sent 32 of his own mares to Bold Lad (Ire) chose not to take up either of the nominations he gets in return for managing and accommodating the stallion. He did, however, make use of the two nominations he receives to the other stallion standing at Kildangan, Karabas, who retired to stud in 1971 but has yet to sire anything dazzling. On the track he won eight races and £27,843 in England and Ireland and two races and 448,860 francs in France, plus $100,000 for his Washington D.C. International victory in 1969, when, as a four-year-old, he enjoyed his best season. At five, he won the Hardwicke Stakes and ran second, beaten a nose, in the Prix Dollar to Priamos, one of the stallions More O'Ferrall now

Above: *The main yard, and Roderic More O'Ferrall*. Right: *Darius, watched by Harry Wragg.*

regularly breeds to. He was also runner-up in the Eclipse Connaught won in record time. A son of Worden II, pre-eminently a broodmare sire, Karabas is out of Fair Share by Tantieme.

The main yard at Kildangan was built by More O'Ferrall's father Dominic for the hunters which .were his principal interest. The present master of Kildangan took out a trainer's licence in 1927, his first step in the development of the thoroughbred breeding side of the business coming in 1932 with the purchase, for 130 guineas, of Straight Sequence (Stratford – Little Flutter, by Happy Warrior, or Flying Orb) on behalf of the diplomat Sir Percy Loraine. Loraine's association with Kildangan continued until his death, in 1961, eight years after he had become an equal partner in the stud; Straight Sequence founded one of Kildangan's most influential dynasties, her daughter, Poker Chip, producing Queenpot, by Big Game, winner of the 1948 1,000 Guineas and half-sister to Quarterdeck, dam of Ambergris, by Sicambre, who won the Irish Oaks and ran second in both the English 1,000 Guineas and the Oaks to Sweet Solera in 1961. More O' Ferrall and Lord Iveagh, who was taken into partnership in 1961, aim to run Kildangan on commercial lines, so when a couple of fillies were kept back in 1976, Ambergris's daughter by Sir Ivor, Istiea, Lancashire Oaks winner of 1973, was sent to the Newmarket December Sales. The mare, who was in foal to Thatch, fetched a record 142,000 guineas. Ambergris who is still on the stud, is also dam of the winners Ambericos (by Darius) and Forever Amber (by Bold Lad), who is now back at Kildangan, too. Also in the broodmare band at the

moment are Ambergris's half-sister by Hill Gail, Quail, and her two daughters Kaku (by Khalkis) and Bold Bird (by Bold Lad).

Poker Chip was the first of Straight Sequence's four foals to race; the second, Khosro, was responsible for the stud's first classic success, in the Irish 2,000 Guineas of 1941. With the death of his father the next year, More O'Ferrall decided to concentrate exclusively on the breeding side, and, in 1947, realised a long-held ambition to secure a representative of the Cantelupe family for his broodmare band, when he paid 310 guineas at the December Sales for Respite, carrying an Ardan foal which was to die at birth. Respite (Flag of Truce – Orama, by Diophon) was barren to Nasrullah in 1948, but returned to him and produced Nearula, sold at Doncaster as a yearling in 1951 to Mr W. Humble, for whom he won seven races, including the 2,000 Guineas, St James's Palace Stakes and Champion Stakes, worth £27,351 5s. The year after Nearula's 2,000 Guineas, the race again went to a Kildangan-bred, Darius, running in the colours of Sir Percy Loraine. Darius's dam, Yasna, had been bought as a foal by More O'Ferrall for 400 guineas and sold to Loraine, at the same price, a year later. She ran second in the Irish 1,000 Guineas of 1939, and produced twelve foals off the reel at Kildangan, Darius, by Dante, winner of nine races worth £38,105 17s 6d being by some way the most distinguished.

No daughters of Yasna or Respite remain at Kildangan, but the other great family introduced to the stud in its early days, that of Laitron, is still represented. Barren when she was purchased, for 400 guineas, at Ballsbridge in 1943, Laitron was by the 1921 Irish 2,000 Guineas and Ayr Gold Cup winner, Soldennis, a full brother to We Kiss, dam of Coronach, winner of the Derby and St Leger for Lord Woolavington in 1926. A miler, out of Chardon, Laitron bred a host of winners, including Dairymaid (by Denturius), dam of the 1962 1,000 Guineas winner Abermaid (by Abernant),

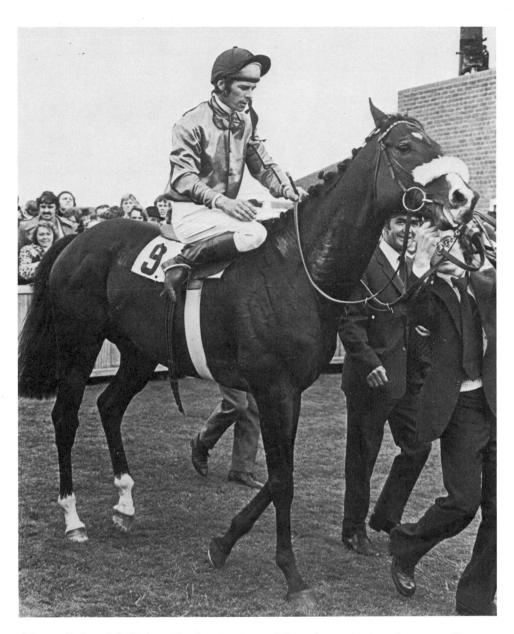

Shantallah, with Brian Taylor in the saddle, after winning the 1975 Cesarewitch. Left: *Recently-built American-style barn and covering yard.*

Silver Thistle (by Sol Oriens), dam of Indigenous (by Mustang) and Nella (by Nearco), dam of Miralgo (by Aureole), Parnell (by St Paddy) and Abanilla (by Abernant), who, at 19, is still on the stud. Nella's non-winning daughter by Democratic, Tiarella, is also at Kildangan, her best-known produce being the 1975 Cesarewitch winner Shantallah (by Levmoss). Tiarella has also bred the winners Psalt (by Psidium), Aubieta (by Aureole) and Lady Esmeralda (by Karabas). The other Kildangan mares tracing to

Laitron are Dinant (Abernant – Dairymaid), Motacilla (Relko – Abermaid) and Arenaria (Aureole – Abanilla) whose son by Bold Lad, Redesdale, ran creditably in 1973, 1974 and 1975.

The 1976 Sandown Park two-year-old winner Claddagh, by Bold Lad (Ire), was the first foal of the Kildangan mare Clarina, by Klairon, whose dam Athanasia (Never Say Die – Hyrcania) and half-sister by Polyfoto, Polycarpa, are also on the stud. Of Kildangan's 19 broodmares, only four are not home-bred, the most expensive purchase being Vela (Sheshoon – Cerentola), who was in foal to Thatch when More O'Ferrall paid 62,000 guineas for her in 1971. She produced a brown filly, which fetched 5,600 guineas at the Newmarket October Yearling Sales. In 1977 she dropped a filly foal to Nijinsky before visiting Nonoalco. Blue Butterfly (Majority Blue – Belle Noisette), Donine (Soleil II – Nanette) and Fighting (Aggressor – Pelting) have also been drafted into the Kildangan broodmare band. Clarina, in 1977, was due to Roberto, sire of her daughter which More O'Ferrall sold at Goffs in 1976 for £14,600. More O'Ferrall, who is a shareholder in Roberto, has made something of a speciality of spotting stallions likely to do well, and was one of the first to breed to a number of influential sires before they became fashionable, among them Fair Trial, Nasrullah, Lyphard, Luthier and Sir Ivor. 'Of course,' he says, 'we've made mistakes as well.'

The Kildangan Stud takes up some 450 acres, with an arable farm supplying oats, hay and straw. In addition to More O'Ferrall's own stock, Gerry Oldham's mares are permanently boarded there. More O'Ferrall relinquished his trainer's licence in 1946, having trained 330 winners of 578 races worth £72,219. He was twice runner-up in the Irish trainers' list, and was responsible for two winners each of the Irish 2,000 and 1,000 Guineas and one of the Irish St Leger.

NORMANDY

H.H. Aga Khan's Studs

Following the death of his father, Prince Aly, in a Paris road accident on May 7, 1960, H.H. Aga Khan spent six months deliberating whether to continue the family's great tradition of horse breeding and racing, a subject of which he claims to have been totally ignorant at the time, and which, naturally, he regards as of negligible importance in relation to his principal mission. His decision to carry on may have been assisted by the run of successes the stable enjoyed in 1960, with Charlottesville winning the Prix du Jockey Club and the Grand Prix de Paris, Sheshoon the Ascot Gold Cup and the Grand Prix de Saint Cloud, Petit Etoile the Coronation Cup and Venture VII the St James's Palace Stakes and the Sussex Stakes, all within a two-month period, but followers of the turf have had good reason since to be grateful he made the time to master the intricacies of bloodlines and the management of a racing empire. That empire has been somewhat trimmed since Prince Aly's day, and the Aga Khan now owns two studs in France, the Haras de Saint Crespin and the nearby Haras de Bonneval, and two on the

Left: *Prince Aly Khan.* Right: *Petite Etoile, ridden by Lester Piggott, led in by Prince Aly after winning the 1959 Oaks.*

Curragh, Sheshoon and Ballymany, as well as a magnificent, ultra-modern training centre in Chantilly. The Haras de Bonneval was established only in 1974, but the other three studs belonged to the Aga Khan's father, who also had Gilltown, Ongar, Sallymount and Williamstown in Ireland, and La Coquenne, Lassy, and Marly-la-Ville in Normandy. Prince Aly, at the time of his death, had a broodmare band of 90; the Aga, having culled quite a few in 1976, now has 65.

'Even so,' His Highness observes, 'I've got too much land, strictly speaking, and I ought either to sell some, or buy some more horses, but I've always been a great believer in having fresh pastures, and, as long as it can be done economically, I'd like to keep things pretty well as they are.' The economics of his operation, of course, got a tremendous boost with the sale of Blushing Groom (Red God – Runaway Bride, by Wild Risk) to America in 1977. Although Blushing Groom was bred by John McNamee Sullivan, his dam used to belong to the Aga Khan and descends from one of his grandfather's famous families. Runaway Bride's third dam, Eclair (Ethnarch – Black Ray, by Black Jester), winner of seven races, was bred by J. B. Joel, and bought from the American Marshall Field by the old Aga in 1942. Her produce for him included Khaled (by Hyperion), unbeaten at two, when he won the Coventry Stakes and the Middle Park Stakes, and successful, the next season, in the St James's Palace Stakes, as well as running second in the 2,000 Guineas and third in the Eclipse, and Emali (by Umidwar), winner of three races as a three-year-old and dam of Aimée (by Tudor Minstrel), whose first foal was Runaway Bride (1962), and whose subsequent produce included the winners Flaming Heart (by Sheshoon), Azardastaan (by Saint Crespin III), and Afayoon and Afara (both by Silver Shark). The Aga Khan had a full-brother to Blushing Groom, called Bayraan, foaled in 1971, but, he now thinks, the horse was spoiled by over-racing. 'We ran him in the Prix de la Forêt after a hard campaign, and that turned out to be a little too much, so we got rid of him,' he says.

The Aga Khan, in fact, fights shy of horses, of either sex, which have been over-extended on the track, but is a firm believer in racing class, when it comes to the selection of breeding stock, and would use, ideally, only group winners. His approach to mating policy is thorough and logical, his exposition of it couched in the vocabulary of the modern businessman. 'We run an ongoing analysis of our stock, and keep an inventory of mares on a system we devised with our trainer Mathet, so that nothing promising will be sold. A committee spends up to a month each year discussing mating problems, and detailed minutes are kept so that we can de-brief on our activities annually – this, we find, is a most useful exercise. Reports on the character and conformation of the fillies are kept from the time they are foals, and we also examine the breeding record of each mare to see if she is in any way difficult. Then we look at the economics of the thing, since there would be no point in

Right: *Louis XIV's stables at Versailles, painted by Jean-Baptiste Martin.*

sending a cheap mare to an expensive stallion. At this stage we might have anything up to 12 stallions as possibilities for a particular mare. Then, if stallions in which I have an interest are involved, we consider whether the mating is going to be good for his career, and this usually brings us down to five or six candidates for the mare. After that, we start comparing pedigrees and looking into questions of outcrosses and inbreeding, and narrow the field down further. It is all done on a group basis, with personal evaluation of the value of the mares an important factor.'

The Aga Khan also hints that the Vuillier dosage system is still confidentially employed, although it is very rare these days to find a horse breeder prepared to place much credence in it. Not only was Colonel Vuillier adviser to the old Aga Khan at the time of his greatest triumphs, though, but his widow was one of the management team at the time of his death, after which the stable's horses ran in her colours for a time. Both she, and the Aga Khan's Irish manager, Major Cyril Hall, died shortly afterwards, however, thus exacerbating the problems of the difficult early years for the present owner.

The year before he was killed, Prince Aly Khan had become the first owner in Britain to win £100,000 in a season – all with horses bred by himself and his father, who had died in 1957. The Prince's 1959 winners included Taboun (2,000 Guineas), Saint Crespin III (Eclipse Stakes), Venture VII (Imperial Produce Stakes and Middle Park Stakes) and Petite Etoile (1,000 Guineas, Oaks, Yorkshire Oaks, Sussex Stakes and Champion Stakes). Petite Etoile, rated by Prince Aly as the best of the family's great fillies, won a total of £73,002 in four season's racing, but was, sadly, beaten by High Hat in the memorial race run for her late owner at Kempton Park on July 4, 1961. It was not until six years later that it was discovered she had been doped that day, when police interrogating some crook for another offence extracted a confession. As a broodmare, Petite Etoile (Petition – Star of Iran, by Bois Roussel) has proved a disaster, producing just three live foals, of which only Afaridaan (1965), by Charlottesville, was a winner.

In 1959 Prince Aly set a record in France too, by winning 212,314,867 francs, including place money, his principal victories there being with Saint Crespin III in the Prix de l'Arc de Triomphe, Ginetta in the Poule d'Essai des Pouliches and the Prix du Moulin de Longchamp and Sallymount in the Prix Jacques le Marois. For good measure, Prince Aly won the Irish 1,000 Guineas that year with Fiorentina as well.

Prince Aly went into formal partnership with the old Aga Khan just after the Second World War, when the quality of horses being bred on the studs was beginning to decline. His judicious purchases were an important factor in the revival of the stable's fortunes, and the partnership did particularly well to acquire the bloodstock empire of the Englishman Mr Harvey and the

Top left: *Boïard*. Bottom: *Sir Alfred Munnings's painting of Hyperion, who won the Derby and St Leger in 1933 for Lord Derby and, as a stallion, exerted an international influence hardly rivalled in the history of the thoroughbred.*

I

American L. L. Lawrence. The Harvey deal, which involved five nominations to Nearco, included Noorani, dam of Sheshoon and Charlottesville, while among the Lawrence stock was Rose O'Lynn, dam of Venture VII and of the 1956 Poule d'Essai des Poulains winners, Buisson Ardent, both by Relic. Prince Aly, who is said to have influenced his father to buy the Haras de Saint Crespin on the death of Edouard Kahn in 1926, was the better practical horseman of the two. He rode 100 winners under rules, and brought a knowledge of conformation to complement the theoretical approach on which the early success of the studs had been based. When the Aga Khan sent Stafaralla (Solario – Mirawala, by Phalaris) to the July Yearling Sales in 1936, Prince Aly, despite parental entreaties, backed his own judgement and gave 1,850 guineas for the filly. She won the Cheveley Park Stakes, and became dam of Tehran, by Bois Roussel, leased, after his third in the 2,000 Guineas, by the Aga Khan.

H.H. Aga Khan III, who was born in 1877, bought his first thoroughbreds at Deauville in 1921, when he acquired Sapience (Gorgos – Sapientia), who, three years later, threw Samya (by Nimbus), a mare sold by the Aga Khan in 1925 and dam of the 1935 Prix de l'Arc de Triomphe winner, Samos, by Brûleur. At the Doncaster Sales in 1921 the Aga Khan bought Teresina (Tracery – Blue Tit, by Wildfowler), dam of eight winners and of the unraced Alibhai, by Hyperion, who did the Americans many favours as a stallion. The next year marked the purchase of the 'flying filly' Mumtaz Mahal in England, where he also bought Diophon, who won the 1924 2,000 Guineas, Salmon Trout, who took the 1924 St Leger, and Friar's Daughter, dam of Bahram. From then on the stream of winners bred by the Aga Khan set new standards, and no man has ever matched the collection of top-class thoroughbreds he owned at the zenith of his career. He was, of course, never reluctant to sell at the right price, an approach in dramatic contrast to that of the other giant of his era, Marcel Boussac. After the 1949 season, when the Aga Khan

Left: *Mumtaz Mahal at Doncaster in 1923*. Above: *Petite Etoile*.

bred the winners of £78,239 and Boussac the winners of £79,419, *Racing and Breeding* computed that, of the Aga's winners, 70 per cent were home bred, nine per cent were by sires bred by him and 33 per cent were out of his mares. The corresponding figures for Boussac were 87, 65 and 67 per cent. Of Boussac's mares 21 per cent were 'highly inbred', as against only four per cent of the Aga Khan's.

When Prince Aly bought the 40 per cent of the bloodstock empire left to his brother, and the 20 per cent left to his sister, he sold 15 leading mares to the Americans. His son, who had to buy the same percentage interests from his own brother and sister, kept the most promising of the mares, but a lot had to go to defray expenses. 'I didn't really know England and France then,' he recalls, 'because I'd been to school in America and Switzerland. I changed trainers pretty soon, since Alec Head had always understood that, if he went into breeding on his own account, it would be impossible to continue his association with my family.'

The Aga Khan's stock today is split more or less equally between his French and Irish studs, and he has about 80 horses in training as well. In France, Saint Crespin is his private stud, the Haras de Bonneval the public, with Zeddaan holding court. Blushing Groom was foaled at Bonneval, as Runaway Bride was visiting that year. The luscious pastures at the Haras Bonneval were not used for horses until the Aga Khan took over the land, and they are grazed alternately by thoroughbreds and Charollais cattle, although the more common Normandy practice is to turn out the beasts together. Few studs can rival the immaculate appearance of the Haras de Bonneval or the attractiveness and efficiency of its new buildings. Zeddaan (Grey Sovereign –

Zeddaan.

Vareta, by Vilmourin) was bred by the Aga Khan, and got, in his first crop, the Ballymany-based stallion Kalamoun (ex Khairunissima, by Prince Bio). Kalamoun, another Aga Khan-bred, won the 1973 Poule d'Essai des Poulains, Prix Lupin and Prix le Marois. His sire won the Poule d'Essai des Poulains, the Prix d'Ispahan and the Prix de Seine-et-Oise in 1968, having already picked up the Prix d'Arenberg.

Although the Aga Khan offered to make shares in Blushing Groom available to French breeders there were, at $180,000 a time, no takers. 'We could keep outstanding stallions in Europe, if only there were financial institutions around to help the industry survive,' he remarks. 'Can you think of any other major industry which functions on a cash basis? It's absurd that there is not the kind of institutional support which every other industry can rely on, because, now, we are an industry before we are a sport.'

The Aga Khan, reasoning that one cannot expect more than one Blushing Groom in a lifetime, exercised the greatest care in selecting the syndicate to sell the horse to. 'What I want,' he said, 'is to get into the leading stallions without damaging the economics of my business. I shall choose whoever gives me the best leverage via Blushing Groom nominations to the American stallions I want to breed to. Meanwhile, I shall continue to conserve the best of my broodmares, and add representatives of good families whenever I can.' Blushing Groom will stand at Gainesway.

Haras du Bois Roussel

Now that Countess Margit Batthyany has sold her Irish and American establishments, she is down to two studs – the Gestüt Erlenhof at Bad Homburg and the Haras du Bois Roussel at Bursard. There was talk, too, of her selling up in France, when Angel Penna, whom she had brought over from America, deserted her in favour of Daniel Wildenstein, but this seems to have blown over. At the moment she has horses in training with George Bridgland in Lamorlaye as well as with Heinrich Bollow in Cologne. The countess has been breeding at the Bois Roussel only since 1970, although the stud itself has been going since 1802, when Napoleon gave it to his Imperial Minister Count Roederer. That the land was excellent for breeding purposes was soon demonstrated, not only in the stream of good thoroughbreds raised there, but in Roederer's prize-winning cattle and the work-horses, which won frequent honours at the Concours de Paris from the Société Hippique Française, various mid-19th century plaques still embellishing their boxes, which now form a yearling annexe. The first great racehorse produced on the stud was Boïard, winner, in 1873, of the Poule d'Essai des Poulains, the Prix Royal Oak, the Prix du Jockey Club and the Grand Prix de Paris,

Haras du Bois Roussel: boxes housing Bold Lad (USA), Caro, Free Round, Gift Card and Gyr.

Sea Bird II (Dan Cupid—Sicalade, by Sicambre), sire of Gyr. Right: *Pia, in foal to Mill Reef in 1977, and No No Nanette.*

adding the Ascot Gold Cup and the Prix du Cadran the following season. Although the stud was later leased out – Léon Volterra bred the 1938 Epsom Derby winner Bois Roussel (ex Plucky Liège) there – it remained the property of Roederer's descendants until the Comtesse de Rochefort sold it to Countess Batthyany.

Pride of the Bois Roussel stallions at the moment is Caro (Fortino II – Chambord, by Chamossaire), tenth in the French sires' list, with only his first two crops racing, in 1976. The winner of the 1970 Prix d'Essai des Poulains and the Prix d'Ispahan, Caro was also third in the Prix du Jockey Club behind Sassafras and Roll of Honour. At four he won the Prix d'Harcourt, the Prix Ganay and the Prix Dollar, as well as running second to Mill Reef in the Eclipse and fourth to him in the Prix de l'Arc de Triomphe. Gyr, a member of Sea Bird's first crop, out of Feria, by Toulouse Lautrec, is at the stud too, a magnificent-looking stallion who is capable of getting winners, but, unfortunately, he doesn't succeed in getting many of his mares in foal. The stallion team is completed by the American Bold Lad, who transferred to France in 1973, Gift Card (Dan Cupid – Gracious Gift, by Princely Gift) and Free Round (Round Table – Fish House, by Porter-

house). The most successful of Bold Lad's get in America have been Niagara, Stage Coach and Rube The Great, in Europe Bold Fascinator, Marble Arch, Gentle Thought, Royal Family and Bold Lady. Gift Card, a foal of 1969, won seven times in 17 outings and earned 868,316 francs on the track. Free Round, winner of 487,350 francs was standing his first season in 1977.

There were 15 yearlings on the stud in 1977, and some 25 broodmares, the most celebrated racer among them being Pia (Darius – Peseta II, by Neckar), bred in Ireland by Countess Batthyany, and winner of the Cherry Hinton Stakes, the Lowther Stakes and the Epsom Oaks of 1967, when she also dead-heated with Pink Gem for the Park Hill Stakes. Her first foal, Palladium, by High Hat, ran fourteenth in Roberto's Derby. Countess Batthyany's good race filly No No Nanette (Sovereign Path – Nuclea, by Orsini), winner of the 1976 Prix de Flore, was in foal to Green Dancer in 1977. Prominent among the Bois Roussel broodmares is Marlia (Crepello – Mirnaya, by Nearco), who was bred in England and achieved one modest success in two seasons' racing in France, retiring to the stud in 1966. She is dam of two classic winners in Mata Hari and Marduk, both by Orsini. Mata Hari won the 1972 Prix d'Essai des Pouliches from a sub-standard field, and Marduk won the German Derby and St Leger in 1974, when he also recorded the first of two victories in the Grosser Preis von Baden Baden. He is now a stallion at the Gestüt Erlenhof. Caro's dam, a half-sister to Krakatao has produced three other winners. She was still on the farm, aged 22, in 1977 and due to visit Gift Card.

Countess Batthyany's most famous win of recent years was not with a horse bred by herself, as the 1972 Prix de l'Arc de Triomphe winner, San San (Bald Eagle – Sail Navy, by Princequillo) was purchased as a foal at the Keeneland dispersal sale of Harry Guggenheim's stock for $15,000. That year – Penna's first in France – the Batthyany stable finished second in the French owners' list.

There are 400 acres of paddocks and 200 acres under cultivation at the Haras du Bois Roussel, which produces almost all its own feed. Equipped with the very latest in agricultural machinery and veterinary aids, the stud has 210 boxes, and an artificially channelled stream meanders through its rich pastures.

Mares and foals at Bois Roussel and (below) *the manager's office.*

Haras d'Etreham
and Haras du Quesnay

Comte Roland de Chambure was 19, and consciously ushering in a new era, when he inherited the 100-acre Haras d'Etreham, near Bayeux, on the death of his father in 1953. The old comte was cast in the mould of the sporting aristocrat of yesteryear, something of a plunger and in the habit of giving away nominations to Verso (Pinceau – Variété, by La Farina), who had won the 1943 Prix du Jockey Club, Prix Royal Oak and Prix de l'Arc de Triomphe for him, and who had turned out, by all accounts, to be a very evil-tempered stallion indeed. Comte Roland, however, saw the writing on the wall, plumped for expansion and the commercial approach, and sold his first yearlings at Deauville in 1954. The stud now covers 600 acres, accommodates Europe's record-breaking stallion Luthier, as well as Lyphard, Tyrant and Tourangeau, and there are 60 mares permanently on the farm, half of them

Verso.

owned jointly with Alec Head, the rest belonging either outright to de Chambure or to patrons of the stud. Alec Head, owner of the Haras du Quesnay, has an equal number of partnership mares, which alternate between the two farms for a change of scenery every couple of years. Owners keeping mares permanently on the studs include Daniel Wildenstein, Sir Robin McAlpine and Mme Volterra.

The Head/de Chambure partnership is the surviving half of 'La Mafia', Paul Chédeville and Louis Champion having loosened their connection with the other two since that nickname was enviously bestowed on the quartet. Head stands Chaparral, Dancer's Image, Green Dancer and Riverman at the Haras du Quesnay, which he bought in 1958. Le Fabuleux is among the many excellent horses he has been responsible for since going into the breeding side of the business. In recent years his lucky race, as a breeder, has been the Prix Hocquart, which he won for the fourth time in 1977 with Montcontour.

The château at Quesnay was built by the Comte de Glanville in the 16th century; the stud was established in 1910 by William Vanderbilt, who spent three years buying up contiguous properties to bring the farm to its present size. Vanderbilt, a refugee from the Hart-Agnew bills, won the Prix du Jockey Club with Sea Sick, in a dead heat with Quintette, and the Grand Prix de Paris with Northeast in 1908. In 1920 Vanderbilt, preparing for the next world, sold his breeding and racing establishments in France to his compatriot A. K. Macomber for 12 million francs. Macomber lost interest in later life, and, by the time Head took the stud over, there had been very little doing there for 20 years.

It was, de Chambure explains, not too difficult to get the money for the purchase of adjacent farms to develop the Haras d'Etreham, because, 'I was working in a merchant bank at the time, and knew funds were available for such purposes.' Although he modestly omits to say so, it may have helped that the bank belonged to his family, but, at all events, the stud soon started to gobble up neighbouring properties. The first stallion installed by the present comte at the Haras d'Etreham was Ferriol (Fastnet – Aisse, by Thor), second in his colours to Darius in the 2,000 Guineas of 1954, and well-fancied for the Derby, in which he broke down. Ferriol achieved little at stud, and was sold to Japan after four years, but the success of the Haras d'Etreham, de Chambure says, is largely due to the stallions which have stood there since. In this department, it has as strong a hand as ever with Lyphard (Northern Dancer – Goofed, by Court Martial), proving France's leading first season sire in 1976, thus emulating the 1973 achievement of Luthier (Klairon – Flûte Enchantée, by Cranach). Luthier, who won four races, including the Prix Noailles, the Prix Lupin and the Prix Jacques le Marois, got 33 winners of 50 races worth 5,241,000 francs in 1976, earnings more than double the figure achieved by the progeny of Carvin, runner-up in the sires' list. Riverqueen, Red Girl, Ashmore, Tip Moss, Twig Moss and Condorcet are among the most distinguished of Luthier's winners so far.

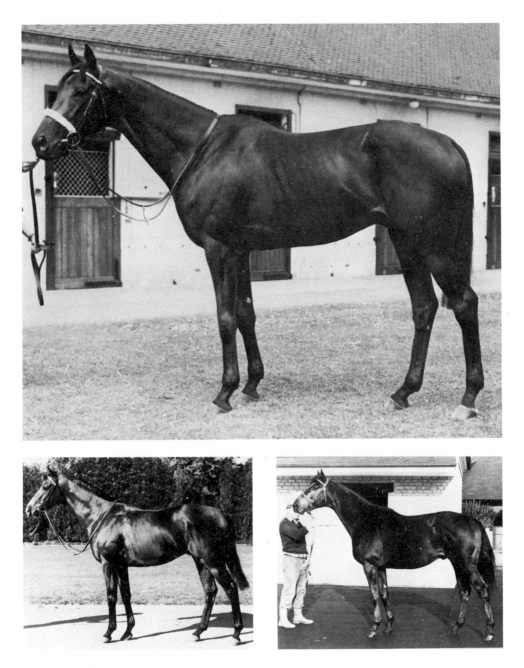

Top: *Luthier*. Above left: *Lyphard*. Above right: *Tourangeau*.

Lyphard, who earned more than 1 million francs in two season's racing and won six times, including the Prix Jacques le Marois, the Prix de la Forêt and the Prix Daru, had both Durtal and Pharly in his first crop. Tourangeau, who has made a fairly encouraging start at stud after a track career cut short by injury, is a home-bred and belongs to the stud's most prolific winner-producing family. He is out of Torbella, by Tornado, a half-sister to the 1965

Above: *Torbella*. Right: *Ferriol*.

French 2,000 Guineas winner Cambremont, by Sicambre, out of Djebellica, who won the Irish Oaks in 1951. Torbella herself finished second in the Irish Oaks seven years later, having won the 1957 Dewhurst Stakes. Retiring to the stud she threw a winner more often than not, her first being Torrefranca, by Sicambre, her second the 1965 Sussex Stakes winner Carlemont, by Charlottesville. She went on to produce the winners Calpé (by Alcide), Belle Carlotta (by Charlottesville), Princess Tora (by Prince Taj), Tourangeau (by Val de Loir), who was successful in two of his three outings and looked classic material, Cambrienne (by Sicambre), Tour Nobel (by Habitat) and Avaray (by Val de Loir). Val de Loir's son out of Aglae, by Armistice, the 1975 Prix du Jockey Club winner, Val de l'Orne, stood at the Haras d'Etreham in 1976, his first at stud, and was then sold to the United States, whereupon Tyrant (Bold Ruler – Anadem, by My Babu) transferred from the Cloghran Stud, County Dublin. The winner of 13 American races, and $198,000, Tyrant got 12 winners of 18 races and £51,612 in his first two crops.

The Société Aland, as the Head/de Chambure partnership is known, makes extensive use of American stallions, keeping the mares, which are generally dispatched for two seasons, at the Hagyard Farm on the Paris Pike, Lexington, which they bought in 1976. Provided barren mares sent abroad return by August 1 of the second year, French regulations permit the foal-at-foot to qualify for the substantial breeders' prizes when they race. Thus,

for instance, Durtal was foaled in Ireland and her dam visited Targowice before returning to the Haras d'Etreham. In 1977 the Société Aland bred to the American stallions Ack Ack, Elocutionist, Empery, Forli, Hoist The Flag, Key to the Mint, Nijinsky, Northern Dancer, Raja Baba, Sir Gaylord, Sir Ivor, Vaguely Noble, Val de l'Orne and Youth. In Ireland they, used Crowned Prince, Habitat, Kalamoun, Nonoalco and Targowice; in England Grundy.

Most of the Haras d'Etreham yearlings are sent to the sales – five or six out of a total of 35 or 40 may be kept back – and they naturally represent a considerable source of revenue. At the 1975 Houghton Sales, for instance, the de Chambure draft of three fetched 128,000 guineas, with Hubert Aillières paying 40,000 guineas for the colt Silver Swan (Reviewer – Swan Dance) and the fillies Diamond Reef (Mill Reef – Dress Uniform) and Valbelle (Val de Loir – Bella Carlotta), fetching 50,000 guineas and 38,000 guineas from Lady Beaverbrook and Bernard Zimmerman respectively.

The mares, of course, represent a means of establishing and consolidating the reputation of the stallions, and the continuous search for the ideal cross results in a 25 per cent turnover of distaff stock at the Haras d'Etreham. De Chambure has been involved in some inspired purchases in recent years, and Pistol Packer, second in Mill Reef's Prix de l'Arc de Triomphe and one of the best middle-distance fillies seen since the war, as well as Riverqueen's dam, Riverside, and Durtal's dam, Derna, were all bought as yearlings by the Société Aland.

Despite the success of the private stud, de Chambure will talk of the Haras d'Etreham as a 'stallion station'. 'People don't realise how much is involved in making a stallion,' he says, 'and I've always been extremely careful in selecting the mares to go to the ones I've managed. Of course, it's not so hard with the French mares, since I know them and the families they belong to, but the business is getting so international these days that there is a great deal of information to assimilate.. At the same time, one achieves nothing without luck.'

The Haras d'Etreham employs some 30 people, and there is a resident veterinary surgeon. A barn of the increasingly popular American type, built in 1976, has 24 boxes for yearlings, and there is also a new stallion yard, completed in 1972. Altogether, the stud has around 150 boxes.

'The Americans will always have to come back to this part of the world to replenish their stock,' says de Chambure, 'because the environment over there constantly makes horses revert to the coarser, sprinting type. Look at the difference in pasture – ours is much more watery than Kentucky bluegrass and grows on a thicker layer of soil. If you drive from Cincinnati to Lexington, where the highway has been cut through the landscape, you see the limestone stratum is just below the surface. This results in a very nutritious grass, which is one of the reasons their horses will always be more forward and bulkier than ours.'

The paddocks at the Haras d'Etreham were laid out in 1928 by Vicomte Foy, who, three years later, leased the stud to the Aga Khan to accommodate foals which were possible candidates for the Deauville Yearling Sales. Mahmoud and Mumtaz Begum thus came to spend their early days on the farm. Comte Roland's father, Comte Hubert, bought the place just after the war. His shrewdest acquisition was Djebellica's dam Nica (Nino – Canalette), when she was a five-year-old in 1939. She produced one colt, Galant Homme, and 11 fillies, including the 1947 Prix de Diane winner, Montenica, Nikitina and Vice Versa.

Green Dancer (left) *and Chaparral, both standing at the Haras de Quesnay.*

Haras de
Fresnay-le-Buffard

There is, even now, such a large number of high class broodmares on the Fresnay-le-Buffard stud that Marcel Boussac may have one or two classic races to win yet, although the dazzling successes of his heyday will remain unrepeatable, and unapproachable. The great stallions Astérus, Tourbillon, Pharis and Djebel are long gone, and neither Faunus (Dan Cupid – Ormara, by Djebel), nor the unraced Kouban (Hauban – Apollonia, by Djebel), who currently stand at Fresnay-le-Buffard, can be expected to show remotely comparable class. The death in 1976 of Boussac's stallion Dankaro (Dan Cupid – Takaroa, by Prince Bio), second in Caracolero's Prix du Jockey Club is, of course, a loss difficult to make up.

Boussac is nervous of sending mares away, because disease was thus once introduced to his stud, so it was inevitable that, with a distaff side almost entirely home-bred, the master of Fresnay-le-Buffard, long pretty well exclusively reliant on his own stallions, should adopt the policies which first made his name synonymous with very close inbreeding some 30 years ago. There was some theoretical basis to these policies as well, however, as Jean Romanet, Director General of the Société d'Encouragement pour l'Amélioration des Races de Chevaux en France, and adviser, like his father before him, to Boussac, explains: 'When you succeed by inbreeding to good horses, you have a purity and a quality not otherwise possible. Too much outcrossing results in a loss of quality, whereas successful inbreeding accentuates the good. The successes of inbreeding are the best, but you do have to kill more horses. M Boussac, though, did not rely as much as people think on inbreeding, and only half his programme was ever based on it.'

As Astérus and Tourbillon came to the end of their stud careers, Boussac stepped up his inbreeding experiments, and got some very fine horses as a result, prominent among them being Coronation, winner of the Prix Robert Papin in 1948, the Poule d'Essai des Pouliches, the Prix de l'Arc de Triomphe in 1949 and second in both the English and the Irish Oaks. She was by Djebel (Tourbillon – Loika, by Gay Crusader) out of Esmeralda (Tourbillon – Sanaa, by Astérus). Soon, though, Boussac was faced with an urgent need for new stallions, and, if it was enterprising of him to turn to the all-conquering Calumet Farm for fresh blood, none of his importations did much to avert the impending decline of his studs. Whirlaway did not long survive in France, Coaltown and Fervent (Blenheim – Hug Again, by Stimulus) were failures, and only Iron Liege achieved anything of consequence. The 1956

season brought a climactic run of scintillating victories in the Poule d'Essai des Pouliches and the Prix de Diane (Apollonia), the Prix du Jockey Club (Philius, by Pharis), the Prix Vermeille (Janiari, by Djebel), the Ascot Gold Cup (Macip), the Prix Hocquart and the Grand Prix du Printemps, but, with that, the Boussac golden age was burnt out. The next year Pharis was dead, and Djebel followed in 1958.

Boussac headed the French owners' list for the 19th time in 1956, since when his success has been modest only by the supreme standards of his own great days. In 1977, at the age of 88, he was still taking an active interest in his string, and winning races. As recently as 1969, he won the Prix de Diane with Crepellana, a daughter of Crepello out of Philius's half-sister Astana, by Arbar. Astana (ex Theano, by Tourbillon) was half-sister to four other winners, and to Anyte II, dam of the 1964 Irish Oaks winner Ancasta. This family derives from Boussac's foundation mare, the Rothschild-bred Zariba (Sardanapale – St Lucre), who was purchased as a yearling in 1920 and who ran 27 times for 13 victories, including the Prix Morny, the Prix Penelope, the Prix Daru, and the Prix Jacques le Marois. Zariba bred L'Espèrance, by Pommern, who in turn produced Theano's dam, Souryva, by Gainsborough. Souryva also bred Pharyva, dam of eight winners, including Djebel's son Galcador, successful in the English Derby of 1950. Zariba's other produce included the good winners Goyescan, Abjer and Goya II, as well as Corrida (by Coronach), who took the Prix de l'Arc de Triomphe in 1936 and 1937 and bred Coaraze (by Tourbillon), first in the 1945 Prix du Jockey Club.

Left: *Coronation*. Above: *Djebel*.

Boussac's involvement in thoroughbred breeding dates from 1914, when he went into partnership with Comte Gaston de Castelbajac, who owned eight broodmares. Five years later Boussac, who has always bred only to race, bought the Haras de Fresnay-le-Buffard, and set about building up a broodmare band with purchases from France, England and America. By 1925 he had 54, and was then, apparently, satisfied, for only 10 more outside mares were drafted in over the next 25 years. His first stallion, Astérus, foaled in 1923 and bred by Rothschild, was bought as a yearling. By Teddy out of Astrella, by Verdun, he won the French 2,000 Guineas, the Prix Greffulhe, the Royal Hunt Cup and the Champion Stakes, and went on to become France's most successful broodmare sire ever, topping the list from 1943 to 1948 inclusive. Astérus, who tended to transmit speed, generally made a good cross with Tourbillon, whose strong suit was stamina. Tourbillon, by Ksar, was bred by Boussac out of Durban (by the 1914 English Derby winner, Durbar II). The dam, a granddaughter of Frizette, was purchased as a yearling from Herman Duryea's widow. After a distinguished racing career, which included victory in the 1931 Prix du Jockey Club, Tourbillon became the centrepiece of the Boussac breeding programme, siring a host of good winners, and Ambiorix, one of the many horses Boussac exported to America, and more influential there than any of the others, although Priam II, Goya II and Djeddah were among them. Pharis,

K

also bred by Boussac, won the 1939 Prix du Jockey Club and the Grand Prix de Paris. He was by Pharos out of Carissima, by Clarissimus, and the highly effective cross he made with Tourbillon accounted not only for Boussac's last victory in the Prix du Jockey Club with Philius, but also for his winning the race four years earlier with Auriban (ex Arriba). Before embarking on his glittering stud career, the home-bred Djebel had won 15 races, including the Middle Park Stakes, the 1940 English 2,000 Guineas and the 1942 Prix de l'Arc de Triomphe.

One of the most successful of the broodmares acquired by Boussac in the early days was Likka (Sardanapale – Diane Mallory, by Nimbus), a foal of 1925. Bred to Astérus, she produced Astronomie, dam of four-time Prix du Cadran winner Marsyas (by Trimdon), unbeaten Caracalla (by Tourbillon), who took the Grand Prix de Paris, the French St Leger, the Arc de Triomphe and the Ascot Gold Cup, Arbar (by Djebel), also successful in the Ascot Gold Cup, and Asmena (by Goya II), winner of the Epsom Oaks in 1950.

For decades Boussac ruled the European roost, winning countless major French and English races and carrying off 11 Prix du Jockey Club, six Prix de l'Arc de Triomphe, five Prix de Diane, one Epsom Derby, one Epsom Oaks, two Ascot Gold Cups, seven Prix de Cadran and two English St Legers. To have achieved so much by deliberately limiting the number of permutations open to him, Boussac must have exhibited a preternatural sagacity when assembling his foundation stock and beginning a truly remarkable chapter in the history of racehorse breeding.

Haras de Meautry

The name of Rothschild first crops up in the history of French racing on the day of the inaugural Prix du Jockey Club, which Lord Seymour won with Frank, at Chantilly on April 24, 1836. Fifteen minutes after that race Frank turned out again to run for a 5,000 franc cup given by Baron Nathaniel de Rothschild, but could finish only third to Lord Seymour's other runner, Miss Annette. The Barons Nathaniel and Anthony de Rothschild soon became the principal patrons of Thomas Carter, who turned public trainer when Lord Seymour sold his stables in 1839, and some good races began to come their way. At first their horses ran in Carter's colours, and it was not until Drummer won five times in 1844 that Baron Nathaniel's name appeared on the official list of winning owners. Two years later Meudon won the stable its first Prix du Jockey Club, and further important successes followed, with Baroncino, in 1855, winning the Prix de l'Empereur, a race later renamed the Prix Lupin, and Gustave and Baroncello taking the Poule d'Essai in 1860 and 1864 respectively.

Following the death of Baron Nathaniel in 1870, his stud at Pont Carré, near Ferrière, was taken over by Barons Alphonse and Gustave, brothers who, three years later, bought the manor of Meautry at Touques, near Deauville and transferred the breeding operation there, retaining the services of Carter as trainer. At the time of the Meautry purchase the Rothschilds also invested 150,000 francs in Boïard as a stallion, but he proved a disappointment at stud. The second Rothschild Prix du Jockey Club was won in 1876 by Kilt, who went on to take the Prix Royal Oak and the Prix de la Forêt. A heavily backed favourite for the Poule d'Essai, he had been beaten into third place, but at the resulting enquiry jockey Wheeler confessed that he had backed against the horse and pulled him.

In 1878 Kilt's sister Brie won the Prix de Diane for the first of 11 Rothschild victories in the race, the most recent coming in 1961, the year of Baron Guy's Hermières (Sicambre – Vieille Pierre, by Blue Peter), a prolific producer at the Haras de Meautry, whose latest foals are Marche Clair (1971), by Sunday, Apanage (1972), by King of the Castle, Caminel (1973) by Blue Tom, Crystal Palace (1974), by Caro, Love Land (1975), by Kautokeino, and Egalière (1976), by Viceregal. The broodmares also include Hermières's daughter by Aggressor, Herminie, dam of Helin (1971), by Timmy Lad, Tartagine (1972), by Blue Tom, Tedscoo (1973), by Exbury, Honeychild (1974), by Tarbes, Saboulard (1975), by Lyphard, and Heurteloup (1976), by Exbury.

Hermières was the last of five fine Meautry mares foaled within a period of eight years – Flûte Enchántée (1950) won the Grand Prix de Deauville and ran second in the Grand Prix de Paris, Dictaway (1952) won the Poule d'Essai, Cérisoles (1954) won the Prix Cléopâtre and the Prix de Diane and Timandra (1957) won the Prix Pénélope, the Poule d'Essai and the Prix de Diane.

When Flûte Enchantée (Cranach – Montagnana, by Brantôme) threw her last foal – Modulation, by Misti – in 1971, her daughter by Blue Peter, Crémone, and her granddaughter by Klairon, Isoline, produced Maria, by Emerson, and Tambourah, by Diatôme respectively. Isoline went on to throw Musique de Nuit (1973), by Reform, Concertino (1974), by Lyphard, and Blue Music (1975), by Blue Tom. The family of Dictaway (Honeyway – Nymphe Dicte) has been maintained through her daughter by Alizier, Celerina, and her granddaughter by Aureole, Citronelle. Dictaway's half-sister by Brantôme, Omphale, also has descendants on the stud. Cerisoles (Tourment – Paix d'Ecosse, by Scottish Union) produced her last foal – a Luthier colt called Fièvre – in 1973, the same year as her granddaughter Artillerie, by Crocket, threw the Diatôme filly Dissuasion. Artillerie has since produced Char (1974), by Reform, and Copperweld (1976), by Jim French, while Cerisole's daughter by Fine Top, Trasimène, dropped a Kashmir II colt named Juvenilia, in 1975. In 1971 Timandra's daughter by Charlottesville dropped an Exbury colt, named Barrymore, and the next year Timandra (Court Martial – Brief Candle, by Brantôme) produced a Misti filly, Barnadine.

The first of the great Rothschild stallions was the 1890 Prix du Jockey Club winner, Heaume, the second Le Roi Soleil, a foal of 1895 who won the Grand Critérium, the Grand de Paris, the Royal Oak and the Prix du Cadran.

Baron Guy de Rothschild with Madame de Rothschild and his jockey Deforge after Exbury's win in the Prix Ganay. Right: *Exbury.*

Baron Alphonse died in 1905 – when Sans Souci II, destined to win the Prix Daru, the Prix Lupin and the Grand Prix de Paris, was a yearling – and his brother followed in 1911, the year his Alacantara won the Prix du Jockey Club. Meautry was taken over by Baron Edouard, whose colours had first appeared when he won a couple of races with Justitia in 1899. La Farina, who was to win the Prix Daru and the Prix Lupin and finish second to Sardanapale in the Grand Prix de Paris, was foaled in 1911, too.

Baron Guy de Rothschild, who succeeded to Meautry just after the Second World War, is President of the French Breeders' Association, and the controversial man who encouraged the authorities to ban non-Common Market horses from the lesser races in France in 1977. All the horses bred by Baron Guy, of course, are retained for racing, and his home-bred Exbury (Le Haar – Greensward, by Mossborough) now stands at the Haras de Meautry, along with Viceregal (Northern Dancer – Victoria Regina, by Menetrier). Unbeaten in eight Canadian races as a two-year-old, Viceregal, who was bred by E. P. Taylor, ran only once at three, finishing lame in the Whitney Purse at Keeneland. Exbury won the 1963 Prix de l'Arc de Triomphe for the third Rothschild triumph in the race after the victories of Brantôme (Blandford – Vitamine, by Clarissimus) in 1934 and Eclair au Chocolat (Bubbles – Honey Sweet, by Kircubbin) in 1938. Both Brantôme and Eclair au Chocolat went on to sterling service at stud, contributing much to the Haras de Meautry's long record of eminent success in breeding racehorses of the highest class.

Right Royal V.

Bachelor's Button.

Haras du Mesnil

Few studs have had so profound a world-wide influence on the racehorse this century as the Haras du Mesnil, where 80 stallions have been bred since it first housed thoroughbred stock in 1908, and where Madame Jean Couturié, widow of the founder, maintains the fiercely uncommercial approach without which it may never have happened. 'Some people think I'm mad, you know,' she says, 'but they are not true breeders, these people who produce horses just for the sales. When I said I wanted to breed stallions, nobody thought I had any chance.' Mme Couturié, who bred, raced and stood the mighty Right Royal V, has managed the stud since the death of her husband in 1949, assisted, in recent years, by her son-in-law, the Comte de Tarragon, and supported by staff all housed on her magnificent 1,000-acre estate, with its tree-ringed lake and five mile of gallops, harrowed every day, running through an exquisite wood.

The creation of the Haras du Mesnil was instigated by the American M. A. Chanler, when he was introduced to Henri Couturié's widow and his son by a previous marriage, Jean. The introduction was effected by M Raoul-Duval, France's leading polo player, brother of Mme Henri Couturié and father of the future Mme Jean Couturié. Chanler, impressed with the milk production of local cows, suggested that the land would be suitable for horse-rearing, and offered to keep his broodmares, and his stallion, Olympian (by Domino) on the farm. Thus, Jean Couturié, until then more interested in English hunting than racehorses, found himself in the thoroughbred business. Olympian proved disastrous as a sire, but, in 1911, the Duc Decazes brought his stallion, Ascot Gold Cup winner, Bachelor's Button, together with his mares, to Mesnil. Just after the First World War Jean Stern transferred his horses, including the stallion Alacantara II, to Mesnil, and Lord Derby and J. E. Widener also began to board stock there.

Jean Couturié bought his first two thoroughbred mares in 1912, and had superb luck with both. The eight-year-old Beattie (Volodyoski – Crusado, by Uncas), imported from England, produced Dark Sedge (by Prestige), who never saw a racecourse but became dam of six winners, and L'Avalanche (by Isard II), winner of five races, second in the Prix Vermeille and dam of Rienze (by Rialto), sire of Sir Winston Churchill's Colonist. Dark Sedge's daughter by Rabelais, Ranai, was sold to Lord Derby for 90,000 francs at Deauville in 1926, won at two in France and retired to the stud in England, where she threw six winners, including Watling Street, who took the Derby in 1942, and Garden Path (1944 2,000 Guineas), both by Fairway. Alta (Alcantara II – Dark Sedge) produced Loët (by Pharos), dam of Lacaduv (by Tornado), winner of the Prix Noailles, second in the Prix Hocquart and third in the Prix du Jockey Club, the Grand Prix de Paris and the Prix du Cadran. Lacaduv's half-sister by Rialto, Lightning, produced Aquarelle (by Daumier), dam of four winners at the Haras du Mesnil.

The second of the Mesnil foundation mares was the American-bred Fair Meddler (Meddler – Fair Star, by Tremont), whose daughter by Rabelais, Red Quill, dropped seven winners. Red Quill's daughter by Scaramouche, Scarlet Quill, did even better with nine winners, and produced Scarlet Skies (by Blue Skies), dam of Tiepoletto, by Tornado. Mme Couturié did not have the best of luck with Tiepoletto, who, after remaining unbeaten at two in 1958, when he won the Prix des Chênes and the Grand Critérium, was injured early the next season and never properly recovered. At stud he has got nothing of consequence, and now stands at the Château du Luc. Another good Couturié racehorse of the same erc, Le Mesnil (Tyrone – Flying Colours, by Massine), foaled in 1960, also unfortunately proved a flop as a stallion. Winner of the Prix de Villebon, and the Prix de Condé at two, the Prix Greffulhe, the Prix Hocquart and the Prix Chantilly at three, and second to Exbury in the 1963 Prix de L'Arc de Triomphe, Le Mesnil is a full-brother to La Chaussée, dam of Mme Couturié's broodmare Quiriquina (by Molvedo), whose best produce to date is Trépan. Flying Colours, a half-sister out of Red Flame, by Vermilion Pencil, to Castel Fusano, is also dam of Fontenay and Dolaincourt. One of the first broodmares installed at the Haras du Mesnil by M. A. Chanler was Simper (Sempronius – Value, by Hanover), who was foaled in America in 1903. In 1910 she dropped Grignouse, by Kilglas, who, eight years later produced La Grêlée, by Helicon, sire also of Hélène de Troie. One of La Grêlée's legs was so bad that there was no hope of racing her, so Chanler decided to have her put down, but on Couturié's offering to pay a butcher's price for the filly, he made him a present of her. Couturié wasted no time and mated La Grêlée, at three, with Verwood, getting a colt of no account called Loung Ma. The next year, however, she threw Rialto (by Rabelais), winner of 17 races in the colours of Jean Stern, and own brother to Roahouga, who won the Poule d'Essai des Pouliches, the Prix Chloé and the Prix La Rochette for M. Esmond. Altogether La Grêlée produced ten winners, including Alcyon (by Alcantara II), who won the Prix d'Ispahan for Esmond in record time, the Princess of Foucigny's high-class racer Roméo, by Rodosto, and Philomela, dam of eight winners, including Philis and Donegal, and second dam of Titien, who earned $5,000 in America. La Grêlée's daughter by Pharos, Phébé, foaled in 1930, won only once, but was third to Bipearl in the Poule d'Essai, produced nine winners and is still making her influence felt at the stud today. Her best runners were Bois Rouaud, by Bubbles, and Doria, by Dogat. Bois Rouaud won three times on the flat, was placed third in the Prix Greffulhe and then went over hurdles, winning five races, including the Gran'de Course de Haies d'Enghien, before retiring to stud. Doria was the second best filly of her generation, running second to Marcel Boussac's Corteira in both the Prix Vermeille and the Prix de Diane of 1948. Doria and her daughters Dorcas, by Sayani, and Dzena, by Tornado, produced winners at the Haras du Mesnil.

Phébé's daughters Phinoola, Gradisca, Tradition and Galatina all distinguished themselves as broodmares. Phinoola, by Rodosto, produced three fillies by Victrix – Catalina, winner of the Prix de la Salamandre and second in the Prix Morny, Kypris (Prix de la Salamandre) and Trinoola, dam of the 1953 Grand Steeplechase de Paris winner, Pharamond III. Catalina's daughter by Neptune II, La Tempête, is now a Haras du Mesnil broodmare, having been once successful on the track. She has so far produced two minor winners in Pupuya, by Le Mesnil, and Sarthois, by Right Royal V.

In 1951 Lord Derby took over Gradisca (by Goya) under an arrangement he had with Mme Couturié whereby each chose one of the other's mares, retaining only an option on any female produce. Amboyna (Bois Roussel – Aurora, by Hyperion) was thus installed at the Haras du Mesnil, where she threw a colt. Mme Couturié had much the better of the deal that year, for not only did Gradisca produce a daughter, by Tornado, but the filly turned out to be the first horse to win a classic in her colours, Tahiti, successful in the Prix de Diane. Tahiti's daughter by Dan Cupid, Abida, is on the stud and is dam of two winners by Right Royal V in Royal Prospect and

Dan Cupid.

Abazie, who is now a member of the broodmare band, too. Abida's own-sister Flèche d'Amour also has a daughter by Blockhaus, Chambre d'Amour, on the stud. Tradition, by Tornado, was sold to England in 1958, but her foal of 1962, Tradsville, by Mossborough, is now among the Haras du Mesnil broodmares. Salamba, by Salvo, one of three winners bred by Tradsville is on the farm too. Galatina, by Galène, produced two fine fillies – Lovely Rose, by Owen Tudor, who dead-heated with Princillon in record time for the 1958 Prix de la Salamandre, and Fougalle, by Djefou, who was foaled after her dam had been exported to England and who was beaten a head in the 1960 Cambridgeshire. Lovely Rose's daughter by Tosco, Danse du Feu, produced Danse d'Irlande (by St Paddy), dam of the Right Royal V filly, Pierre Précieuse, who entered training with Yves de Nicolay at Yvre-l'Evêque in 1976, when he contested two provincial races without reaching a place.

The year after Lovely Rose was foaled Mme Couturié, anxious to introduce more Hyperion blood to her stud, sent another mare, Bastia, to Owen Tudor. Bastia, Tahiti's pacemaker in the Prix de Diane but never a winner herself, was out of Barberybush, who, together with Flying Colours, was given to the Couturiés by P. A. B. Widener when, seriously ill just after the Second World War, he decided to ship home to Kentucky all his stock except for the two mares excused the long journey on grounds of superannuation. Barbery-bush had been a good racefilly, and had produced a number of winners for Widener, including Blue Berry (by Blue Skies), Basileus and Ber-geronnette (both by Victrix) and Flying Fortress (by Fair Copy). There was originally some doubt as to whether Bastia had been sired by Tornado or Victrix, but the happy outcome of the Owen Tudor mating, Right Royal V, settled the issue when his racing plates, mounted and sent to Mme Couturié, displayed the same deformity in one foot as the latter stallion. 'Nothing,' Mme Couturié observes, 'is as hereditary as feet.'

As a two-year-old Right Royal V won the Prix Frisky Matron, the Prix de II Salamandre and the Grand Critérium, suffering defeat only in the Prix d'Aumale at Chantilly, on the eve of which he was running a temperature. He started the next season by finishing second when badly ridden in the Prix de Fontainebleau to Mme Widener's Aerodynamic, a regularly inferior work companion. After winning the Prix du Jockey Club, from Match, the King George VI and Queen Elizabeth Stakes from St Paddy, and the Prix Henry Foy, Right Royal V met his only other defeat in the Prix de L'Arc de Triomphe, when he ran a close second to Molvedo. He was syndicated as a stallion, and stood at the Haras du Mesnil until, at the age of 15, he fell, fractured his leg and had to be put down. His get included Prince Regent, Salvo, Ruysdael, Roi de Perse, Right Noble, Monarca, In The Purple, Aranas, Ricardo, Royal Warrior, Royal Garland, Prince Consort, Wenceslas, Rangong, Falkland, Ormindo, Politico, Royal Falcon, Royal Sword, Sang Bleu and Golden Eagle, and the mares Right Away, Lastarria, Royal Display, Clef Royale, Beychevelle, Reine Berangère and Jaffa.

The Haras du Mesnil permanently boarded large numbers of mares, owned by Jean Prat, Lord Derby and the Wideners, until after the Second World War, when it was decided that the strain of coping with visitors during the season was quite enough. Even so, there is still a tenuous connection on the farm today in the shape of the mares Polamịa (Mahmoud – Ampola, by Pavot) and Sly Pole (Spy Song – Ampola), jointly owned by Mme Couturié and Mrs E. W. Wetherill, formerly Mrs Peter Widener. Scores of good horses, and several successful stallions, were reared at the Haras du Mesnil on behalf of its clients between the wars, including Stern's Scaramouche (Durbar – Saperlilpopette), Lord Derby's Nepenthe (Plassy – Frisky) and Widener's Victrix (Kantar – Victory), Tornado (Tourbillon – Roséola) and Wild Risk (Rialto – Wild Videt). The first notable stallion bred at the Haras du Mesnil was La Grêlée's half-brother, Grand Guignol (1920), by St Simon's most successful son in France, Rabelais, who stood just down the road at the Haras de Montford, whither Jean Couturié dispatched many a mare.

In 1929 Widener bought a filly by Nicéas out of Doniazade, called Dogaresse, at the Deauville Yearling Sales. From three outings at two, she won three races, including the Prix d'Arenberg, and was then retired to stud, proving sterile, so Widener gave her to an English friend for a hunter. A few years later an injury put a stop to that activity, and Widener was notified that Dogaresse was about to be put down. With inspired optimism, Couturié arranged a reprieve for the mare, took her over for breeding purposes and was rewarded, in consecutive years, with Roi de Naples, Déesse, Don de Roi and, in 1940, Dogat, by Rodosto, winner of the Poule d'Essai des Poulins, the Prix Jean Prat and the Prix Jacques le Marois before retiring to stud.

Until the last couple of years Haras du Mesnil stallions were mostly home-bred. In Right Royal's early days at stud there were five stallions there – the others were Dan Cupid, Tiepoletto, Tyrone, and Tosco – and all were regularly ridden for exercise. This unusual method of keeping stallions fit has now been discontinued at the stud, and the two currently standing there, Roybet and Versailles, are got up by more conventional means. Versailles, a son of Right Royal V and a half-brother out of Décor III, by Court Martial, to Forum, winner of $205,550 in America, is owned jointly by Mme Couturié and Mme A. Gaulin. Injury necessitated his retirement from the track after his two-year-old campaign in 1966, when he won the Prix Magister at Saint Cloud, beating Topyo. Roybet (Le Fabuleux – Rush Floor, by Guersant) retired to the stud in 1974, after racing only as a four- and five-year-old, winning the Prix Regain at Longchamp, the Grand Prix de Marseille and the Prix du Carrousel at Longchamp.

The Haras du Mesnil is situated at Savigné-l'Evêque at the southern tip of Normandy. 'We are fortunate in having a stream running through our paddocks,' Mme Couturié observes, 'and the water is good, rich in iron. The pastures here, though, cannot be compared with those on the studs further north. Because our grass isn't particularly good, we have to feed our horses much more than the other breeders.' The result is that her yearlings are impressively big, a good two months forward.

Mme Couturié has attracted a deal of international interest recently with her experiments inbreeding white horses. She started by sending a grey mare to Mont Blanc, who, in due course, twice covered the resulting filly. This produced a brother and sister, who were twice mated, and, in 1977, there was a two-year-old colt and a yearling on the farm, both pure-white, blue-eyed and, apparently, of normal temperament, Mme Couturié, who is of the opinion that we don't inbreed enough these days, is prepared to make a present of the two-year-old to any breeder interested in continuing the experiment. The colt is ridden every day at the Haras du Mesnil.

White full brother and sister : the third generation of Mme. Couturié's experiment. Bottom: *the original grey mare with her Mont Blanc filly.*

Haras du Petit Tellier

'The commercial breeder may have ideas and theories of his own, but it is virtually impossible to implement them since he must bow to the fashions of the time and concentrate on popular bloodlines. One tries to breed classic winners, but the market wants precocity and the problem of striking the right balance is a ticklish one. One often hears French racing described as well-organised, but there aren't the horsemen in this country that you find in England, and the sport just represents a betting medium for lots of people who don't even know who Blushing Groom is.

'Our bloodstock sales can't be compared to the English, although, over there, you just have to go through an agent – otherwise you find your lots coming up at the beginning or the end of the day when there's nobody around. It's not so easy for us to consign to the Newmarket Sales as it is for people like Roland de Chambure, who is well-established internationally, so we generally have to go to Deauville. French bloodstock agents are a disaster for the breeders, because, although we pay their commissions, it is the purchaser who engages them, so they are not so interested in our welfare as they might be.'

Having unburdened himself of these unchauvinistic views, Patrick Chédeville, owner of the Haras du Petit Tellier at Sévigny, near Argentan, has a sideswipe at the French breeders: 'Oh, we get plenty of tears when a good stallion, like Blushing Groom, leaves the country, but when breeders have got a chance to send mares to a classic winner, they just aren't too keen. Last year I had Roi Lear here, but he didn't fill, and he only had 28 mares, including the ones my family sent. Now he's in Australia. I just don't understand it – he was a Prix du Jockey Club winner, had a good pedigree and conformation and was very cheap – 10,000 francs for the cover, and 10,000 francs more if the mare got in foal. I wish I knew what people had against him.'

Roi Lear (Reform – Kalila, by Beau Prince), who wore blinkers, got first run in the Prix du Jockey Club of 1973 and then never reappeared on a racecourse, so it may not have been all that odd for breeders to be a little chary of him. Although he was only once beaten, when running third to Kalamoun in the Prix Lupin at Longchamp, he had only four races, winning the 1972 Prix Sicambre at Saint Cloud, and the 1973 Prix Greffulhe at Longchamp. There is, furthermore, a feeling in some circles that his family's temperament is suspect.

At all events the three young stallions at the Haras du Petit Tellier in 1977 were all attractive prospects. The oldest of them, Satingo (Petingo – Saquebute, by Klairon), foaled in 1970, had a winner with his first runner when Citingo (ex Civette) took the Prix du Debut at Saint Cloud in May 1977. Unbeaten as a two-year-old, when he won the Prix de Tancarville, at Deauville, the Prix La Rochette and the Grand Critérium at Longchamp, Satingo added the Prix de la Jonchère in 1973, when he also ran third in the Poule d'Essai. He is a son of the speedy Petingo (by Petition), winner of £30,993 in six victories, including the Middle Park Stakes and the Craven Stakes at Newmarket, the Gimcrack Stakes at York and the Sussex Stakes at Goodwood. Chédeville also stands Caracolero, who won three races in addition to his Prix du Jockey Club, and Red Lord (ex Dame de Grace, by Armistice), winner of the 1976 Poule d'Essai, and the only son of Red God at stud in France.

Below: *Caracolero*. Right: *Satingo*.

Chédeville, the breeder of Président (Luthier – Peisqueira, by Free Man), who won the 1977 Prix de Guiche and burst the Général bubble, has been running the Haras du Petit Tellier for the last six years. The stud, where the French 2,000 Guineas winner, Adamastor, and the French 1,000 Guineas winner, Rajput Princess, were bred, was established by Chédeville's parents in 1960 on land owned by his mother right next to the Haras du Tellier, which belongs to his grandfather, André Chédeville. Chédeville works in conjunction with his father, Paul, who is some 15 miles away at the Bois Barbot. Chédeville père keeps the young stock until the yearlings are transferred to the Petit Tellier to be prepared for the sales, when the mares are transferred to the Bois Bardot. There are 20 mares of Paul Chédeville's and 13 of Patrick's, while Gerry Oldham and Van Jysel also have permanent boarders there. Van Jysel's Comeram and Pharly were both reared at the Haras du Petit Tellier.

The Chédevilles have been in the thoroughbred breeding business since 1850, when Paul Chédeville set up at the Haras La Coquenne, which eventually became part of the Aga Khan/Prince Aly Khan empire. Paul Chédeville bred the 1860 Cambridgeshire winner Palestro at the Haras de la Tuilerie, and established the Haras du Tellier in 1894. William Vanderbilt's Tchad, who dead-heated with J. Hennessy's Sourbier for the 1919 Prix du Jockey Club, was among the horses bred there in its early days, and Radio (Prix Vermeille), Minamoto and Galèrien (both second in the Prix du Jockey Club) are probably the best horses bred there since. Prince Rose spent the last six years of his stud career at the Haras du Tellier, and was killed there during the hostilities of 1944. While the fighting was going on, an attempt was made to move Prince Rose to a safer box, but he refused to enter the corridor of the barn chosen for him, and was returned to his normal quarters. Almost immediately there was an explosion outside and the stallion was mortally wounded. At the time, of course, nobody had any inkling of his importance to the breed. The current stallion at the Haras du Tellier is Bourbon (Le Fabuleux – Biobelle, by Cernobbio), who started second favourite for Mill Reef's Derby and whose first crop ran in 1976.

Right: *St Simon* (top) *and Bold Lad (Ire)*.

KENTUCKY

The Godolphin Arabian
The Byerley Turk

Early Importations

By around 1840 Kentucky had superseded Virginia as America's leading state for the importation and breeding of racehorses, and so it has remained to this day. The concentration of thoroughbreds now to be found within a 30-mile radius of Lexington is one of the finest the world has ever seen, and it is barely conceivable that the Blue Grass region should ever relinquish its pre-eminent position, *pace* the traditional rivals in California, those preserving the noble and ancient equine traditions of Maryland and Virginia, and the admirable band of dedicated horsemen who have succeeded in turning the classic limelight on that parvenu, Florida. Long before Kentucky had even been explored by the white man, however, Virginians were shipping quality horses from England, and, to a much lesser extent, from Spain and the West Indies, so that, by the time of the Revolution, a spectacular improvement had been wrought in a horse population, which, for the first decades of the 18th century, had consisted mainly of mixed blood North European breeds like stots, rounceys, hobbies, bidets and hart dravers, brought from England, France and Holland during the preceding 100 years, and chicasaws, inherited from the conquistadores by the southern Indians and passed on to white traders. Of the importations on which Virginia's pre-Revolutionary breeders relied to upgrade their stock, the first recorded was Bully Rock, a son of the Darley Arabian out of an unidentified mare, possibly by the Byerley Turk, foaled in 1709 and brought over as a 21-year-old by a merchant mariner called James Patton. In 1733 a half-bred yearling filly by the Godolphin Arabian was imported by Alexander Clarke, and thereafter transatlantic traffic in horseflesh grew apace. This eagerness to acquire the best blood was accompanied by a mounting enthusiasm for long distance sport in the English manner among the colonial tidewater planters, who had long been keen promoters of quarter racing. On September 30, 1737, the *Virginia Gazette* announced: 'We have advice from Hanover County that on St Andrews Day the 30th of November next there are to be horse races and several other Diversions for the Entertainment of the Gentlemen and Ladies at the Old Field near Capt John Bickerton's in that County. . . . It is proposed that 20 Horses or Mares do run round a Three Miles Course for a prize of the Value of Five Pounds according to the usual rules of Racing.' The additional attractions included 'a hat to be cudgell'd for; a violin to be played for; a Quire of ballads to be Sung for; a pair of shoes to be danced for; a pair of silk stockings for the handsomest young country maid.' A footnote added: 'As this Mirth is designed to be purely innocent and void of offence, all Persons resorting there are desir'd to behave themselves with Decency and Sobriety, the Subscribers being resolv'd to discountenance all Immorality with the utmost Rigor.'

It seems likely that 'course' racing had been introduced to Virginia as early as 1691, since, whereas quarter races were mostly matches, Francis Nicholson, the Governor, that year offered 'first and second prizes to be run for by Horses on the 22nd day of April next St George's Day being Saturday'. More typical of 17th century Virginia, in more ways than one, however, was the event mentioned in the York County Court records for September 10, 1674: 'James Bullocke, a Taylor, having made a race for his mare to runn with a horse belonging to Mr Mathew Slader for twoe thousand pounds of tobacco and caske, it being contrary to Law for a labourer to make a race, being a sport only for Gentlemen, is fined for the same one hundred pounds of tobacco and caske. Whereas Mr Mathew Slader and James Bullocke, by condition under the hand and seal of the said Slader, that his horse should runn out of the way that Bullocke's mare might win, w'ch is an apparent cheat is ord'ed to be putt in the stocks and there sitt the space of one hour.'

In 1745 a group of young planters (Ralph Wormeley IV, Marmaduke Beckwith, Joseph Morton, Benjamin Tasker junior, John Colvill, John Tayloe II, John Spotswood and William Byrd III) assumed charge of racing on the Rappahannock and Potomac and agreed to procure from English racing studs mares suitable for mating with their compatriots already in America. The first known 'thoroughbred' mare in America had appeared 10 years before the establishment of this confederacy, according to a pedigree certificate for Queen of Sheba, bred on the Rappahannock and foaled in 1746, which was signed by James Caruthers of Richmond County on May 15, 1757: 'Got by *Dabster: Bulle Rock, out of Gower's imported mare got by Whitefoot: Bald Galloway: Old Smales: Darley's Arabian: Mr Burdet's Young Child mare, by the Harpur Barb: Old Child mare by Sir Thomas Gresley's Bay Arabian: her dam by the Helmsley Turk: her dam was also the dam of Old Dodsworth. I do hereby certify that the above imported mare was foaled in 1732 and got by (the Godolphin) Whitefoot and bred by Lord Middleton. The pedigree there given is true and correct and I imported her in the year 1735.'

Three of the most influential mares to be imported to 18th century Virginia came over with Joseph Morton's great sire Traveller in 1748 – Mary Grey, a daughter of the Bolton Starling (by Bay Bolton) out of an unknown chestnut, bred at the Crofts stud in Yorkshire and owned in America by Ralph Wormeley IV, Muslin Face, of unknown breeding, purchased by Joseph Morton, and Marmaduke Beckwith's Primrose, a bay mare, foaled in 1739, which raced in 1745 and 1746 for R. Shafto in Northumberland and Durham. By the Wyvill Belgrade Turk, or his son Young Belgrade, out of Sir R. Milbank's Doll by Lord Darcy's Woodcock, she produced two known fillies, the sixth dams of *Monkey's son Herod and of one Fraxinella by an unidentified imported stallion. Mary Grey was 'remarkable for her speed', according to a 1776 advertisement for Jolly Roger, a son of *Jolly Roger out of Mary Grey's daughter by *Dabster, foaled in 1755, or thereabouts. Her only other known produce was Poll Flaxen by *Jolly Roger, foaled approximately ten years later. Muslin Face, who had a *Traveller filly around 1752, was chiefly notable during her racing career in Durham for shrinking from $13.3\frac{3}{4}$ in 1745 to $13.2\frac{1}{2}$ in 1748, according to Cheny.

Fairfax Harrison in *Early American Turf Stock* mentions five other mares of consequence imported by this group of Virginia and Maryland planters. Of these, four – Miss Colvill, Jenny Cameron, Creeping Kate and the Randolph-of-Chatsworth mare – went to Virginia, the exception being Selima, a bay foaled in 1745 by the Godolphin Arabian out of Lord Godolphin's Shireborn by Hobgoblin, which Benjamin Tasker imported into Maryland in 1750. Two years later she won a $10,000 race from horses owned by William Byrd III, John Tayloe II and their fellow Virginian Francis Thornton. Of her ten foals, nine were to prove of great merit. Three of them were by *Traveller and three by Tasker's *Othello. John Colvill bought a mare of uncertain breeding from Lord Tankerville in 1750, called her Miss Colvill and got, two years later, a colt by *Barb, who was owned by Governor Samuel Ogle, founder of the great Belair stud. Miss Colvill passed into the ownership of Benjamin Tasker, brother-in-law and successor at Belair to Governor Ogle, who bred her repeatedly to *Spark, getting the fillies Bessy Bell, Shadow and Moll Brazen. Her last identified foal was a son of *Traveller, known as Young Traveller. In 1751 John Tayloe bought Jenny Cameron, a bay (1742) by Quiet Cuddy, a son of Lord Portmore's Old Fox out of a 'high bred mare of Mr Witty's'. At the time of her importation she was in foal to Blaze, producing a chestnut filly called Betty Blazella. She is also known to have dropped four colts – Little David by John Tayloe II's *Childers, a son of Blaze, Smiling Tom by Marmaduke Beckwith's *Tom Jones, Silverlegs and Lloyd's Traveller, both by *Traveller. A maiden fifty at Beverley in 1749 was won by a mare called Creeping Kate, probably the grey, foaled in about 1745, by Badger, a son of Partner, out of a mare by Lord Portmore's Fox which was sent to America, together with Jolly Roger, in 1751. Imported by John Spotswood and his brother-in-law Bernard Moore, she had fillies by *Jolly Roger in 1758, *Traveller around 1759 and *Janus a year later. In 1761 she had a colt, Flagatruce, by *Sober John, and a filly called Dolly Fine by *Silvereye the next season.

One of America's most influential taproots was imported in 1751 to William Byrd III's Westover Stud, from where, soon afterwards, she was bought by Peter Randolph of Chatsworth. Never, apparently, otherwise identified than by the name of her second American owner, the Randolph-of-Chatsworth mare, through her daughters by *Tryal, established both the 'Piccadillas' and the 'Fluvias', the families which dominated racing in the

Roanoke Valley after the Revolution. The Randolph-of-Chatsworth mare ended her days at 'Bollingbroke', near Petersburg in Dinwiddie, a stud owned by Randolph's brother-in-law, Robert Bolling.

Of the English-bred stallions which stood in colonial Virginia, Janus, Fearnought, Traveller, Jolly Roger and Dabster seem to have been the most prolific and prepotent. *Janus, who raced in England for Anthony Swymmer under the name Stiff Dick, was by Janus, a son of the Godolphin Arabian, his dam by Fox, grandam by Bald Galloway. He was said in England to have 'foul sinews', which presumably encouraged his owner to release him for export after three seasons at stud in Morton, Oxfordshire. *Janus arrived in Virginia, aged 10, in 1756, was consigned to Mordecai Booth and raced successfully. A chestnut of $14.0\frac{3}{4}$ and a good four-mile horse, he proved a fertile sire of fast runners who tended to be lacking in 'bottom', and many of his get were put to quarter racing. His name appears frequently in quarter horse pedigrees, although that thickset, short-coupled breed otherwise owes little to thoroughbred influence. *Janus's offspring were said to be instantly recognisable, and it became common practice for him to be bred not only to his own daughters but to the fillies resulting from such matings. By the time of his death he had achieved legendary status, idolised particularly south of the James River, where he stood most of his stud career, and where quarter racing was still popular. Of *Fearnought (bay colt, 1755, by Regulus, a son of the Godolphin Arabian: Silvertail by Whitenose, a son of Hall's Arabian) 'Advocate' in *Annals of the Turf* (1826) wrote: '[He] holds the first claim prior to the day of Medley, and is therefore entitled to the palm of preference to any stallion that had preceded him in giving the Virginian turf stock a standing equal to that of any running stock in the world.' *Fearnought was imported in 1764 by John Baylor of Caroline County, who had chosen him from a list of 20 candidates provided by his English agent in answer to the stipulation that he should find 'a most beautiful strong bay at least 14.3 high, as much higher as possible, provided he has beauty, strength and sp't with it, and one that had won some Kings plates with a pedigree at full length and cert of age under a nobleman's hand as most of the list belong to noble'n.' To this Baylor added: 'As I expect one of the above I think it advisable to send a groom with him either by the trip to deliver him here to me or to agree with him for a years wages, for I must confess I am not fond of such troublesome fellows on my plan'n.' *Fearnought, who was one hand taller than the minimum specified, commanded £8 at stud, or £10 no foal no fee, at a time when *Janus was fetching a mere £4 to insure. *Traveller (bay colt, 1746, by Crofts' Partner: Crofts' Bay Bloody Buttocks by Bloody Buttocks) crops up as a cross in many an ancient pedigree. He got Ariel (1754), Partner (1755) and Bellair (1761) on *Selima, as well as a large number of good colts on imported English mares and their American-bred daughters. *Jolly Roger, who cannot quite be ranked with *Traveller and *Fearnought, either in the quality or the quantity of his get, was owned in England by the Duke of Kingston. A chestnut (1743) by Mogul, a son of the Godolphin Arabian out of a Partner mare, he was eventually sold by John Spotswood to Ralph Wormeley. *Dabster (by Lord Portmore's Old Fox: Hobgoblin, Spanker: Hautboy), a chestnut foaled in 1736, was imported in 1742 by John Carter.

During the War of Independence, the British cavalry, never fully mounted in any case because of the hazards involved in shipping horses from England, were relieved of a good many well-bred mounts, which eventually became crosses in American pedigrees. The dashing Colonel Banastre Tarleton, for instance, lost an Eclipse mare, second dam of a horse called First Consul. After the War two firms of Virginia merchants, Hart and McDonald and Benjamin Hyde, revived the business of importing English horses to such good effect – their purchases included Medley, Clockfast and Shark, and the mares Mambrina and Gunilda – that their buyers in England were soon joined by hordes of others anxious to jump on the bandwagon. Around the same time Messenger was imported to Pennsylvania, proving a spectacular success. By September 1803 William Lightfoot II was writing in the *American Turf Register*: 'I am sorry to inform you that there are so many Americans here, from Boston to Charlestown, endevoring to purchase horses that gentlemen who have them hold them at prohibitive prices, from 800 to 2,000 guineas.' During this period the Americans managed to get their hands on five Derby winners (Diomed, Saltram, Spread Eagle, Sir Harry and Archduke), as well as some outstanding mares, including Peggy, Psyche and the blind Castianira, dam of the immortal Sir Archie (by Diomed), but many of the late 18th century importations, albeit rich in the blood of Herod and Eclipse, were of indifferent quality. Colonel John Tayloe III, writing to J. S. Skinner, editor of *The American Farmer*, in 1823, observed: 'It is a fact well known to the amateurs in this favourite animal of the Virginians that we abounded much more in a fine race of horses for the saddle and harness thirty years ago than at this day. This was precisely the period when the descendants of some of the best of the English stock which had been early imported into the colony had become acclimated and fully naturalized, and I have but little doubt had we proceeded upon the rational plan of breeding solely with an eye to qualities for service, Virginia would now have had the most valuable race of horses in the world: but, unfortunately, about twenty-five or thirty years ago, the late Colonel Hoomes of the Bowling Green, of well known racing memory and many others [principally William Barksdale, Walter Bell, Hart and McDonald, Benjamin Hyde, Lamb and Younger, William Lightfoot II, Thomas Reeves, William Smalley, William Thornton, James Turner, and A. Walke and Sons] availing themselves of the passion for racing inundated the state with imported English race horses, well nigh to the extinction of the good old stocks of Janus, Fearnought, Jolly Roger, Mark Anthony, Selim and many other but little less tried and approved racers. The difficulty of getting a fine saddle horse has of late become a general remark; and when you do find one, with the exception of now and then a Diomed or a Bedford cross, you rarely hear

of any other of the late imported blood in his veins. The descendants of Cormorant and Stirling and Spread Eagle and Dare Devil and Oscar and Saltram and twenty others which might be added, are either extinct or still languishing through the probationary term of over pampered exoticks. Such as have the stamina to go through the trial and become naturalized to corn and fodder in log stables, may form the basis of some future good stock; but, I dare say, we shall never hear of many of them again.'

The diatribe against what Colonel Tayloe, in the same letter, dubbed the 'worthless garrans' brought over from England in the late 18th and early 19th centuries was somewhat overdone. Although Diomed's success at stud in America had been a turn up for the book, the inaugural English Derby winner (by Florizel, a son of Herod, out of Sister-to-Juno, by Spectator, a son of Crab) had already proved himself as influential a sire as had been seen in the country up to that time. At the time of his importation Diomed had been accurately described, in a letter to Tayloe from James Weatherby, as 'a tried and bad foal getter', and there was certainly more disingenuous sales-manship than prescience in an advertisement signed by Hoomes in the *Fredericksburg Virginia Herald* for June 16, 1798: 'The celebrated English horse, just imported from London, late the property of Sir Thomas Charles Bunbury was not only a capital racer in his days, but has proved himself to be an excellent stallion as will appear by the certificates below. . . .' Neverthe-less, by the time Tayloe was penning his querulous letter, Diomed's dis-tinguished get included such as Ball's Florizel, Potomac, Stump-the-Dealer and Duroc. The 1795 Epsom Derby winner, Spread Eagle, a son of Volunteer, is said to have had 234 mares booked to him in 1801 – Hoomes was again the importer – while Shark, brought over in 1786 after setting a record for prize money won on the English turf, had a distinguished stud career in America, mainly as a sire of fillies. His best known offspring were Virago, Annette, the elder Black Maria, Black-Eyed Susan, Betsey Lewis, Betsey Baker and Narcissa. Moreover, the success of Tayloe's own stable, which won 113 races in 141 starts from 1791–1806, leaving out the year 1802 for which records have been lost, had owed a lot to four sons of Medley (Gimcrack-Arminda, by Snap) – Bellair, Calypso, Grey Diomed and Quicksilver. Harrison observes that there is a 'constant recurrence in persisting American turf pedigrees of the names not only of Diomed, Medley and Shark, but of Alderman, Bedford, Buzzard, Citizen, Dare Devil, Expedition, Gabriel, Y. Highflyer (2), Knowsley, Oscar, Paymaster (2), Precipitate, Robin Redbreast, Royalist, Sourcrout, Speculator, Spread Eagle, Stirling, Y. Trumpator and Whip, all of which were "sent to America" between 1784 and 1805'.

Even so, dissatisfaction with the general run of horses recently imported must have been one of the factors which caused the trade with England to dry up around 1805, while the end of the Tripolitan War that year instituted a fashion for Oriental stock, mostly brought back by officers of the United States Navy or American diplomatic and consular agents returning from posts in the Mediterranean, which went on long enough to have a profound effect on numerous American pedigrees. Among the first of the exotic creatures to find their way into America during this period was the pure Arab Selim, reputedly General Sir Ralph Abercromby's battle charger,

Left: *Shark(e) 'got by Marsk, His dam by Snap'*. Below left: *Banastre Tarleton, Colonel in Cornwallis' army, by Joshua Reynolds*. Below right: *the death of Sir Ralph Abercromby*.

brought over to Virginia in March 1805 by Captain James Barron, U.S.N. With him came a certificate signed in Malta by N. Ramsay in 1802: 'Selim, a thoroughbred Arabian horse seven years old 14 hands and a half high . . . was got by Achmet a favourite horse of the Mameluke chief Murad Bey; out of an Abyssinian mare. He was procured and presented to the late general Sir Ralph Abercromby by the Grand Vizier on his arrival in Egypt. Sir Ralph gave him to an officer of high rank; of whom I obtained him.'

Reproduction of the map of Kentucky in the Voyages of Nicholas Cresswell in America.

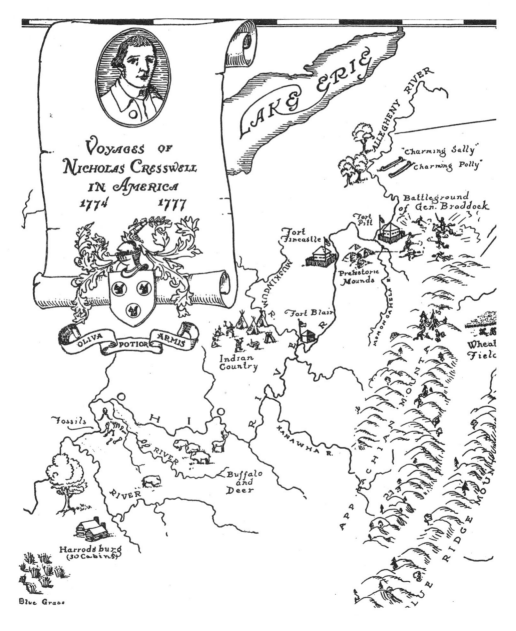

The Blue Grass

In 1808 Thomas Jefferson's embargoes on trade with England were introduced, putting the tidewater planters of Virginia and Maryland under severe economic pressure and foreshadowing the end of their long dominance of American racing and breeding. The renewal of organised racing after the 1812–14 War was not immediate, and by the time it was once again in full swing, in the early 1820s, the sport was run on more or less a national basis, as it was to be until the Civil War, with financial support from the commercial cities of the Atlantic seaboard and valuable publicity from *The American Farmer*. Breeders put their faith largely in the best of the stock against which Colonel Tayloe simultaneously inveighed, and the produce of Medley mares and the get of Diomed's sons were much in evidence around the Roanoke Valley and the newer communities of Kentucky and Tennessee. New York, too, where America's first formal racetrack, a two-mile circuit on Hempstead Plain, Long Island, had been laid out as long ago as 1665, continued to have its share of the action. It was at that city's Union Course in May 1823 that the equine hero of the epoch, the unbeaten American Eclipse, by Duroc out of the Messenger mare Miller's Damsel, in the first of the great North–South matches, dashed Virginian hopes by beating Sir Archie's son Henry in three four-mile heats. When, around 1830, demand for English stock was suddenly renewed, William Jackson of New York was the first to import on a serious scale, but it was not long before most of the English horses sent to America were once more going to Virginia. Merritt and Company of Hicks Ford on the Roanoke River in Brunswick County included the 1830 Derby winner, Priam, in the large number of horses they imported between 1835 and 1837, but with the distribution of the last of their stock, Virginia yielded its position as America's racehorse centre.

And no wonder, if the effusions of Senator John James Ingalls of Kansas are anything to go by. That worthy's collected writings, published in 1902, contained the following paean:

'There is a portion of Kentucky known as the "Blue Grass Region", and it is safe to say that it has been the arena of the most significant intellectual and physical development that has been witnessed among men or animals upon the American continent, or perhaps upon the whole face of the world. In corroboration of this belief, it is necessary only to mention Henry Clay, the orator, and the horse, Lexington, both peerless, electric, immortal. The ennobling love of the horse has extended to all other races of animals.

The reflex of this solicitude appears in the muscular, athletic vigor of the men, and the voluptuous beauty of the women who inhabit this favored land. Palaces, temples, forests, peaceful institutions, social order, spring like exhalations from the congenial soil. All these marvels are attributable as directly to the potential influence of bluegrass as day and night to the revolution of the earth . . . [Bluegrass] is the healing catholicon, the strengthening plaster, the verdant cataplasm, efficient alike in the Materia Medica of Nature and of Morals.'

Bold claims, these, for a smooth-stalked meadow grass, properly called *Poa pratensis*, which grows extensively in England and Europe, as well as North America, but most Kentucky horsemen attribute much of their success to the good grazing. Indeed, when the experts suggest, as they generally do, that bluegrass is not native to Kentucky, passions can be aroused. The late Judge Samuel Wilson, a Kentucky historian, for instance, wrote in the magazine *Kentucky Progress* for December 1933: 'Let no true son of Kentucky ever doubt or waver in his faith that "bluegrass", "Kentucky bluegrass", genuine *Poa pratensis* is a native product of the soil.' To substantiate his claim the judge cited Christopher Gist, who did indeed report 'quantities of bluegrass' in 1751, but that was north of the Ohio River, his brief from the Ohio Land Company being to 'go out westward of the great mountains in order to search out and discover the lands upon the river Ohio down as low as the Great Falls thereof; and to take an exact account of all the large bodies of good land, that the Company may the better judge where it will be most convenient to take their grant'. Reliable references to bluegrass in Kentucky not long after Gist's time survive aplenty, however. The map of Kentucky in the *Voyages of Nicholas Cresswell in America, 1774–1777* shows bluegrass, while several other sources quoted by Judge Wilson confirm its presence. Dr Jeremiah Morse, the geographer, spoke in 1789 of a Kentucky 'covered with clover, blue grass and wild rye', while the *Kentucky Gazette* for February 16, 1793 offered for sale a farm, owned by Peter January and son, 'about 400 yards from the courthouse', which had 17 acres sown with clover, blue grass and timothy. Moreover in the 1806 case of Higgins' heirs versus Darnell's devisees twelve witnesses testified to the existence, up to 30 years earlier, of 'English grass', 'Blue Grass' or 'English Blue Grass' on Grassy Lick at a point near the junction of the present three counties of Bourbon, Clark and Montgomery. The Kentucky Historical Society in Frankfort also has a transcript of an interview with one Daniel Spohr, who lived at Strode's Station near Grassy Lick in the 1780s and recalled: 'The first blue grass seed I ever saw came from that place. Not the same kind that grew in Virginia; more productive. It was not as green as the Virginian, and the stem ripens and dies when the head does, while of the Virginia bluegrass the stem is green when the head is dry and ripe.'

The experts, nevertheless, tend to deny that bluegrass is indigenous to America at all. Robert Buckner, Professor of Agronomy at the University of Kentucky and the man who developed the Kenwell Fescue, states that it is of

Eurasian origin. J. S. McHargue, Professor of Chemistry at Kentucky, who did extensive research on bluegrass in 1926, not only arrived at a similar conclusion but followed Dr W. J. Beal, author of *Grasses in America*, published in 1887, in suggesting that the genuine bluegrass is not *Poa pratensis* at all, but its coarser Canadian relative *Poa compressa*. The Canadian strain, described in 1824 by Dr John Torrey as 'short, linear, carinate, smooth and glaucous' was, according to Professor D. L. Phares, quoted by Beal, 'blue, the true blue grass from which the genus received its trivial name.' 'The only time *Poa pratensis* possesses any blueness of colour during its growth,' wrote McHargue, 'is when the grass is in full bloom. The anthers have a purplish hue and when the grass is tall and thick on the ground a bluish cast may be seen in looking over a considerable expanse of the grass. However, the purplish color is very transient and is more pronounced if the weather happens to be warm and dry previous to and at the time of blooming, which is usually the latter part of May for Kentucky.' Colonel George Chinn, grandson of the gambler Colonel Chinn for whom Jesse James's brother Frank used to act as commission agent, now working with the Kentucky Historical Society, guesses that, in the early days when Kentucky was still forested, the grass, growing in the intermittent light filtering through the leaves, was actually blue.

What is more important, though, is that, as Professor Buckner puts it: '*Poa pratensis* is a most nutritious cool season grass which needs soils rich in phosphorus and calcium, and, ideally, a pH range of 6.5 to 6.7'. Central Kentucky, with its rare outcropping of Ordovician limestone at the apex of the Cincinnati anticline, has the perfect soil, although it is in Wisconsin, because of the equable climate, that *Poa pratensis* flourishes best. It is a grass free, in Professor Buckner's words, of 'the anti-quality components found in other types – the alkaloids which occur in the tall fescue, the prussic acid in Sudan or Johnson grass or the tannin in alfalfa and lespedezas, for example'. Or, as Kentucky-breds are supposed to remark to their Californian rivals in the back stretch at Churchill Downs: 'You might as well quit now. I was raised on bluegrass, not cactus.' On the other hand, there are one or two good horses coming out of Florida these days, and even Bob Green, manager of

John Hay Whitney's Greentree Stud on the Paris Pike, just outside Lexington, surely one of the handsomest and best-kept horse farms in the world, has been heard to voice vague and heretical doubts as to whether the local grazing really is a *sine qua non* for the production of the best American thoroughbreds. Over on the Frankfort Pike, Olin Gentry, who runs Darby Dan Farm for John W. Galbreath, expounds the conventional view with the fervent exaggeration of a man who has spent decades perfecting the art of the outrageous remark. 'Now timothy is for poor people and poor horses,' he explains, 'but if you've got bluegrass in your fields, it doesn't matter if you feed them anything else.' Well, there is the hay he gets from Northern Michigan, where 'I've got a good man to find the best and damn the expense', alfalfa and clover, the grain which is denied only the barren and maiden mares, and so on, but Gentry may safely be regarded as a believer in the efficacy of *Poa pratensis*.

While the breeding and racing of horses was burgeoning into quite a business in Virginia, Kentucky was still talked of as the untrod paradise over the mountains, and it was not until 1750 that Cumberland Gap was named, in honour of the Duke, by Dr Thomas Walker of Castle Hill, Albemarle County, as he passed through it leading the first expedition into the territory. Even then, a legend carved on a tree indicated that some nameless white man had already ventured there alone. Lewis Evans produced the first map of Kentucky in 1752, and 17 years later Daniel Boone and John Finlay arrived with a hunting party only to lose their horses immediately to the Indians. It was in 1775 that Boone brought settlers along the Wilderness Trail to Boonesboro, and Lexington was named the same year. The hazards of frontier life notwithstanding, the early denizens of the town did not waste much time before getting down to some serious sport, and a sign erected on what is now South Broadway by the Historical Marker Society reads: 'Near this spot pioneers in 1780 established the starting point of the first race path in Kentucky, extending southward one quarter mile.'

The newly-explored region was organised as Kentucky County, Virginia, in 1776, and six years later Lexington received its town charter. There were horse races at Humble's race-paths and Haggin's race-paths outside Harrodsburg, near Lexington, in 1783, the records of the Oyer and Terminer Court for August that year showing that one Hugh McGary was found guilty of backing a mare there. It was decided that 'the said H. McGary, gentleman, be deemed an infamous gambler, and that he shall not be eligible to any office of trust or honor within this state – pursuant to an act of assembly entitled an act to suppress excessive gaming.' The first newspaper west of the Alleghenies, the *Kentucke Gazette* was started in 1787, and on February 16 the next year it carried the earliest known pedigree published in the region: 'The famous horse PILGARLICK of a beautiful chestnut colour, full fourteen hands three inches high, rising ten years old, will stand the ensuing season on the head of the Salt River . . . Pilgarlick was got by the noted imported horse Janus, his dam by Silver-eye, and is the swiftest in the district

Above: *Daniel Boone*. Top right: *Stallions in Kentucky, from Harper's New Monthly Magazine, September 1889*. Above right: *'Concluding a bargain'*.

of Kentucke from one to six hundred yards, Darius only excepted.' The invincible Darius was one of those horses who had *Janus as sire, grandsire and great grandsire. Around this time 'course' racing was introduced to Lexington, although the location of the circuit is unknown. The first announcement of a formal meeting appeared in the *Kentucke Gazette* for August 22, 1789:

'A purse race at Lexington on the 2d Thursday in October next, free for any horse, mare or gelding, weight for age, agreeable to the rules of New Market (three mile heats) the best two in three; one quarter of an hour allowed between heats for rubbing. Each subscriber to pay one guinea, and every person that enters a horse to pay two guineas including his subscription. One guinea for every horse starting to be considered as entrance money for the second best horse. Judges to be appointed by a majority of the starters on the day of running. The horses to be entered the day before running with Mr John Fowler, who will attend at Mr Collins' tavern on that day. The age of the horses to be ascertained to the satisfaction of the judges appointed before they can be admitted to start, even although they have paid the entrance money etc., and the money paid remain for the good of the purse. But the starter may be admitted to start his horse at

Court House Square, Lexington in 1889. Right: *Charles Baskerville's picture of Richard Ten Broeck from an original by Reinhardt.*

the age adjudged by the judges, agreeable to the rules of New Market. The horses to start precisely at one o'clock: Any horse not starting agreeable to the appointment to be adjudged a distanced horse. All disputes arising to be left to the decision of the judges. Subscriptions taken in by Nicholas Lafon, Lexington.'

Quarter racing along the town's thoroughfares was still popular, however, so much so that, in October, 1793, the Trustees 'feeling the dangers and inconveniences which are occasioned by the practice, but too common, of racing through the streets of the in and out lotts of the town, and convinced that they are not invested with sufficient authority to put a stop to such practices, recommend it to the people of the town, to call a public meeting, to consider of the means which ought to be adopted for applying a remedy to the growing evil.' The resulting prohibition on 'jockeys racing their horses through the streets' was rescinded for July 4, 1976, as part of Lexington's bicentenary junket. By 1791, when the free population of the whole of Fayette County was still only 3,517, a three-day October meeting had become an annual event in Lexington. Kentucky's first Jockey Club was formed in 1797 – a year after the state had been admitted to the Union – with Henry Clay as a member. The same year the first of the 'blooded' stallions to cross the Alleghenies in response to the shift from quarter to 'course' racing in Kentucky was advertised to stand at Colonel Robert Sanders' farm near Georgetown. This was Benjamin Wharton's Blaze, by Vandal, foaled in 1786 and imported to Virginia in 1793. Many more followed, and in the first decade of the 19th century, race meetings were being held not only in Lexington itself but nearby in Maysville, Winchester, Paris, Versailles, Flemingsburg, Harrodsburg and Richmond.

Woodburn Farm in the 19th century

The Kentucky Jockey Club was abolished in 1809 to be replaced by a Lexington Jockey Club with Dr Elisha Warfield as a member. Dr Warfield was to become the state's leading authority on pedigrees and the rules of racing but his principal claim to immortality is as the breeder of the most successful sire in American history, Lexington. Foaled on March 17, 1850, Lexington was by Boston out of the *Sarpedon mare Alice Carneal. Boston, a son of the Florizel mare Sister to Tuckahoe, was by Timoleon, who is generally said to have been by Sir Archie out of a *Saltram mare. However, in his account of the Jersey Act in the monumental *Bloodstock Breeding* Sir Charles Leicester wrote that Timoleon's 'parentage was open to the gravest suspicion. Some authorities aver that he was at stud under three different pedigrees within a period of eight years. The only animal of this name to be found in the pages of the English stud book was a mare. It is therefore plain that in the English terminology Lexington could only be described as of unknown pedigree – or in other words as a "half-bred".' Whatever doubts may have been entertained about the impurity of their blood, Boston, winner of 40 of this 45 starts, and Lexington, who won $56,000 for his six victories, including one against the clock, were certainly racehorses of the highest class. As far as Timoleon's dubious parentage is concerned, it may possibly be significant that both Boston and Lexington, like Sir Archie's dam, went blind.

It was with Lexington's arrival at R. A. Alexander's Woodburn Farm in Woodford County that the foundations were laid of that confident, well-informed and opulent Blue Grass society which today has custody of so much of the world's best bloodstock. Alexander, in the words of John Hervey in *Racing in America (1665–1865)*, was 'the first gentleman of great wealth and high social position who deliberately engaged in breeding as his life-work with the avowed purpose of introducing the most intelligent and approved methods, the end in view being the "improvement of the breed of horses".' Pre-Civil War Kentucky, bestrewn with buildings in the classical style erected by gentlemen with literary tastes, had become America's most important breeding region in any case, but, after Alexander, the Blue

Left: *Lexington, by Edward Troye.* Bottom: *'The First Futurity' by L. Maurer, 1889, showing Salvator losing by half a length to Proctor Knott at Sheepshead Bay.*

M

Above: *Alice Carneal*, Below: *Boston*. Right: *Lexington in 1872*.

Grass had the permanent and prescriptive right to be the principal arena for the development of the American racehorse. Lexington, originally named Darley because Dr Warfield discerned some resemblance, when he was foaled, to the Sartorius painting of the Darley Arabian, began his racing career at three – by which time his owner-breeder was 72 – on lease to a negro called Burbidge's Harry. He ran in the Warfield colours (light blue cap, white jacket), racing, at the time, being a sport only for white men, and took the Association Stakes and the Citizens' Stakes at Lexington before he was sold to Richard Ten Broeck, a former Mississippi gambler and estranged member of a distinguished Albany, New York, family. Ten Broeck took in three Kentuckians (General Abe Buford, Junius R. Ward and Captain Willa Viley) as co-owners of the colt, renamed him and shipped him to the trainer J. B. Pryor at Natchez. Lexington had cost $2,500, plus the same again in the event of his winning the Great State Post Stake at the New Orleans track, Metairie, which was to be the scene of all his remaining appearances and where the principal shareholder was Richard Ten Broeck. His first race for his new owners was a match against Sallie Walters on December 2, 1853, which he won handsomely, the *New Orleans Picayune* remarking: 'Upon stripping, the fine form of Sallie and the apparent excellence of her condition challenged the admiration of all. Lexington's appearance violates all laws of horsemen in the purchase of a horse – four white legs, glass or "wall" eyes, and is a blazed young rip. His style of going, however, is poetry in motion and the horse that outruns him in a sticky, heavy track, like that of yesterday, must be some sort of steam engine in disguise.' On April 1 the next year he won the Great State Post Stake for Kentucky from the Mississippi representative Lecomte, another son of Boston, who, in two four-mile heats four days later, gave Lexington his only taste of defeat. There had been some disagreement among the syndicate members about the wisdom of running Lexington that day, and Ten Broeck had bought his partners out. The time for the first heat, 7:26, was a new record, which Lexington, given a flying start and the assistance of pacemakers, duly beat by six and a quarter seconds on April 2, 1855. His last race, 12 days later, was something of a hollow victory over Lecomte, who was suffering from colic and who was withdrawn by his owner, General Thomas Wells, after being all but distanced in the first heat.

'In introducing this establishment to the notice of the public,' wrote R. A. Alexander in Woodburn's first catalogue, issued in 1857, 'I may say that I have been actuated not only by the interest I feel in all sorts of good stock, which has induced me to attempt myself the breeding of thoroughbred horses, but by the desire to afford those who have the same taste as myself, but who are not so advantageously located for the purpose, the opportunity of having their breeding stock properly kept. . . . For my own convenience in breeding, and with the view of giving every facility to those breeders who are disposed to avail themselves of the opportunity here offered, I have purchased the celebrated horse LEXINGTON; and have also imported a young horse, SCYTHIAN – both of which will serve mares at Woodburn Stud Farm.' Lexington's fee was $100, *Scythian's $75. Robert Aitcheson Alexander was born in Frankfort, Kentucky, on October 25, 1819. Woodburn, '2,000 acres, more or less, situated in the county of Kentucky, on the waters of Elkhorn Creek', had been bought 29 years earlier by his father, Robert, who was born in Scotland, the son of a prominent banker and Lord Provost of Edinburgh, and who, as a youth, served as Benjamin Franklin's secretary in France. When Robert senior died in 1841, he left Woodburn jointly to R.A., his younger brother Alexander John and their two sisters, but R.A., after completing his education at Trinity College, Cambridge, and remaining some years in Scotland and Europe, returned home in 1849 intent on devoting himself to the improvement of American livestock. He bought up all the shares in Woodburn, and, after two years studying agriculture and breeding in Europe, took up residence early in 1852, extending the estate to some 4,000 acres by 1860. Alexander's enduring fame as a breeder by no means rests entirely on his achievements with horses, and his contributions to the establishment of Shorthorn and Jersey cattle, Cotswold and Southdown sheep and Berkshire swine in the United States were a vital factor in the evolution of America's best livestock. The development of the standardbred horse – trotting was in its infancy when Alexander took over Woodburn – also owed much to his efforts, but it was with his thoroughbreds that he achieved a dominance over his contemporaries which has never, and hardly ever can be, equalled. At Lexington's 1856 Autumn meeting George Harrison and the filly Novice recorded Alexander's first successes on the turf, but the owner was not around to see them, having gone to England looking for a couple of decent stallions. There he bumped into Ten Broeck, who sold him Lexington for the unheard-of price of $15,000. By 1861 Lexington was champion sire – as he was for the 14 remaining years of his life, besides

Glencoe, engraved from a painting by Hancock.

winning the title twice more posthumously, while his crop that year included three super-colts out of *Glencoe mares in Asteroid, Norfolk and Kentucky. None was ever beaten, apart from the Jersey Derby in which Kentucky ran second to Norfolk, who had just been sold to the Californian Theodore H. Winters for $15,001. The odd buck was one in the eye for those who had predicted that Alexander would never get as much for a son of Lexington as he paid Ten Broeck. Norfolk's dam, incidentally, was none other than Novice, out of Chloe Anderson by Rudolph. In 1862 Lexington's get included the speedy filly Maiden, out of Kitty Clark by *Glencoe, who became a highly influential mare. Her granddaughter Saluda, mated with the imported English stallion Sailor Prince, winner of the 1886 Cambridgeshire, produced Sibola, first in the 1,000 Guineas and second in the Oaks of 1899 for Lord Beresford and third dam of Nearco.

Racing opportunities were naturally limited during the Civil War, yet only two of Alexander's horses failed to win between 1861 and 1865. Three-quarters of them were by Lexington, and if the most spectacular performers were the result of a nick with *Glencoe mares, this was by no means the whole story. Notable sons of Lexington during the period also included Bay Flower and Beacon, both out of Bay Leaf by *Yorkshire, and Bay Dick, out of Alabama by Brown Dick. In 1862 the four-year-old *Australian, who had been raced under the name of Millington for A. Keene Richards of George-

West Australian.

town, Kentucky, joined the stable. A son of the 1853 English Triple Crown winner West Australian and the *Young Emilius mare, *Emilia, he was to prove a stallion second only to Lexington in the years from the end of the Civil War to 1880. Alexander, who in his 1857 catalogue had requested that 'all patrons sending mares to Lexington and Scythian send their pedigrees that they may be recorded' was the first in America to achieve a systematic and comprehensive documentation of equine genealogies. The donkeywork was done by Sanders D. Bruce, compiler of the first *American Stud Book*, published in 1862, whose efforts were fiercely denigrated in J. H. Wallace's *The Horse in America* (1897), where he was described as 'not a pedigree tracer, but a pedigree maker'. Bruce's fallibility, according to Wallace, was matched only by Alexander's gullibility: 'Thus the acts of an incapable and dishonest employee were given the endorsement of an honorable and eminent name; falsehoods were made to appear as truths; counterfeits put in circulation that are still circulated as genuine coin by many people.' Whatever mistakes there are to be found in the early Woodburn catalogues, none of Kentucky's horse dealers and sharpers, at any rate, claimed it was easy to put one over on Alexander.

During the Civil War, Woodburn, initially immune because Alexander flew the British flag, suffered two raids. In the first, on October 22, 1864, four Lexington two-year-olds were taken as well as, even more disastrously, Asteroid. He was recovered by Major Warren Viley for $250. The second band of guerrillas to plunder Woodburn almost caused it to close down as a horse breeding establishment. The raid, during which Alexander was involved in a brawl with one of the bandits, occurred on February 2, 1865. Alexander's own account of events that day, contained in a letter from Chicago, dated March 4, to his brother-in-law Henry Deedes, read, in part:

'They asked for Asteroid but in the dusk of the evening the trainer gave them an inferior horse and so saved the best horse in my stable. They got Norwich, brother to Norfolk, a four-year-old mare that was a good one, and a three-year-old filly by Lexington which we think well of, besides the colt they mistook for Asteroid, making four from my race stable. They also got four from my trotting stable and four from my riding horse stable and three more from various places, making 15 horses in all. The most valuable of the whole was the trotting horse the Captain of the band seemed to be so anxious to get hold of and he was worth fully as much as any horse I own except Lexington himself, and I doubt if I would have touched fifteen thousand dollars in green backs for him. The second most valuable was my trotting stallion Abdallah. Both these are dead, the first from a wound in the back; the second, being captured by the federals, was ridden to death by a federal soldier. The third in value, Norwich, was still in the hands of the guerrillas when I heard last from home. Six horses and mares are still missing, including the two which are dead, and their value is not less than $32,000. We can console ourselves with the idea that it might have been far worse. . . . The uncertainty of matters in general and of life and property in my portion of Kentucky as illustrated by the raid of which I have given you an account has at last induced me at a very heavy expense to change my abode and to remove almost all my stock to Illinois.'

Lexington and 48 other thoroughbreds, as well as 43 trotters, were duly transferred, but, on April 9 that year, the War ended, and it was not long before there was talk of a great match between Asteroid and Kentucky, representing the New York stable of John Hunter, W. T. Travers and George Osgood. Alexander, writing to his brother on August 5, reported:

'In his trial Asteroid ran his miles as follows: $1:51\frac{1}{2}$, $1:51\frac{1}{2}$, $1:49\frac{1}{2}$ and $1:51$, a final time of $7:23\frac{1}{2}$. This over a track which was good but not extraordinarily fast. The weight carried was the proper weight for a four-year-old, viz 104 pounds. He ran at his ease and would have done better if he had been urged, but this trial was made with 11 pounds more weight, comparing ages and weights, than Lexington carried. Lexington's proper weight as a five-year-old would have been 114 pounds, whereas he carried 103 pounds. If I can judge of the effect of 11 pounds overweight from the little experience I have had it will be equal to a little over 10 seconds in the four miles, thus bringing his time to $7:13\frac{1}{2}$, and this too on a track that had no extra work on it to prepare for a fast run. You see what I think of this horse, and in some measure I have shown you why I think so well of him; as it is possible that our Yankee friends may desire to try his mettle, I wish this to be kept quiet, indeed I wish you to burn this on receipt after reading it.'

The great race never came off, as Asteroid went lame, and early the next year, with the horse market in a depressed condition, Alexander offered his entire stud for sale. In New York looking for a buyer, he bumped into the trainer Harry Belland, who, four years earlier, had been given charge of 34 Woodburn horses to race and sell in Canada. Belland was on his way to Kentucky to report profits of $300,000, and Woodburn was withdrawn from the market.

Alexander appointed Daniel Swigert, one of the greatest horsemen of his generation, as manager of Woodburn in 1862. Relinquishing this position in 1869 Swigert established his own stud, Stockwood, and then, in 1881, bought the Preakness Stud from Milton H. Sanford and renamed it Elmendorf, the maiden name of his wife's paternal grandmother. Swigert's daughter Mary in 1876 married Leslie Combs Junior, grandfather of the present proprietor of Spendthrift Farm. When the bachelor R. A. Alexander died on December 1, 1867, Woodburn passed to his brother. A. J., although he carried on his brother's work in thoroughbred and standardbred pedigrees, was more interested in cattle than horses and had little to do with running the stud, which now functioned purely as a commercial operation. Swigert was succeeded by his brother-in-law Lucas Brodhead, who maintained Woodburn's outstanding record, and there was never a threat to the farm's supremacy until the early 1880s. Lexington died in 1875, and the *Kentucky Livestock Record* owned and edited by Benjamin Gratz Bruce, brother of Sanders D., then in its first year of publication, carried a long obituary on September 7, which began:

'We need not we are sure make any apology for the space devoted this week to the memoir of Lexington, the most remarkable horse this country, if not the world, has ever seen. He was not a passing meteor that rushes through the air, dazzling our eyes with its brilliant light, leaving little or no impression, but a blazing sun whose influence interpenetrated and has become identified with all our stock. No horse was his equal upon the American turf, and none can compare with him as a stallion.'

Brodhead's account of Lexington's demise was also printed:

'[He] had suffered from nasal catarrh for about three years, but the discharge was not very copious or annoying to him until within the last two months, when it became very copious, as you saw when you were down. His appetite continued good, and his general health in every particular was excellent with the exception of the catarrh. The day before his death, he was breathing with great difficulty, and refused his feed for the first time. The bones of his face had become diseased, and the skull was pressed out between or a little below his eyes, I suppose by the accumulation of matter. A few hours before his death the skull was eaten through by the poisonous matter and became soft. The Old Hero was game to the last, and hardly laid down, and seemed perfectly conscious. He died about 12 o'clock Thursday night of July 1st, finishing the season of 1875. I think we have about ten mares in foal by him. He retained his sexual vigor up to a few days of his death; but the catarrh would not permit him to mount a mare. Drs Herr and Harthill were called in some months ago and after a careful examination concluded that there was no chance to cure his disease. We buried him in the open space just opposite his stable door, putting him in a coffin made to receive him. We have received many applications for his bones, but we felt like an old friend had departed and could not bear to see him cut up by unfeeling hands. We had him buried carefully so that none of his bones can be lost, and in the future expect to have them mounted.'

On November 19 the same year, the *Kentucky Livestock Record* reported: 'The bones of Lexington, the grandest race horse and sire of them all, were exhumed last week and forwarded to Prof H. A. Ward of Rochester N.Y., who will immediately proceed to set the skeleton for the Smithsonian Institute. The skeleton will be exhibited at the Centennial next year.' Today, it is still on display at the Institute.

Lexington, the *Kentucky Livestock Record* computed, had covered 925 mares, apart from trotters, in his time, getting 236 winners of $1,159,321 despite the fact that the Civil War was fought in his prime as a stallion and many of his progeny were lost. A comparison of doubtful validity with Herod (497 winners, $970,000), Matchem (345 winners, $531,000) and Eclipse (344 winners, $548,520) emphasised Lexington's claims to the crown. *Australian did not long survive his illustrious colleague, and the *Kentucky Livestock Record* for September 18, 1897, reported that he had been 'found dead in his box having broke a blood vessel.' Their assessment of his career at stud went:

'The following are among the best of his get: Fellowcraft, Rutherford, Abd-el-Kader, Abd-el-Koree, Dickens, Helmbold, Maggie B.B., Joe Daniels, Mate, Mozart, Silent Friend, Springbok, Wildidle, Waverley, Baden Baden, Zoo Zoo, Spendthrift and a host of others. *Australian has not been a prolific sire, but rather an uncertain foal getter, but from his sons and daughters he stands second only to Lexington as a sire. He has more colts that have run four miles under 7:35 than any sire that has ever stood in America, namely: Abd-el-Kader, 4 yrs, 7:32$\frac{1}{2}$; Abd-el-Koree, 3 yrs, 7:33; Helmbold, 4 yrs, 7:32$\frac{1}{2}$; Fellowcraft, 4 yrs, 7:19$\frac{1}{2}$; Silent Friend, 4 yrs, 7:30$\frac{1}{2}$; Rutherford, 4 yrs, 7:34$\frac{3}{4}$; and Wildidle, 5 yrs, 7:25$\frac{1}{2}$ . . . Lexington must share part of the honor with Australian, as Abd-el-Kader and Abd-el-Koree are out of a half sister to Lexington, and Helmbold is out of another half sister. Wildidle is out of Idlewild by Lexington, and Fellowcraft and Rutherford, own brothers, are out of Aerolite, sister to Idlewild by Lexington. So it will be seen that the old blind hero's name and fame are closely interwoven with Australian's seven great sons. The four yearlings that were sold at Woodburn in June, 1879, are the last of Australian's get, as he had been unable to serve any mares for the past two seasons. They did breed Aerolite to him this year, but she failed to catch.'

Although Woodburn was to produce many a good horse before the stud

ceased operations around the turn of the century, the golden age was inevitably coterminous with the careers of Lexington and *Australian. From the end of the Civil War to 1880, Woodburn-bred horses – in any average year, about three per cent of the country's total – maintained a stranglehold on the top stakes races, taking the Belmont eight times (General Duke 1868, Kingfisher 1870, Harry Bassett 1871, Joe Daniels 1872, Springbok 1873, Duke of Magenta 1878, Spendthrift 1879, Grenada 1880), the Travers nine times (Maiden 1865, Merrill 1866, Kingfisher 1870, Harry Bassett 1871, Joe Daniels 1872, Attila 1874, Baden Baden 1877, Duke of Magenta 1878, Grenada 1880), the Jerome seven times (Bayonet 1868, Kingfisher 1870, Harry Bassett 1871, Joe Daniels 1872, Acrobat 1874, Duke of Magenta 1878, Grenada 1880), the Saratoga Cup eight times (Lancaster 1868, Bayonet 1869, Helmbold 1870, Harry Bassett 1872, Joe Daniels 1873, Springbok 1874, Springbok/Preakness dead heat 1875, Tom Ochiltree 1876), the Dixie six times (Preakness 1870, Harry Bassett 1871, Hubbard 1872, Tom Ochiltree 1875, Duke of Magenta 1878, Grenada 1880), and the Kentucky Derby twice (Baden Baden 1877, Fonso 1880).

If no year passed during this period without Woodburn producing top-class horses, there was still, even by the stable's own high standards, the

Left: *Spendthrift as a three-year-old.* Below left: *Springbok as a five-year-old.* Below: *Preakness.*

PREAKNESS.

GARRICK

DUKE OF MAGENTA

TROUBLE

occasional *annus mirabilis*. While R. A. Alexander was contemplating selling out and moving to Illinois, one of the stud's best-ever crops was produced, foals of 1865 including Asteroid's brother Ancroid, out of Nebula, who fetched $7,000 at the yearling sales, and five excellent performers in General Duke, Vauxhall, Bayonet, Abd-el-Kader and Pat Malloy, all of whom, however, failed to reach their reserves at auction. They were disposed of privately as two-year-olds, although Pat Malloy (Lexington – Gloriana, by American Eclipse) finished his days as a Woodburn stallion, siring a large number of fast runners, including the 1879 Kentucky Derby winner, Lord Murphy. The last Woodburn crop before R. A. Alexander's death turned out to be a good one too, including three of Lexington's best colts. Daniel Swigert bought two of them, Kingfisher, out of Eltham Lass by Kingston, for $490, and Foster, out of Verona by *Yorkshire, for $585. The third, out of Bay Leaf, was knocked down for $2,000 to Milton H. Sanford, who, apparently out of habit, called him Preakness. From him, of course, the second leg of the American Triple Crown took its name. The next year Woodburn again produced more than its far share of champions, with, among the yearlings sold at the 1869 auction, Harry Bassett, by Lexington, out of Canary Bird by *Albion, Monarchist, by Lexington out of Mildred by *Glencoe, Wanderer, by Lexington out of Coral by Vandal and Lexington's daughter, Salina, out of the *Glencoe mare Lightsome, who became dam of Salvator. The 1871 yearling sale set new records for Woodburn, which was not surprising since among those on offer were Wildidle, Fellowcraft, Springbok, out of Lexington's daughter Hester, and Lizzie Lucas (*Australian – Eagless, by *Glencoe). Perhaps the most notable of the other great race-horses bred by Brodhead for Alexander in the 1870s were Tom Ochiltree (1872, Lexington – Katona, by Voucher), Baden Baden (1874, *Australian – Lavender, by Wagner), Duke of Magenta (1875, Lexington – Magenta, by *Yorkshire) and Spendthrift, a full brother to Rutherford and Fellowcraft, foaled in 1876. Swigert bought Baden Baden for $1,010 and Spendthrift for $1,000. The latter was so named by Swigert as a comment on one of his wife's shopping trips. She retaliated the next year by bestowing the name Miser on the colt's full brother. Both were sold in 1869 to James R. Keene, Spendthrift, after his Belmont win being sent to race, unsuccessfully, in England. He did well at stud, though, and is best known as the sire of Hastings, winner of the 1896 Belmont and grandsire of Man o' War. The last of Woodburn's classic winners was Chant (1894 Kentucky Derby), who had one grandam by *Australian and one by Lexington, but by this time the farm was in decline. When A. J. Alexander died on December 2, 1902, there were neither thoroughbreds nor standardbreds left at Woodburn, and it was not long before Lexington's long-term influence on the breed was being impugned – not, of course, that such posthumous indignities are uncommon for American stallions. *The Thoroughbred Record* – the magazine founded in Lexington by Benjamin Gratz Bruce had carried a new legend on its mast-head since February 2, 1895 – printed the following iconoclastic lines from a correspondent on March 18, 1905:

'Whatever may be the cause – tainted blood, climatic conditions, or just plain not good enough – the fact remains that Lexington blood in tail male has just about played itself out. Once in a while an occasional flicker is seen from some California-bred descendant of old Norfolk, but no really prominent stallion of today or even for some years past, can boast of tracing in direct mail line to the famous Woodburn stallion. To say the least of it this is rather an extraordinary happening, for Lexington has not been dead for so very long and numbers of his sons were freely used . . . How different the case of imported Glencoe, a pure bred horse in whose case climatic influence does not as yet appear to have got in its work, for just now the line of Glencoe in tail male is in a remarkably healthy and flourishing condition, and every one knows the chances afforded to the sons of Glencoe (I understand he got but few) in the stud was nothing to those accorded to the sons of Lexington. Both Glencoe and Lexington are of Herod descent, so we cannot attribute the failure of the latter to the effeminacy of the line. Although Lexington has to all appearances played out in the male line his blood is highly prized and lives on in the female line, for many of the pedigrees of our most famous race-horses of today show a dash of Lexington not far from the surface. But in almost every instance, Lexington mares that have attained marked success in the breeding paddock are found to have an imported horse as the sire of her dam . . . Imported Glencoe is responsible for not quite one third of the dams of the successful Lexington mares. Imported Yorkshire, imported Albion and imported Margrave all did their part and materially aided Lexington to acquire fame as a broodmare sire, and from whatever angle you may view it the fact remains that Lexington was not a success as a progenitor of sires, and also that his best efforts in the broodmare line were from mares whose sires were of imported blood.'

Early results of the Kentucky Derby, first run in the year of Lexington's death, seem to substantiate this contention. *Glencoe, who won the 1834 2,000 Guineas for the first of Lord Jersey's four consecutive victories in the race as well as becoming the first three-year-old to win the Goodwood Cup, was a broodmare sire par excellence, yet four of the first twelve heroes of Churchill Downs were direct tail male descendants of his – Vagrant (1876), Day Star (1878), Hindoo (1881) and Ben Ali (1886). *Glencoe, imported in 1836 by James Jackson of Tennessee, has 481 foals credited to him in the *American Stud Book*, only 144 of which are described as colts, although there are 20 of unspecified sex. By the time Lexington's impact on succeeding generations was being questioned in *The Thoroughbred Record*, his tally was probably three – Lord Murphy, Apollo (1882) and Manuel – although Apollo may have been not by Lexington's son Lever but by *Ashtead. Manuel was a grandson of Pat Malloy. Nevertheless, in the first decades of Kentucky Derby history the winner's pedigree included Lexington more often than not, albeit almost always in the bottom half. Indeed, not two months after *The Thoroughbred Record* published those observations on the relative merits of Lexington and *Glencoe blood, the race went to Agile, whose second dam was by Pat Malloy out of Penelope. If, as *The Thoroughbred Record* correspondent persuasively argued, the daughters of imported stallions had played an important part in bolstering Lexington's reputation, it is, given the fashions of the time, just as remarkable that, of the 31 broodmares listed in the 1857 Woodburn catalogue, none was imported, and all but two had first dams foaled in America.

Airdrie Stud Farm

The original tract at Midway on the Old Frankfort Pike just outside Lexington is now divided into three farms – Woodburn, Lanark and Airdrie. Woodburn House, built in about 1850, is occupied by Dr A. J. Alexander, a doctor. On Lanark A. B. 'Gus' Gay has, over the years, kept a number of broodmares and a few stakes winners have been bred there, but on the Airdrie portion racehorses are once more being commercially bred in earnest. Airdrie's 1,200 acres are farmed by Brereton Jones and his wife Elizabeth, daughter of General Arthur Alexander Lloyd. Since setting up in 1971, Jones has built up his stock to 52 foaling mares and six stallions, including 1976 Preakness winner Elocutionist (Gallant Romeo – Strictly Speaking, by Fleet Nasrullah), syndicated for $1,080,000. Elocutionist's total racetrack earnings were $343,150 (12 starts, 9 wins). The first stallion Jones bought and syndicated was Speculating, whose virtues are more in his pedigree (Bold Ruler – Rash Statement by *Ambiorix) than in race-course performance. He started 12 times as a three-year-old in 1970, the only season he raced, winning an allowance race at Aqueduct and a maiden at Belmont. One third place brought his total winnings to $12,475. The

Yearlings at Airdrie. Right: *Brereton Jones at Aidrie with his family.*

sire of winners Speed Monger, Ready Runner, Ishtar, Money Plays, Linda Joy, Three Carat Sue, Another Runner, Big Tishie, Run and Play and Linda Silvia, Speculating has, however, gone some way at stud towards vindicating his distinguished pedigree. In addition to a famous sire, he has a strong female line – Rash Statement won eight races and $218,022, her dam Hipparete won four times at three-years-old for $8,850 and her second dam Alcibiades was champion filly at two and three-years-old, winning seven races, including the Kentucky Oaks, and $47,860. Of her eight foals, seven were winners. Also standing at Airdrie are Nalees Man, whose first foals were yearlings of 1976, Torsion, whose first foals were produced in 1976, and Accipiter and Key to the Kingdom, both 1976 debutants at stud. Nalees Man is out of Nashua's daughter, Nalee, by Gallant Man, winner of 14 races, including the 1957 Belmont, and $510,355. Gallant Man, bred by the Aga Khan in partnership with his son Aly, was bought in Ireland by Fasig Tipton President and General Manager, Humphrey S. Finney, in 1955. Nalee won eight races and $141,631 at two and three years old, her dam, Levee, registered the same number of victories in two seasons and earned $223,305 and her second dam, Bourtai, twice a winner at two years old, produced 12 winners from 13 foals. Torsion is by Never Bend out of Prince John's daughter, Fairway Fun, who won 11 times from two to four years old and earned $103,816. Accipiter (Damascus – Kingsland, by Bold Ruler) won $192,073 in 35 starts, with nine wins, while Key to the Kingdom represented Jones's boldest outlay before the Elocutionist deal. By Bold Ruler out of Fort Marcy's dam, the *Princequillo mare Key Bridge, he fetched a record public auction price at the conclusion of his racing career in 1975 when he was knocked down to the master of Airdrie for $730,000.

Left: *Elocutionist*. Above: *Key to the Kingdom*. Below: *mares at Airdrie*.

He raced four seasons, starting 38 times, winning seven, finishing second six times and third once for total earnings of $109,590.

Jones's occasional, disarming references to the modesty of his outfit may make English breeders feel like refugees from a gypsy camp, but they also testify eloquently to the vast resources behind the huge and high-powered farms in the locality which currently have the whip hand. The Airdrie stallions, with some of the best American blood in their veins and more than a leavening of racetrack ability, have obviously been painstakingly selected to give the best chance of a rich return on investment. Like most breeders, Jones is a believer in nicks, and fancies some mild inbreeding, ideally 3 by 3, but looks first and foremost for good-producing mares. Using a close study of pedigrees as the basis for some shrewd percentage play, Jones is often talked of as the coming man around Lexington, and the day may not be too far off when he will be able to realise an ambition and retain the whole of a crop. 'So long as you have to sell your yearlings,' he says, 'you'll never know just how good you are. So much depends on what happens in training.' Airdrie may not be the only smart and efficiently run stud in Kentucky, but only a young man aiming for the top could match Jones's enterprise in the rewarding art of keeping patrons sweet. Once, the owner of a recalcitrant mare, due to be covered at Airdrie, telephoned to say he had abandoned all hope of loading her. Jones sent the stallion round.

Elmendorf Stud Farm

For all that Brereton Jones is working on hallowed ground and there are R. A. Alexander-commissioned Edward Troyes on the walls of Airdrie, whatever successes he enjoys in the future will owe nothing to the dead glories of Woodburn. But for almost a century, one name, Elmendorf, has never departed the Blue Grass scene, although the size of the farm bearing it has varied from the 231 acres Swigert bought to the 8,700 acres of James Ben Ali Haggin's heyday early this century. Sanford had already bred one Kentucky Derby winner there in Vagrant (Virgil – Lazy by *Scythian) before Swigert came along with a bankroll and the new name. Swigert won the Kentucky Derby with the Woodburn-foaled Baden Baden, besides breeding three more colts to win the race. Two were out of Lexington mares (Hindoo, by Virgil – Florence, and Ben Ali by Virgil – Ulrica, by Lexington out of *Emilia, who won in 1881 and 1886 respectively). The other was Apollo.

James Ben Ali, owner of the last Swigert-bred Kentucky Derby winner, bought Elmendorf in 1897, at $100 the acre, from Con J. Enright, whose fairly brief tenure of the farm had as its high point the breeding of Hamburg, after whom the farm on the Winchester Pike, Lexington, now worked by the great John E. Madden's grandson Preston, was named. Haggin was something else. Born in Harrodsburg, Kentucky, in 1821, he made a fortune as a lawyer in California in the aftermath of the Gold Rush. At his Rancho del Paso near Sacramento he eventually established what is generally described as the largest thoroughbred stud in world history. His 1903 catalogue listed 30 stallions, 562 broodmares and a total of some 2,000 thoroughbreds. At 74, Haggin, a widower, married Pearl Voorhies, a 28-year-old Kentucky belle, who encouraged him to set up a stud in his home state. Haggin began by buying what was then the 544 acres of Elmendorf, and soon set about building himself a palatial residence there, at a cost of $250,000, which was unfortunately demolished in 1929. The pillars of the portico, the steps to the front entrance and the ornamental lions are the only relics on Elmendorf today of the Haggin splendours. Nancy Lewis Greene in her *Country Estates of the Blue Grass,* published in 1904 and reissued in 1973, wrote of Elmendorf:

'In erecting a white palace in the Blue Grass Region of Kentucky, and in preparing a site for it, Mr J. B. Haggin did for the state what Mr George Vanderbilt did for North Carolina – took the natural features of a land-

Green Hills in James Ben Ali Haggin's time, and its present-day remains.

scape rich in possibilities and, sparing no expense of labor, developed it to the highest point of which art and invention is capable. A succession of terraces and sloping hills spreads out in a panoramic vista as one approaches the dwelling, so vividly green that the place seems to have been christened by Nature herself – 'Green Hills'. The stock farm, which is known as Elmendorf, under the management of Mr C. H. Berryman, has helped to give Mr Haggin the reputation of being the most extensive breeder of fine stock in the world. The whole estate comprises over 6,000 acres of the best blue grass land and absorbed several historic homesteads in its boundaries. Among the latter was 'Elk Hill', ancestral home of the Carter Harrisons, and this colonial building stands back of the Haggin mansion today, unmolested. 'Green Hills' may be said to be one of the most complete homes in the world, having its own electric and ice plant, greenhouses, dairy, poultry yards, butcher shops, and every convenience to make an independent existence possible.'

James Ben Ali Haggin, grandson of a Turkish army officer called Ibrahim Ben Ali, was one of the most successful breeders in the history of American

Salvator.

racing, and so, with his vast broodmare band, he should have been. The most famous horse he ever raced, Salvator, however, was bred by Swigert at Elmendorf 11 years before Haggin bought the farm. Salvator set an American record for the mile when he clocked 1:35½ at Monmouth Park on August 28, 1890, assisted by two pacemakers who went half a mile each. The record stood until Roamer returned 1:34⅘ in 1918. A son of *Prince Charlie, Salvator won four of his six races as a three-year-old, seven out of eight at three and was unbeaten at four. He was successful at stud, too, *The Thoroughbred Record* notice of his death published on October 30, 1908, recording: 'The first of Salvator's get appeared in 1894 as two-year-olds, and among the good ones he sent to the races are: Sallie Clicquot, Silver II, Salvable, Miss Rucker, Salabar, Salmera, Salvation, Salaire, Pearl V (dam of Water Pearl), Savable (Futurity), Ronald and others.' Haggin continued to expand Elmendorf, so that in 1905 he was able to sell his Rancho del Paso stud at auction and concentrate on his Kentucky holding. For the 1909 Futurity Haggin nominated no fewer than 284 mares. 'Once, when he owned both Rancho del Paso Farm in California and Elmendorf in Kentucky, he named more mares for the Futurity but never were as many as 284 (nominated) from just one farm,' *The Thoroughbred Record* reported in its issue for January 12, 1907.

One of Haggin's more bizarre breeding triumphs was the result of the English Grand National of 1908. Major F. Douglas-Pennant's 10-year-old

Rubio in 1908.

chestnut gelding, Rubio, the winner by ten lengths, had been bred at the Rancho del Paso, and sent to the Newmarket Yearling Sales, where he fetched 15 guineas. Rubio was a son of Star Ruby, a decent sprinter, but lousy sire, by Hampton, whose many distinguished sons included three English Derby winners in Merry Hampton, Ayrshire and Ladas, out of Ornament, a full sister to the unbeaten English Triple Crown winner Ormonde, and dam of the wonder-filly Sceptre. Rubio was hunted as a four-year-old and raced with modest success under rules before breaking down. He was then lent to the landlord of a Towcester hotel to see if road work under harness would get him sound again. Eventually, Rubio was ready to return to training, which he did with Fred Withington at Danebury, who thus had the distinction of preparing the first American-bred horse to win the Aintree race. However, even while Rubio was covering himself with glory, plans were afoot to stifle American racing, and in June, 1908, the notorious Hart-Agnew bills, which prohibited betting in New York, were passed. This presaged the end of Elmendorf's golden age under Haggin, and, on April 1, 1911, *The Thoroughbred Record* reported:

'The curtailment of James B. Haggin's Elmendorf Stud of thoroughbred horses has been rapid and certain, and the process of abbreviation is to be carried further. When Governor Hughes succeeded in having the Hart-Agnew bills passed . . . Mr Haggin had on his magnificent farm near this city more than 1,000 thoroughbreds, possibly 1,200 . . . Mr Haggin's perspicacity brought him quickly to a realization of the havoc that would be brought to the horse-breeding industry by the enactment of those repressionary laws and he at once laid plans for the systematic dispersal of the stud. Exportations to England, France, Germany and the Argentine Republic were made at intervals and the horses were sold by public auction in those countries. John Mackey, the veteran turfman, who has been identified with the Haggin racing and breeding interests since and before the first thoroughbred set hoof on the great Rancho del Paso, now a sugar-beet farm, was here last week and made a count of the thoroughbreds at Elmendorf. There are, including the foals of this year, 225 head. Of the broodmares 28 are at or above the age of 18, and they are virtually pensioners upon the farm. They are not to be bred again, and under Mr Haggin's orders, they are to be well cared for until they die of natural causes.'

Early in 1914, Haggin, fancying there might be a revival of racing, paid $40,000 for the stallion Ballot, who had been champion handicapper of 1908. In August, however, Haggin's long and fabulous life came to a peaceful end and the dispersal of his estate, the largest expanse of Blue Grass ever owned by one man, began. The original 213-acre Elmendorf was bought by John E. Madden, but sold in 1920 to Joseph E. Widener. Three years later Joseph E. Widener and his nephew George D. Widener bought 'Green Hills', in order to pull it down, as well as another 530 acres of Elmendorf land. Elmendorf remained in the ownership of the Widener family until Joseph E.'s

Above: *Ballot*. Right, top left: *August Belmont I*. Top right: *John E. Madden*.
Below: *Payne Whitney (left) in conversation with Joseph E. Widener*.

grandson Peter A. B. III sold it in 1950 to Tinkham Veale II and Sam A. Costello. It changed hands again in 1952 when Maxwell H. Gluck, the present owner, who served as Eisenhower's ambassador to Ceylon, bought what had become a 505-acre farm. Included in the deal were 27 broodmares, their foals and 15 yearlings.

Joseph E. and George D. Widener, millionaire sportsmen from Philadelphia, became two of the most respected figures in American racing and breeding. George D. Widener, owner of Erdenheim Farm near his home town, bred 100 stakes winners, and was chairman of the American Jockey Club for 14 years. He died on December 8, 1971. Joseph E. was master of Elmendorf until he died on October 25, 1943, and was also largely responsible for the development of Belmont and Hialeah racetracks. His colours were familiar not only to American racegoers but to followers of the sport in France and England. Among his more celebrated winners in England was Seminole, who took the Cesarewitch in 1933, while his vast number of winners in his own country included the Belmont victors Chance Shot (1927), Hurryoff (1933), and Peace Chance (1934). At the dissolution sale of the Nursery Stud a month after the death of its owner, August Belmont, in December 1924, Widener bought Fair Play, then aged 20, for $100,000. Fair Play (Hastings – Fairy Gold, by the 1880 Epsom Derby winner Bend Or) was already world-renowned as the sire of America's most famous racehorse ever, Man o' War. This stirp, Sir Charles Leicester observes, was 'an exclusively American branch of the Matchem sire line'. Widener also imported high-class stallions to Elmendorf, notably Sickle, Sweeper II and Stefan the Great. Sickle, who ran third for Lord Derby in the 1927 2,000 Guineas and earned a total of £3,915 in England, was by Phalaris, a top handicapper and

Left: *Sickle*. Below left: *Sweeper II*.
Above: *Pharos and* (right) *Pharis*.

highly influential sire, out of Selene, a daughter of Chaucer (by St Simon). This makes Sickle a product of one of the best-known nicks in the history of racehorse breeding in England. Fairway, who won £42,722 in stakes, Colorado (£30,358), Pharos (£15,694), Fair Isle (£13,219), Caerleon (£11,210), Warden of the Marches (£8,422), Meadow Rhu (£4,175), Burnt Sienna (£3,705), Pharamond (£3,695), Sargasso (£2,160) and Phalarope (£2,116) were the other most successful representatives of the Phalaris/ Chaucer nick. Pharos, moreover, got Pharis II, French champion sire, and Nearco, while his full brother, Fairway was four times champion sire in England, his sons including the Derby winners Blue Peter, who won the race in 1939, and Watling Street (1942), as well as the champion sire Fair Trial, who got the 2,000 Guineas winners Lambert Simnel (1941), Court Martial (1945) and Palestine (1950). Sweeper II, a son of Broomstick out of Ravello II by Sir Hugo, was owned by the American, H. B. Duryea, when he won the 2,000 Guineas in 1912. Stefan the Great, after a successful stint at Elmendorf, was returned to stud in England, but was of little account once back home. His breeding was of the most patrician – his sire was The Tetrarch, his dam Perfect Peach, by Persimmon, winner of the Derby, St Leger, Eclipse and Ascot Gold Cup, and a son of St Simon.

For an American, Widener bred and owned a considerable number of steeplechasers, with Bushranger, Duettiste, Arc Light, Fairmount, Lorenzo, Neap Tide, McCarthy More, Relluf, Compliment, Skibbereen, Barleycorn and Lizzard among the best known of them. He won the Manly Memorial seven times, and was successful every year from 1925 to 1930 in the Temple Gwathmey Memorial. However, in 1931, with *Sickle's first American yearlings looking exceptionally promising, Widener gave up the jumping game to concentrate on the flat. *Sickle had been bought from Lord Derby as a replacement for Fair Play, who died in December 1929, 'as he lived, game to the core', according to *The Thoroughbred Record*. Apparently, a

Verbatim.

group of men working nearby saw him 'gallop towards his barn, stop suddenly, raise his beautiful head, neigh two or three times and then topple over dead'. He had, however, vindicated Widener's judgement, heading the sires' list in 1927, as he had in 1920 and 1924. Fair Play's major successes at stud were with daughters of *Rock Sand, English Triple Crown winner of 1903 – Man o' War himself, out of Mahubah, was a product of this nick. Of the host of good racers got by Fair Play, *The Thoroughbred Record* obituary listed Mad Hatter, Stromboli, Mad Play, My Play, Ladkin, Dunlin, Messenger, Sporting Blood, How Fair, Blind Play, Chance Shot, Chatterton, Chance Play, Display and Catalan. Widener, who was America's champion breeder in 1940 with $317,961 earned, was in the fortunate position, as Gluck is today, of being able to keep and race as many of the horses foaled at Elmendorf as he cared to. This meant that practically all yearlings were broken at Elmendorf and appeared at two in the Widener red and white stripes. However, following Joseph E.'s death, when his son P.A.B. II purchased the farm from the estate, it was announced that the entire crop of 1944 yearlings would be offered for sale. Elmendorf was to remain primarily a commercial breeding operation until the successes of the late 'sixties, when Verbatim was on the track, enabled Gluck to disdain the sales. It was also announced, in December 1943, that 'Elmendorf stallions, headed by the classic *Sickle, and including Chance Shot, Haste, Roman and Unbreakable . . . in addition to their service to Elmendorf broodmares will continue to be available at stud to other thoroughbred breeders.' *Sickle did not long survive his importer, however, and on Boxing Day, 1943, America's champion sire of 1936 and 1938 succumbed to an enlarged spleen.

In 1954 Gluck made a wise investment, with far-reaching consequences for Elmendorf, when he gave $14,300 for the yearling Prince John, by *Princequillo out of Not Afraid, an unraced daughter of 1943 Triple Crown winner, Count Fleet. Prince John became the cornerstone of modern Elmendorf's success, and the unremitting search for mares likely to make suitable outcrosses to him – Gluck professing himself no great believer in inbreeding – involved frequent importations from England and Ireland. Gluck, advised by John Bricken, still purchases mares at the European sales, while of the three stallions now standing at Elmendorf, two, High Tribute and Speak John are sons of Prince John. The fourth, Verbatim, is by Speak John. Prince John's racing career was cut short when he broke loose from his groom at Hialeah and injured himself at a time when he appeared a live contender for the 1956 classics after winning three stakes races and $212,818. He was syndicated in 1961 and now stands at Spendthrift. The sire of more than 40 stakes winners, he got Speak John, now Elmendorf's top stallion, commanding $7,500 a live foal, in 1958. Speak John, out of Nuit de Folies, by Tornado, raced only at three years old, when he won four times from twelve starts and earned $36,480. His successful offspring includes the stakes winners Hold Your Peace, Speak Quick, Proposal, Happy Chant, Speak Action, Talking Picture and Verbatim, who was foaled in 1965 and picked up $415,702 in four racing seasons, involving 51 starts, 11 wins, 10 seconds and seven thirds. Out of the Never Say Die mare Well Kept, Verbatim has had encouraging results from his first few

Prince John.

crops. High Tribute, a year older than Verbatim, was just off the top class as a racer, winning $143,022 in five seasons. He, too, has started nicely at stud, and, outbred à la Gluck, might well go on to transmit more of the virtues to be found among the distinguished names in his pedigree:

Prince John	*Princequillo	Prince Rose	Rose Prince Indolence
		Cosquilla	Papyrus Quick Thought
	Not Afraid	Count Fleet	Reigh Count Quickly
		Banish Fear	Blue Larkspur Herodiade
En Casserole	War Relic	Man o' War	Fair Play Mahubah
		Friar's Carse	Friar Rock Problem
	Beanie M.	Black Toney	Peter Pan Belgravia
		Betty Beall	*North Star III *Macaroon

Perhaps the saddest sight of all on the Blue Grass farms, until his death late in 1976, was Protagonist, out of *Hornpipe II by Hornbeam, the champion two-year-old of 1973 whose racing career was brought to an end when he fractured a foreleg. In 1976, he was thought up to covering 15 or so mares, and, fine racehorse that he was, he remained game to the end, of course. It may be neither here nor there that so sick a member of a less expensive species would long ago have been despatched, but as, covered with sores, he tottered shivering round his stall, Protagonist served as a harrowing witness to the ingenuity of his ambitious masters. There is also a goodly amount of Prince John blood in the 100 or so broodmares resident at Elmendorf. Several of his daughters seem to have the happy knack of upgrading their stallions, so that, for example, one of the farm's favourites, Rare Bouquet, out of Forest Song by Mr Music, in 1969 produced My Old Friend, winner of $156,150, by Outing Class, and the next year dropped Fresh Pepper, by B. Major, who went on to earn $109,960 on the track. Farm manager Jim Brady, who took Elmendorf to the top of the American breeders' list in 1973 with winnings of $2,128,080, has seen the farm into the top ten ten times in the last dozen years. Like most professional breeders he is disinclined to allow theories to obtrude

Left: *Speak John.* Below: *Elmendorf manager Jim Brady.*

on the day-to-day business of producing and rearing good stock. 'I've had good results from inbreeding and good results from outcrosses,' he says. 'You can't draw any conclusions.' Even when it comes to the time-honoured Kentucky pastime of musing on the relative merits of sire and dam in a foal's make-up, Brady is less dogmatic than most, going to the unusual lengths of allowing some flexibility in his percentages: 'I'd say it's 30–35 the stallion, 40–45 the mare and the rest environment.'

Brady was emphatically not pleased in 1974 when 17 of Elmendorf's best mares, together with two weanlings, were sold to Gainesway. The mares included *Hornpipe II, in foal to Hoist The Flag, Lover's Quarrel by Battle Joined and Poster Girl by *Nasrullah, both in foal to Speak John, Manta by *Ben Lomond and Red Damask by Jet Action, both in foal to *Herbager, and Imsodear, by Chieftain, who got in foal to Hoist The Flag. Lover's Quarrel and Red Damask produced bay colts, the others bay fillies. Feeling that, even if a good workman does not blame his tools, he has every reason to complain if they are taken away from him, Brady came close to resigning, which, though understandable, would have been a sad end to an association which has added an era of consistent and phenomenal success to the many triumphs associated with the name of Elmendorf. Just what alchemy is worked with the horses Gluck chooses to keep on the farm, however, is a mystery. One of America's top horsemen, known to dealers throughout the world, remarked: 'Jim Brady is a hell of a good horseman, but no-one's that good a horseman, and Elmendorf's fine land, but no land's that good.' Standing just across the road from the well-ordered serenity of Greentree, Elmendorf, with its mobile homes parked near the foaling barns, looks not unlike a number of other Kentucky working farms, manned by industrious professionals, but, in the last decade or so, some magic has been involved.

Elmendorf Farm.

Hamburg Place
Stud Farm

'As to breeding, a stallion is 75 per cent of the stud. The mare contributes the vitality. Her control of form is slight. If you have any doubt in regard to this, take the result when a mare is mated with a jack. It always is a mule. The only change is color and size. Race mares rarely produce great performers. Their daughters seldom fail when properly mated.' Thus, in 1922, John E. Madden, running, jumping, fighting and betting man, the 'Wizard of the Turf' and one of the greatest-ever breeders of both runners and trotters, who set himself up at Hamburg Place in February 1898. The 235-acre farm, where Henry Clay is reputed to have been married, had been known as Overton, but was renamed after the colt, by Hanover, out of Lady Reel by Fellowcraft, which Madden had sold the previous December to Marcus Daly for what was then the record price for a horse in training of $40,001. Hamburg went on to become the leading three-year-old of 1898 and champion sire of 1905. Madden wasted no time in building up his farm to its present size of 2,000 acres. By the time Nancy Lewis Greene came to write her survey, it covered 'about 1,600 acres of choice blue grass land, stretching along the Winchester Pike, with the C. & O. Railroad in the rear.'

Mare and foal at Hamburg Place.

Hamburg.

'Hamburg Place,' Miss Greene went on, 'differs from many others in that it is not only a breeding but a training ground as well for the horses which it sends forth. Mr Madden has given the turf such stars as Hamburg, Irish Lad, Yankee, Blue Girl, Heno, Prince of Melbourne and David Garrick. None of these, it is true, are products of Hamburg Place, and all of them were bought as yearlings by its owner. But here they were developed and here they were given the preliminary work which enabled them to win the richest stakes in the east. To the rear of the handsome residence on the place is a paved court around which the barns and other outbuildings are grouped. Most prominent of them are the stallion barn and the two large training stables, all three models of their kind. Near them is the three-quarter mile training track. There are many famous thoroughbreds at Hamburg Place at the present time. Most notable among them are the Futurity winners, Ogden and Yankee.'

In each of the first 11 years for which breeders' statistics were kept in America, Madden was responsible for more winners than anyone else, with totals, starting in 1917, of 334, 213, 311, 313, 424, 366, 419, 318, 383, 368 and 362. No-one came within 40 of his two best years until 1974, when Rex C. Ellsworth was credited with 415. Money totals for breeders were first published in 1919, when Madden, with $561,490 was top of the list as he was every year up to and including 1923 ($507,715, $627,577, $568,785, and $632,630) as well as in 1925, when Hamburg-bred horses earned $535,790. In his book on Madden, Kent Hollingsworth, editor of *The Blood Horse* lists 182 stakes winners bred by Madden and notes: 'Madden owned and trained Plaudit when he won the 1898 Kentucky Derby, and he bred five other winners of that classic: Old Rosebud (1914), Sir Barton (1919), Paul Jones (1920), Zev (1923) and Flying Ebony (1925). He bred five winners of the Belmont Stakes: Joe Madden (1909), The Finn (1915), Sir Barton (1919), Grey Lag (1921) and Zev (1923). When Madden died in 1929, he had credit for breeding America's only Triple Crown winner in Sir Barton, America's leading money-earner in Zev ($313,639), and America's leading money-earning filly in Princess Doreen ($174,745).' By the time *Daily Racing Form* began to publish the annual statistical returns, Madden's status as one of the all-time greats, whether it be in the breeding, training or selling of racehorses, was assured. Born in Bethlehem, Pennsylvania, of impecunious Irish immigrant parents on December 28, 1856, and gifted with considerable athletic prowess, he graduated from the boxing booths, foot-racing and trotting tracks of the local fairs to become a highly successful dealer in standardbreds. At the age of 30, he arrived in Kentucky with a fair-sized bankroll and a shrewd eye for a horse, which he first turned to the thoroughbred market in 1888. For the first ten years or so he was in the thoroughbred business, many of the horses Madden owned raced in his colours, but thereafter he was exclusively a market breeder, acting also, around the turn of the century as adviser, and then trainer, to W. C. Whitney, who bought Hamburg at the Marcus Daly dispersal sale in 1901. When Whitney died in 1904, his son, Harry Payne, paid $70,000 at a Madison Square Garden auction, held on October 11 and 12, to keep the stallion in the family. Harry Payne Whitney, in partnership with Herman B. Duryea, had, in 1902, bought the two-year-old Irish Lad (*Candlemas – Arrowgrass, by Enquirer or Bramble) from Madden for $17,500, plus $10,000 from any future winnings. Irish Lad won the Great Trial Stakes as a juvenile for his new owners, and, at three, took the Saratoga Champion, the Brooklyn Handicap and the Broadway Stakes. Not long before he died, Madden was to write: 'I may say that I developed at least two great horses, Hamburg and Sir Martin (*Ogden – Lady Sterling, by Hanover, winner of $78,590 in America, as well as a number of good races in England, including the 1910 Coronation Cup) and some others, but it is in the turfmen that I developed that I take great pride, among them two champions, Harry Payne Whitney and Herman B. Duryea . . . They were exceptionally keen observers – learned the ropes quicker than any men I ever knew. Harry Payne Whitney has few, if any, equals in this line.' The master of Hamburg Place was no less generous in paying tribute to what might be termed the competition: 'August Belmont junior was unquestionably the most successful student of thoroughbred lines in America. Indeed, I do not exaggerate in asserting that he had more success in breeding good horses than any breeder in the world.' As the explosive and violent young man mellowed into the rich autocrat,

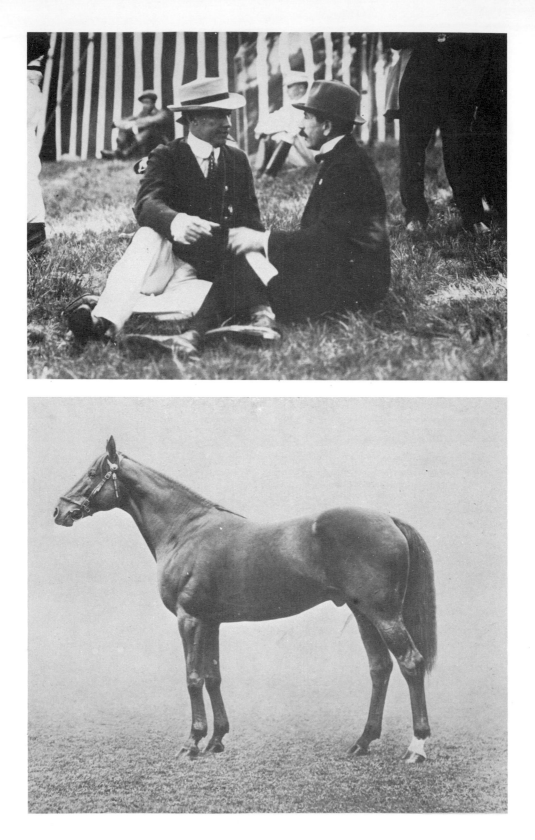

Madden's gruff commonsense made him into the most quotable of horsemen, a tough hombre and self-made man, untroubled by self-doubt, but not easy to gainsay either: 'Determining the quality of a horse by size or color is a matter of fancy. My experience has taught me that a good horse, like a good gamecock, has no bad colour. As to size, many big turnips are hollow,' he remarked in 1924, for instance. The most fetching statement of Madden's philosophy was probably made in a press interview which, unusually expansive, he gave in 1903: 'It seems to me that nature is mainly responsible for our kings and queens of the turf. Racehorses, like poets, are born . . . It is this glorious uncertainty, which enables a poor man to get hold of a great horse, that makes racing the most fascinating and exhilarating sport in all the world . . . What would a rich man care for the turf if he could win all the races? . . . It is true that experience and judgement go a great way in making success on the turf, as they do in all other pursuits. You have heard a great deal, perhaps, about my success on the turf; you have never heard of my many failures. It is just the same on the turf as it is in other lines of endeavor. A man must work if he hopes to win success, but on the turf luck plays a more prominent part than it does in other lines of work. My success has been due largely to luck. In breeding horses it is my aim always to mate what appear to be the horses best suited to each other, but one can never tell what the outcome will be. As to the so-called intricate science of breeding, by so blending the blood of sire and dam that winners may be produced in large numbers, though doubtless of absorbing interest to the student and theorist, it is, I believe, of little value. The practical man need confine himself only to the formula of breeding good mares to great horses, taking into due consideration the varying qualities of each and putting his trust into the possibility of like producing like or the likeness of some good ancestor. He will have his due share of the winners, his good years as well as his bad years, and the experts will tack figures on to the pedigrees of his winners and tell you how it all happened.' Not the least of Madden's skills was as a salesman, and he naturally had an aphorism for it: 'A man is a fool to spend three years raising a horse, and less than 15 minutes wooing the buyer.' Perhaps, however, he came closer to defining the salesman's art when he said: 'In my youth, it was a word and a blow, and I could knock down most of those with whom I argued. After a while it dawned on me that while I could knock a man down, I never could make him like it. So I changed my tactics, and instead of knocking them down I began slapping them on the back. And, you know, I began making money from that hour.'

Today, Hamburg Place, with John E. Madden's grandson Preston in charge, is once again an important nursery for thoroughbred stock, although there was quite a hiatus after the death of the 'Wizard of the Turf', since neither of his sons, Joseph or J. Edgar, took any interest in horseracing.

Harry Payne Whitney (left) with Foxhall Parker Keene. Below: *Sir Martin, favourite for Minoru's Derby, in which he fell, and winner of £3,248 in England.*

Never Say Die, ridden by Lester Piggott, after the 1954 Derby.

Edward kept polo ponies on Hamburg until his death in 1943, after which part of the land was leased to Jonabell Farm. It was here that Never Say Die, out of Singing Grass, by War Admiral, winner of the English Derby and St Leger in 1954, was foaled and broken by John A. Bell III before being shipped across the Atlantic as a yearling. At the time of his Epsom success, Humphrey S. Finney was racing manager for the owner, Robert Sterling Clark, who was in hospital for his annual check-up on Derby Day. After the race Finney went to visit the victorious owner and congratulated him on having set up a record by becoming the first American to breed and own an Epsom Derby winner. 'Say,' said Clark, his mind still on the enema he had undergone, 'What time was that race?' 'About eleven, our time, I suppose,' Finney replied. Clark mused for a while and announced: 'In that case I may have set up two records . . . I could just be the first man to win the English Derby with a pipe up his arse.'

Preston Madden, who stood Man o' War's sons War Admiral and War Relic at Hamburg Place for the estate of Samuel D. Riddle in the early years of the farm's revival, was only 26 when, in September 1961, he bought T. V. Lark, who promptly won the Washington D. C. International for him in record time, beating Kelso, American Horse of the Year from 1960 to 1964 inclusive, and top money-earner of all time with $1,977,896. More important for the Hamburg breeding set-up, T. V. Lark, until his untimely death from some unidentified allergy in 1975, consistently managed to transmit much of the toughness and soundness which brought him 19 wins from 72 starts in four seasons, and racetrack earnings of $902,194. Having thus far sired 38 different stakes winners, T. V. Lark, America's leading sire of 1974, has played an important part in the perpetuation of the *Nasrullah line in the United States. His pedigree to three generations is:

*Indian Hemp	*Nasrullah	Nearco
		Mumtaz Begum
	*Sabzy	Stardust
		Sarita
Miss Larksfly	Heelfly	Royal Ford
		Canfli
	Larksnest	*Bull Dog
		Light Lark

If Preston Madden has gone some way towards restoring the prestige Hamburg Place enjoyed in his grandfather's day, his approach is nothing like John E.'s. Even as an old man, the 'Wizard' was obsessed with physical fitness, diving into cold brooks, jumping fences, bringing down runaway horses and exercising daily in his gymnasium. He never smoked, and rarely took a drink. Preston, hurtling across an unmown field at the wheel of one of his Cadillacs, draws whimsically on a cigarette, and contradicts the suggestion that there is some pretty impressive livestock on the place: 'No – it's the best.' Back at the house he points to the large structure with the red bulbous top:

'I suppose you think that's a water tower?'

'Well, isn't it?'

'No. It's the biggest martini in the world.'

Preston Madden with Buffalo Lark.

Inside the champagne and bourbon flow, people keep turning up, some talking horses, some playing guitars and singing songs, all apparently familiar with the magnificent hospitality of Hamburg Place, where a huge portrait of Preston's wife, Anita, by the court painter, adorns one of the walls. The Madden eve-of-the-Kentucky Derby parties are a byword for wildness, and a couple of years ago they even hired some dim students to streak. Of course, this is only one side of Preston Madden, a big man who looks a bit like Elvis Presley, is rumoured to take his exercise by running with the horses in his fields and reckons he will achieve enough as a breeder to overcome the handicap of his name.

A new interstate highway was built in 1964, cutting across Hamburg Place, despite vigorous representations from Madden, and impinging on a field, which is nevertheless still the best part of 200 acres, where a dozen or so yearlings are generally left to run together. In this policy, Madden is following one of his grandfather's precepts, and, indeed, American breeders altogether are supposed to be more inclined to expose their young horses to the elements than their English counterparts in what seems the logical belief that the result will be hardier animals on the racetrack. Although it remains to be seen how Hamburg Place recovers from the unexpected demise of T. V. Lark, Madden, who breeds primarily for the yearling sales, can

Left: *Buffalo Lark*. Above: *Chris Evert with her Secretariat foal*. Above right:
Mickey McGuire.

point to fair success so far. Of T. V. Lark's progeny, the best have been
Bwamazon Farm's Quack, out of Quillon, by *Princequillo, winner of eight
races and $514,400, and Buffalo Lark, out of Chance Gauge, by Degage,
foaled at Hamburg Place and sold as a yearling, who went on to earn $499,715
on the track. He has now been syndicated as a stallion, and stood his first
season, at Hamburg Place, in 1976. Miss Carmie, by T. V. Lark, dam of the
1974 champion filly Chris Evert, was also sold as a yearling by Madden,
while a filly which caught many an eye in 1976, when she won nine stakes
races, was T. V. Lark's three-year-old daughter T. V. Vixen, out of Crimson
Lass, by Crimson Satan. Her career earnings, by the end of that season,
totalled $324,441.

Mickey McGuire, a 1967 son of T. V. Lark out of Edie Belle, by Deter-
mine, now stands at Hamburg Place – his first foals were three-year-olds of
1976 – after a racetrack career spanning three seasons, with 15 starts, five
wins, two seconds and two thirds ($83,080). Mickey McGuire, who had 16
winners of 32 races and total progeny earnings of $223,412 in 1976, had
his fee doubled to $2,000 a live foal in 1977, when the stallion's joint owners,

Madden, J. E. Johnson and George Green, repeated their offer of the previous year to pay a $5,000 reward to the breeder of the first foal in the ensuing crop to win a $1,000-added race. Madden also stands Amber Morn (*Ambiorix – Break o' Morn, by Eight Thirty), who ran 100 times in five seasons to earn $150,720 and who is the sire of a number of stakes winners, the best of which are probably Royal Chocolate, Amber Herod, Good Port and Amber Prey. He still costs $1,000 for a live foal, whereas another stallion in which Madden has a major interest, Lt Stevens (Nantallah – Rough Shod II, by Gold Bridge) holds court at Gainesway for $7,500. Lt Stevens is own brother to two two-year-old champions in Ridan, who died in Australia early in 1977, having been sent from Ireland to cover for the antipodean season, and Mocassin, dam of Apalachee. Chou Croute, champion sprinter and winner of $284,662, is the most prolific stakes winner so far sired by Lieutenant Stevens, who made something of an impact in Europe through his son Sky Commander (ex Star of Wonder, by Dark Star), winner of the Prix Robert Papin in 1974. At the end of 1976 Avatar's half-brother by *Prince Royal II, Unconscious, moved to Hamburg Place from Spendthrift. The sire of five winners in his first crop to race, Unconscious (1969) won the Californian Derby, the San Felipe Handicap, the Santa Catalina, Charles H. Strub and San Antonio Stakes and a total of $373,300.

Below: *Moccasin.* Below right and bottom: *mares and foals at Hamburg Place.*

Spendthrift Stud Farm

Leslie Combs junior and Mary Swigert had three sons, Brownell, Lucas B. and Daniel Swigert, father of Leslie II, current owner of Spendthrift, who was born in 1901. Leslie junior, son of Henry Clay's law partner, was ambassador to Peru from 1906 until 1911, when he retired to operate Belair Farm, near Lexington, where he bred a number of good thoroughbreds. He died there in 1940, aged 88. Just three years before the death of his grandfather, Leslie Combs II bought 127 acres on the Iron Works Pike, which had once been part of Elmendorf, from F. A. Rowland and named it after his grandfather's famous horse. 'Cuzin Leslie', as he is widely known, had begun his working life in Guatemala with a plantation company but was invalided home with malaria after a year. He then worked for American Rolling Mills in Ashland, where in 1924, he married Dorothy Enslow, daughter of the founder of the Columbia Gas and Electric Company. Later, at Huntingdon, West Virginia, Combs became a partner in an insurance agency and served on the first two West Virginia Racing Commissions. Leslie Combs II's decision to sell up his insurance interests and return to the real family business coincided with the retirement from the track of the

Left: *Brownell Combs*. Right: *his father, Leslie Combs II*.

Top: *Myrtlewood*. Bottom left: *Blue Larkspur*. Right: *Sir Gallahad II*.

sensational Myrtlewood, who won 15 races and $40,620. In the Lakeside Handicap at Washington Park she equalled the track record for a mile, 1:35⅗, which was also the fastest time ever recorded by a mare. She set new track records for six furlongs and eight and a half furlongs at Detroit, while her time of 1:09⅖ in the six-furlong Great Lakes Purse at Arlington Park stood for 14 years. Her rivalry with Clang, a gelding owned by John F. Clark, junior, of New Orleans, caught the public imagination when they were three-year-olds in 1935. Two matches were staged, both desperately close, with Myrtlewood winning the first at Hawthorne, Clang the second at Cincinnati's Coney Island track. Myrtlewood (Blue Larkspur – *Frizeur, by *Sweeper) ran in the colours of her breeder, Leslie II's uncle Brownell, who retired her, at the end of the 1936 campaign, to Belair Farm. Her dam was bred by Herman B. Duryea in France and brought to America by his widow, who sold her to John E. Madden. *Frizeur was out of Hamburg's American-bred daughter Frizette (ex *Ondulee), who figures in Sir Charles Leicester's list of ten taproot mares at stud this century to have founded 'great long-term Classic winner-producing families', and whose great grandson Tourbillon, French Derby winner of 1931, was three times champion sire in France and a significant factor in the successful French raids on England of 20 or 30 years ago. Brownell Combs, who, as Duryea's guest in France in 1914 had first conceived an admiration for Frizette as a broodmare, paid Madden $6,000 for *Frizeur, in foal to Runnymede. In the words of one of Spendthrift's own brochures, 'The fabulous success of

Spendthrift—the residence.

Myrtlewood's offspring is responsible to a great degree for the success of
Spendthrift Farm. Such brilliant stakes winners as Flag Raiser, Mr Brick,
Kentucky Derby winner Jet Pilot, champion filly Myrtle Charm and literally
dozens of other brilliant stakes winners trace their family to Myrtlewood.'
It in no way detracts from the importance of the mare to ask what Jet Pilot
is doing in that list, since the conventional view is that he was by *Blenheim II
out of Black Wave, by *Sir Gallahad III. His third dam, admittedly, was
*Frizeur, but it is difficult to give Myrtlewood much credit for that. Of the
76 Spendthrift broodmares to have produced stakes winners, a dozen currently represent the foundation family of Myrtlewood, while Seattle Slew
also descends in tail female from her. Combs has made several other significant acquisitions on the distaff side, notably Gay Hostess, by Nearco's son
*Royal Charger out of *Alibhai's daughter Your Hostess. Her sons by Raise
A Native (1961, Native Dancer – Raise You, by Case Ace) are the best
known, of course – Majestic Prince, who won nine races, including the 1969
Kentucky Derby and Preakness, and was beaten only once, when he ran
second to Arts and Letters in the Belmont, earned $414,200 on the racetrack,
while Crowned Prince, after a surprise defeat on his debut in a maiden race
at Newmarket, looked a world-beater in winning the 1971 Champagne and
Dewhurst Stakes. Unfortunately, a soft palate prevented his running after
his Craven Stakes flop on his reappearance. Both these fetched world record
prices at the Keeneland Yearling Sales, as did their full brother, Elegant
Prince, in 1975, when he was knocked down to Mr and Mrs Franklin Groves

Left: *Raise A Native*. Above: *Majestic Prince*.

of Minneapolis for $715,000, breaking the record set the previous year by another Spendthrift-bred colt, Mr Prospector's full brother, Kentucky Gold (Raise A Native – Gold Digger, by Nashua), who went for $625,000. Combs has made such a habit of breaking world records at yearling sales that there have inevitably been sour suggestions of rigging, but $715,000 did not seem all that high a price by the time a Nelson Bunker Hunt-bred Secretariat colt out of Dahlia's dam, Charming Alibi (by Honeys Alibi, by *Alibhai) was led out of the Keeneland ring in 1976. Canadians John Sikura and Joe, Jack and Ted Burnett had just bid $1,500,000 for him. Gay Hostess's produce, incidentally, also includes Betty Loraine, by Prince John, dam of Caracolero, by Graustark, winner of the 1974 Prix du Jockey Club, and now standing at the Haras du Petit Tellier. Track performances, of course, do not always bear much relation to yearling prices, and Wallace Gilroy's Kentucky Gold, with one modest success and earnings of $5,950 to his credit, is now back at Spendthrift, where he covered his first mares in 1977 at a fee of $1,500. His poor showing on the track has been put down to respiratory troubles, which necessitated an operation.

At Keeneland's 1976 November Breeding Stock Sales, Spendthrift disposed of 96 broodmares, but there will still be around 400, counting boarders, on the farm, which still spans about 5,500 acres, although it was decided to sell off some land at the same time as the broodmare population was reduced in 1976. Thirty four stallions currently stand at Spendthrift, where some 3,000 matings are effected every year. Up to 300 foals are dropped each season in the modern and well-equipped sheds humorously known as the 'maternity ward'. Full-time trainer Dick Fischer has tracks on the farm itself and in Florida to provide year-round exercise facilities, and Spendthrift even has its own milling station. Over the last 33 years Spendthrift has been the leading seller at the Keeneland Summer Yearling Auction 18 times, including 15 on the trot, taking approximately $15 million in the last ten years, during which period the farm has bred more stakes winners than anyone else, and the winners of more money than anyone else. Figures for North America's four leading money winning breeders, 1967–1976, are:

	Combs with partners $	E. P. Taylor $	Elmendorf $	Claiborne with partners $
1967	1,190,476	870,671	648,257	1,157,839
1968	1,290,298	888,155	759,620	1,506,908
1969	1,467,664	1,004,057	1,300,324	1,341,157
1970	1,685,692	1,069,553	747,611	1,063,984
1971	1,869,477	1,168,777	1,239,895	820,344
1972	1,916,337	1,433,489	1,502,406	1,270,224
1973	1,582,644	1,283,967	2,128,080	1,545,321
1974	1,998,419	1,926,937	1,867,015	1,327,409
1975	1,883,695	2,366,571	1,888,641	1,878,336
1976	2,354,547	3,022,181	2,306,864	1,837,046
Total	17,239,249	15,034,358	14,388,713	13,748,568

As Leslie Combs II's son, Brownell, who manages the farm, observes, such a comprehensive thoroughbred service as Spendthrift provides amounts to 'one-stop racing', and if the farm cannot quite match its big rival Claiborne for the sheer quality of its stock, it is still an awe-inspiring operation. Such spectacular development in a mere 40 years has clearly required more than the good luck of finding a successful foundation mare, and Leslie Combs II, usually described as 'the man who perfected the art of stallion syndication', has proved as smart a businessman as he is a horseman. Although, as early as 1926, A. B. Hancock senior formed a partnership of four to buy Sir Gallahad III for importation, it was Combs's post-war deals which set the fashion in America for selling shares in high-priced stallions. He began in 1947 by paying the film magnate Louis B. Mayer $100,000 for the successful Australian stallion Beau Père, but the horse died shortly after arriving at Spendthrift from California. Undeterred, Combs went back to Mayer the next year and shelled out $500,000 for ★Alibhai, by Hyperion out of Tracery's daughter Teresina, bred in England by the Aga Khan. ★Alibhai was brought to America as a yearling in 1939, but broke down on both forelegs before he ever saw a racecourse. By the time he died on June 9, 1960, he had sired the winners of

Bull Lea.

more money than any stallion in American history up to that time, apart from Bull Lea. The first million-dollar syndication deal came in 1955 with the dispersal of the stock from the Belair Stud in Virginia following the death of its owner, William Woodward, from a shotgun blast when his wife mistook him for an intruder. The break-up of Belair came with the stable, which had sent out such horses as Gallant Fox, Omaha, Flares, Granville and Fenelon, at the height of its distinction. The star that year was Nashua (*Nasrullah – Segula, Johnstown), winner of what was then a record for a season of $752,550, and he it was who, auctioned by sealed bid, broke the million dollar barrier. Combs, leading a syndicate of Christopher J. Devine, John W. Hanes, P. A. B. Widener III, Harry Warner and Mereworth Farm, bid $1,251,200. Altogether Leslie Combs II has arranged a dozen million-dollar syndications, the others being Raise A Native for $2,625,000 in 1967, Exclusive Prince for $1,920,000 in 1972, Majestic Prince for $1,800,000 in 1970 and Unconscious for the same figure two years later, Kennedy Road for $1,440,000 in 1973, Bald Eagle for $1,400,000 in 1960, Gallant Man for $1,333,333 in 1958, Never Bend for $1,225,000 in 1964, Creme Dela Creme for $1,200,000 in 1966 and Cornish Prince for the same amount in 1972, and Fleet Nasrullah for $1,050,000 in 1965. The biggest syndication deal ever brought off, however, was engineered by Brownell, and great was the rejoicing on November 19, 1975, proclaimed 'Wajima Day' by Kentucky's

Governor Julian M. Carroll, when the son of Bold Ruler out of *Iskra by Le Haar, winner of $502,792 from 15 starts, with nine wins, arrived at Spendthrift at the conclusion of his three-year-old campaign. The sum involved was $7,200,000, which, one way or the other, is just too much. In addition to Majestic Prince, Nashua, Kentucky Gold, Prince John, Raise A Native and Wajima, Spendthrift stands the following stallions:

Alto Ribot, 1964 (Ribot – Parlo, *Heliopolis)

Bold Hour, 1964 (Bold Ruler – Seven Thirty, Mr Music)

Cabildo, 1963 (Round Table – Delta, *Nasrullah)

Cornish Prince, 1962 (Bold Ruler – Teleran, Eight Thirty)

Crewman, 1960 (Sailor – *Twelve O'Clock, Hyperion)

Delta Oil, 1969 (Delta Judge – Grey Oil, Oil Capitol)

Exclusive Native, 1965 (Raise A Native – Exclusive, Shut Out)

Fleet Nasrullah, 1955 (*Nasrullah – Happy Go Fleet, Count Fleet)

*Gallant Man, 1964 (*Migoli – *Majideh, Mahmoud)

Goal Line Stand, 1970 (Graustark – Dinner Partner, Tom Fool)

Intrepid Hero, 1972 (*Forli – Bold Princess, Bold Ruler)

Jungle Savage, 1966 (*Indian Hemp – Foolspoint, Tom Fool)

Kennedy Road, 1968 (Victoria Park – Nearis, Nearctic)

List, 1968 (*Herbager – Continue, Double Jay)

Marshua's Dancer, 1968 (Raise A Native – Marshua, Nashua)

Native Royalty, 1967 (Raise A Native – Queen Nasra, *Nasrullah)

Orbit Dancer, 1973 (Northern Dancer – Triple Orbit, Gun Shot)

Pretense, 1963 (*Endeavour II – *Imitation, Hyperion)

Princely Native, 1971 (Raise A Native – Charlo, Francis S)

Proud Clarion, 1964 (Hail to Reason – Breath o' Morn, *Djeddah)

Rainy Lake, 1959 (*Royal Charger – Portage, War Admiral)

Sham, 1970 (Pretense – Sequoia, *Princequillo)

Traffic Cop, 1969 (Traffic Judge – Flight Bird, Count Fleet)

Triple Bend, 1968 (Never Bend – Triple Orbit, Gun Shot)

Turn to Mars, 1967 (*Turn-to – Marshua, Nashua)

West Coast Scout, 1968 (*Sensitivo – Dandy Princess, Bull Dandy)

Above: *Wajima*. Below: *Fleet Nasrullah*.

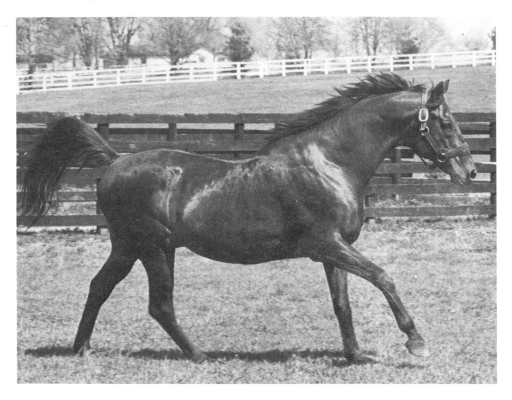

Sham.

There are no Triple Crown winners in this list, but Majestic Prince is not the only one with two legs of it to his credit – Nashua won the 1955 Preakness and Belmont – while Gallant Man won the Belmont two years later, and Proud Clarion took the Kentucky Derby in 1967. Moreover, Sham, syndicated by Brownell Combs for $2,880,000 after running second in the 1973 Kentucky Derby and Preakness, might be reckoned unlucky to have come along at the same time as Secretariat, but he still won $204,808 from 13 starts, with five wins. Nashua's career total was $1,288,565 (30 starts, 22 wins), *Gallant Man's $510,355 (26, 14) and Proud Clarion's $218,730 (25, 6). Of the rest of the Spendthrift stallions, the vast majority of which were big money winners of the track, the most successful were Bold Hour with $548,190 (31 starts, 11 wins), Cabildo, $267,265 (75, 22), Crewman, $315,843 (29, 9) Fleet Nasrullah, $223,150 (29, 11), Kennedy Road, $481,007 (45, 17), List, $279,327 (71, 17), Native Royalty, $304,517 (40, 10), Pretense, $494,602 (31, 13), Prince John, $212,818 (9, 3), Triple Bend, $366,760 (29, 10) and West Coast Scout, $543,191 (33, 9). Most of them have a very impressive record at stud, too – even if the farm's familiar boast to having five of America's top six living sires of stakes winners has a lot to do with longevity, as well as quality – and the most recent champion among them is Cornish Prince, who headed the juvenile list in 1975 with 19 winners. The great thing about the Spendthrift stallion list is that it has something to suit every taste and pocket, as it were, with a choice from, say, the well-bred, but unraced Goal Line Stand, whose fee is $1,000 for a live foal, through a successful young stallion like Cabildo (two crops, 49 starters, 40 winners) who is twice as expensive, to the aristocrats of the breeding shed like Nashua and Fleet Nasrullah. One of Spendthrift's greatest stallions, Never Bend (*Nasrullah – Lalun, by *Djeddah) died at the farm early in 1977 aged 17. Five times champion sire in America, he also headed the English list in 1971, when his son Mill Reef was a three-year-old. Seven of Mill Reef's yearlings were sold at auction in 1976, when they fetched an average of $84,000. J. O. Tobin, Iron Ruler, Never Bow and Riverman are among the best-known of his stakes-winner progeny.

'Breed the best to the best and hope for the best.' That celebrated saw has been heard more than once around Spendthrift, although Leslie Combs II has been quoted, expanding it somewhat, thus: 'First of all, we try to follow the pattern of successful matings of the past. Some blood nicks very well with another cross, and once this has been proved on the track, it's a good idea to follow along. Then we take conformation into account. You want to have a certain compatibility in conformation between sire and dam or you can produce a freak. We also try to breed out faults at Spendthrift. We try to get favourable characteristics of the parents in the offspring. It just doesn't make sense to me to spend $10,000 for a stud fee, and then send a $5,000 mare to that stallion hoping for the best.' All unexceptionable stuff, but the *Daily Racing Form,* discussing the breeding of Tumiga, foaled in 1964, who raced four seasons and won 11 races and $220,740 from 26 starts, moved

Nashua.

on to more contentious ground: 'It is perfectly obvious that 'Cuzin Leslie' bred Tumiga on purpose, with deep concern for the Dosages Diagram and the stampede of cluster mares involved.' Here's how it all works:

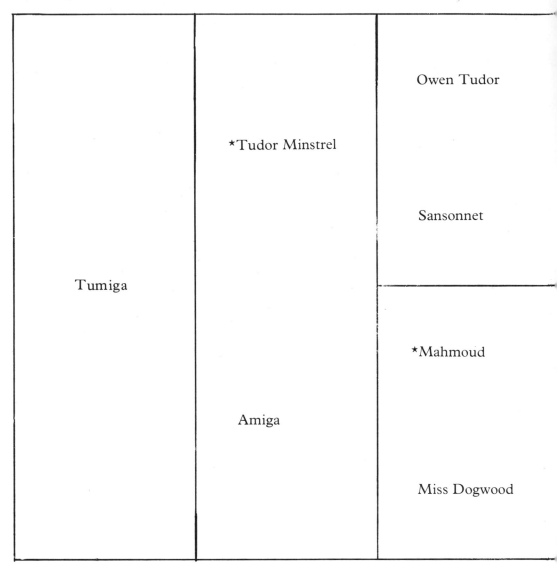

Tumiga	*Tudor Minstrel	Owen Tudor
		Sansonnet
	Amiga	*Mahmoud
		Miss Dogwood

'Nashua mares have done well with Raise A Native at Spendthrift,' Brownell Combs remarks, 'and the My Babu/Creme Dela Creme nick also seems to be a good one.' My Babu, incidentally, was the most expensive piece of horse-flesh ever to have set foot in America when he came over from the Maharani of Boroda's County Kildare stud in 1956, Leslie Combs II having the previous year put together a $600,000 syndication deal for the French-bred winner of the English 2,000 Guineas, Craven Stakes, Sussex Stakes and Victoria Cup. He was by Tourbillon's son Djebel out of Perfume II, by Badruddin. Of the stakes winners produced by his daughters to Creme Dela Creme, the best are probably Silent Beauty, winner of the Kentucky Oaks, and the Miss Suwanee Stakes, and Without Peer, winner of the Breeze-A-Lea Stakes and the Wings of Man Stakes. Creme Dela Creme (Olympia – Judy Rullah,

Hyperion	Gainsborough	Bayardo *Rosedrop
	Selene	Chaucer Serenissima
Mary Tudor II	Pharos	Phalaris Scapa Flow
	Anna Bolena	*Teddy Queen Elizabeth II
Sansovino	Swynford	John O' Gaunt Canterbury Pilgrim
	Gondolette	Loved One Dongola
Lady Juror	Son In Law	Dark Ronald Mother In Law
	Lady Josephine	Sundridge Americus Girl
*Blenheim II	Blandford	Swynford Blanche
	Malva	Charles O' Malley Wild Arum
Mah Mahal	Gainsborough	Bayardo *Rosedrop
	Mumtaz Mahal	The Tetrarch Lady Josephine
*Bull Dog	*Teddy	Ajax Rondeau
	Plucky Liège	Spearmint Concertina
Myrtlewood	Blue Larkspur	Black Servant Blossom Time
	*Frizeur	*Sweeper Frizette

by *Nasrullah) died in 1977, aged 14. In talking of nicks, Brownell Combs enters the familiar caveat: 'Of course, it may just be a question of opportunity, the fact that those particular good mares are available to that stallion.' Such reasonable caution stops some way short of the position adopted by the late Joe Estes, editor of the Lexington-based magazine *The Blood Horse*, who is remembered, *inter alia*, for the apophthegms with which he bombarded Kentucky horsemen, and who was once bold enough to assert: 'Nicks are the bunk. They are the most universally accepted bunk in the whole business.' Until someone finds out why certain crosses have proved consistently and particularly successful, however, horsemen will have to go on believing there is something in nicks. The 'official' tour of Spendthrift is deeply impressive. Hooper Roff, superintendent of the stallion complex, a most engagingly voluble enthusiast, bustles round his immaculate domain, showing off the horses and the ultra-modern breeding shed, with its glass-fronted viewing gallery and the paraphernalia of scrupulous hygiene and veterinary services. Farm manager Harry Schmidt has a few tourist attractions, too, showpieces including the fine foaling sheds and the milling station, where all the feed is produced, except for the 26 per cent lactose paste pellets, now manufactured by Kraft, but originally developed at Spendthrift anyway. Until a few years ago, the feed used to include 'AG' pellets, made, from soybean grass and alfalfa, at the Abbey of Gethsemane, Kentucky, by the Trappist monks, but they suddenly stopped supplying them, without, presumably, saying why.

Left: *Stallion man Hooper Roff.* Right: *Spendthrift paddock.* Bottom: *Yearlings.*

Claiborne Stud Farm and Stone Farm

Leslie Combs's rise to the top has been assisted by a great deal of entrepreneurial legerdemain, and a certain amount of razzamattazz, while the rival, giant outfit – the older-established Claiborne Farm at Paris, Kentucky, owned by the Hancock family – has tended to rest confident in the undoubted quality of its horses, men and land. The Hancocks have traditionally never bothered all that much with tarting up horses for the sales ring, or producing the kind of glossy, but helpful, promotional literature that Spendthrift brings out, although the late A. B. 'Bull' Hancock, by all accounts, was nevertheless fairly forthcoming, and when he died, in September, 1972, he was liked as well as respected by horsemen all over the world. The running of the farm passed to his younger son, Seth, who is still a mere 27, and, no doubt, any young man inheriting such awesome responsibilities might expect a certain amount of attention from the prophets of doom and some sniping from the envious. On the other hand, even people owning shares in

Left: *Arthur Boyd Hancock Senior*. Right: *Seth Hancock*.

Previous four pages: *Claiborne Farm. The foals* (left) *are by Herbager and Tell.*

233

Claiborne stallions or breeders sending mares to them, do not always feel they have been mistaken for the flowers in May by the new President of Claiborne. In the incidental art of public relations at least, Spendthrift is way ahead.

To account for the consistent success of the Hancocks in horse breeding Seth vouchsafes the modest, but unenlightening, explanation: 'It's all luck, I guess.' The luck started with Richard Johnson Hancock, born in Limestone County, Alabama, on March 22, 1838, and named after the hero credited with killing the Shawnee chief, Tecumseh. After the Civil War, in which he served as a captain, Hancock opened the Ellerslie Stud at Charlottesville, Virginia, which was to remain the headquarters of the family breeding business even for some years after his son, Arthur Boyd senior, established the Paris operation in 1910 on a portion of Marchmont Farm inherited by his wife Nancy. The name Claiborne happened to be available, Mrs Clarence Lebus, owner of a nearby farm, which had been known thus, having developed a passion for all things Japanese and rechristened her spread Hinata, meaning sunshine. Since Nancy Hancock was née Clay, the name seemed a suitable one to adopt. In 1912 the Hancocks took up permanent residence in Kentucky, and Arthur Boyd senior began to build up the equine side of the farm – he had been principally concerned with tobacco and cattle in the beginning – and in 1915 he went to England in search of a stallion. Good luck attended him and with the importation of Wrack at the end of

Wrack, with Whalley up, in England. Right: *Robert le Diable.*

234

that year's English flat racing season, Claiborne's development as a major force in thoroughbred breeding began. Wrack, foaled on April 22, 1909, was a tough, indomitable racer, trained by Frank Hartigan and owned and bred by Lord Rosebery, with an impressive pedigree:

Robert le Diable	Ayrshire	Hampton	Lord Clifden Lady Layden
		Atalanta	Galopin Feronia
	Rose Bay	Melton	Master Kildare Violet Melrose
		Rose of Lancaster	Doncaster Rouge Rose
Samphire	Isinglass	Isonomy	Sterling Isola Bella
		Deadlock	Wenlock Malpractice
	Chelandry	Goldfinch	Ormonde Thistle
		Illuminata	Rosicrucian Paraffin

At the time of his sale the *Bloodstock Breeders' Review* commented: 'Both sire and dam are by Derby winners and four other winners of the great

Left: *Wrack in America*. Right: *Sam Hildreth*.

Epsom classic are found in the next two removes, *viz* Melton, Galopin, Doncaster and Ormonde. Robert le Diable will be remembered as the winner of the City and Suburban, the Doncaster Cup and other good races, who after spending some years at Lord Carnarvon's stud was sold to Austria. Wrack's second dam Chelandry won the 1,000 Guineas in 1897, and is not only dam of the 2,000 Guineas winner, Neil Gow, and of Traquair: she is also half-sister to Gas, whose son Cicero won the Derby. This is, of course, the famous Paraffin family, which includes Glare (a grand-daughter of Paraffin), dam of Flair (sold for 12,000 guineas and winner of the Middle Park Plate and 1,000 Guineas), Lady Lightfoot (dam of Prince Palatine, winner of the St Leger, and sold for £40,000), Lesbia (winner of the Middle Park Plate and sold for 9,000 guineas), Menda (sold as a two-year-old for 5,600 guineas and dam of Rossendale) and other winners. That the Paraffin line continues to produce successful sires is proved by Traquair's record in Australia. He had only been at the stud there a few years when he died as the result of an accident, but his stock have made for him an enduring name . . . Wrack has been in training five seasons and he is the winner of ten races on the flat and six over hurdles. In eleven other races he finished second and won £6,869 in first place money and £600 in place money.' At stud, ★Wrack was an immediate success, and in 1919 his first two-year-olds included seven individual winners. Sam Hildreth, at any rate, was sufficiently impressed with ★Wrack's early progeny to pay the Belair Stud $10,500 for his bay son out of Medora II at the year's Saratoga Yearling Sales. The best of ★Wrack's first crop was certainly Blazes, who raced in the colours of Ral Parr and who, after a hurried preparation, finished sixth in the 1920 Kentucky Derby to his owner's other runner, Paul Jones. In the autumn of his three-year-old campaign Blazes managed to pick up two $10,000 handicaps on consecutive Saturdays. The end of the 1921 season found *Wrack sixth in the sires' list, with 38 winners or placed horses netting $153,401, and 83 races going to his progeny. One of America's top three-year-old fillies that season was his daughter Careful, out of Mindful, by Star Shoot, who ran 21 times, winning ten and running second four times and third twice. *Wrack's 14 two-year-old winners in 1921 earned $32,894 and made him the top sire of juveniles in America. After *Wrack had been put down in October, 1934, the *Bloodstock Breeders' Review* noted; 'From the time his progeny began racing in 1919 to the end of 1934 they won $2,455,708. The best of [his] get were Petee Wrack, Little Chief, Flying Cloud, Knobbie, Single Foot, Cloudland, Bulls Eye, Devastation, Golden Rule and Careful.' The year *Wrack died, *Sir Gallahad III was champion sire for the third time. By *Teddy out of Plucky Liège, the Claiborne stallion had already headed the list in 1930 and 1933, as he was to do again in 1940. He was also leading broodmare sire twelve times. Of the other great sires to have stood at Claiborne in the heyday of A. B. Hancock senior, perhaps the most influential was *Blenheim II, English Derby winner of 1930, who was imported in 1936,

Blenheim

the year his son *Mahmoud repeated his Epsom triumph. His American get included Whirlaway, out of Dustwhirl, by Sweep, Triple Crown winner in 1941 and formerly the world's leading money winner, and the good stakes winners Fervent, A Gleam, Mar-Kell, Bryan G, Thumbs Up, Free America, Miss Keeneland, Saratoga, Battle Mom, Duke's Lea, Air Hero, Proud One, Ocean Wave, Halberd, Nellie L, Dustman, Saguro, Copper Beech, Adaptable, Darby Dunedin, Hail Victory, Prognosis, Rapier, Tailspin, Owners Choice, What's New, Blentigo, Risque Rouge, Swift Sword and Quick Lunch. *Blenheim II headed the sires' list in 1941, was second once, third once and finished in the top ten seven times. He was also a successful broodmare sire, and when he died at Claiborne on May 26, 1958, he had been in the top ten in that category nine times in succession. Calumet Farm, which had a 25 per cent share in *Blenheim II, found a rich nick between his daughters and Bull Lea, producing such talented runners as Coaltown, Mark-Ye-Well and Hill Gail. A. B. Hancock senior was nine times America's leading breeder in the number of races won with 292 in 1935, 314 in 1936, 279 in 1937, 300 in 1938, 302 in 1940, 333 in 1942, 346 in 1943, 322 in 1944 and 350 in 1946. In terms of money won, horses bred by A. B. Hancock senior five times led the list in 1935 ($359,218), 1936 ($362,762), 1937 ($416,558), 1943 ($619,049) and in the year of his death, 1958 ($1,414,355) although, for official purposes, the honour was shared with 'Bull'. Born in Paris, Kentucky, a few months before his mother came into the Marchmont land, 'Bull' Hancock took over the managership of Claiborne in 1948, Ellerslie having finally been sold two years earlier. A Princeton graduate in genetics, 'Bull' Hancock spent his entire working life in the family breeding business, apart from his wartime service in the United States Army Air Corps, and was leading American breeder in his own right in 1959 with $1,322,595, 1968 with $1,493,189 and 1969 with $1,331,485.

'A good bull is half the herd, but a bad bull is all the herd' runs a favourite Hancock slogan, and no man has done more than 'Bull' to bring stallions representing the most distinguished European bloodlines to America. In December 1949, at a time when the cosmopolitan Nearco branch of the Phalaris male line was represented in America by only one stallion, *Rustam Sirdar, he paid $372,000 for *Nasrullah on behalf of a syndicate, which included William Woodward, John S. Phipps, Harry Guggenheim and John D. Hertz. *Nasrullah's son Noor (ex Queen of Baghdad, by Bahram), winner of four races worth £4,705 in England and third in the 1948 Derby, had been imported that autumn by Californian Charles S. Howard, for whom he had finished second once and third twice in handicap company, giving no hint of the glories to come. In 1950 he beat Citation four times in winning the Santa Anita Handicap, the San Juan Capistrano Handicap, the Forty Niners Handicap and the Golden Gate Handicap – in the last case actually giving one pound to Bull Lea's greatest son – and also took the Hollywood Cup and the American Handicap. He earned $356,940 that season, and was voted Handicap Horse of the Year. Under the terms of his

Bold Ruler.

sale, *Nasrullah completed his 1950 stud season in Ireland before coming over to Claiborne. Bred by the Aga Khan, by Nearco out of Mumtaz Begum by *Blenheim II, he ran third in the 1943 substitute English Derby at Newmarket and retired to stud as a four-year-old, having won five races, including the Coventry and Champion Stakes, worth £3,348. His last crop sired in Ireland included Never Say Die, his first in America Nashua, and, as champion English sire in 1951, and champion American sire in 1955 and 1956, he became the first horse to have headed the list on both sides of the Atlantic. He had 245 American starters, of whom 192 were winners and 53 stakes winners. *Nasrullah, whose sons and daughters won a total of 1,088 races and $12,810,228 in America, died in 1959, the same year as his son Bold Ruler took up stud duties at Claiborne. *Nasrullah was three times champion sire posthumously. The last occasion was 1963, whereupon he was succeeded by Bold Ruler, who then headed the list for an unprecedented seven years in a row. He was champion in 1972 as well. Out of Miss Disco, by Discovery, Bold Ruler raced three seasons, winning 23 times from 33 starts and earning $764,204. He was Horse of the Year in 1957 and Champion Sprinter in 1958. By a coincidence amazing even by Claiborne standards, Bold Ruler and Round Table were both foaled at the farm on April 6, 1954. Round Table (*Princequillo – *Knight's Daughter, by Sir Cosmo), whose racetrack

Round Table.

earnings of $1,749,869 constituted a world record at the time of his retirement, has proved one of the all-time great stallions at Claiborne, where he is now equipped with a muzzle to prevent him from taking lumps out of his flanks. His racetrack earnings total was duly passed by Kelso, while Forego, by Claiborne's Argentinian stallion *Forli, out of Lady Golconda, by Hasty Road, was on the $1,655,217 mark at the end of 1976. When Bold Ruler died on July 12, 1971, *The Thoroughbred Record* had no hesitation in calling him 'the most remarkable stallion of his era, if not of all time', although, of course, his greatest son, Triple Crown winner Secretariat, out of *Princequillo's daughter, Somethingroyal, was still only a yearling and Wajima still *in utero*. From his first crop, which included the talented Lamb Chop, out of Sheepsfoot, by Count Fleet, he consistently got a high proportion of quality horses, and, by the end of 1976, his 13 crops had produced 267 starters, 224 winners and 77 stakes winners. His progeny have earned a world-record $17,930,305, compared with the $13,589,021 won by the sons and daughters of the previous most successful sire of all time, Bull Lea, who was represented by 24 crops, and who was largely responsible for the long period of post-war ascendancy enjoyed by Calumet Farm. Comparisons between great stallions of different eras are as unreliable as they are invidious, no doubt, and the important consideration is that both Bold Ruler and Bull Lea were, in their heydays, undisputed champions, but the statistics of Bold Ruler's stud career and the sheer quality of his progeny are hardly to be rivalled. As a grandsire, Bold Ruler is faring well, principally through his

Florida-based son What a Pleasure, out of Grey Flight by *Mahmoud, who had six wins in two racing seasons. What a Pleasure was champion sire in 1975, when his son Foolish Pleasure, out of Fool-Me-Not, by Tom Fool, won the Kentucky Derby, and in 1976, when Honest Pleasure (What a Pleasure – Tularia by Tulyar) was fancied for the classics. The best Honest Pleasure could manage, however, was second in the Kentucky Derby to Bold Forbes, although, by the end of 1976, he had taken his earnings total to $815,776. Bold Forbes, another grandson of Claiborne's greatest stallion, subsequently ran third to Elocutionist in the Preakness before winning the Belmont. Like Honest Pleasure, Bold Forbes's sire, Irish Castle, is one of the best products of the nick between Bold Ruler and Tulyar mares, in this case Castle Forbes, champion filly at two years old and winner of $359,366. His dam, Comely Nell is by Bull Lea's son Commodore M out of *Blenheim II's daughter Nellie L.

The names of *Nasrullah and *Princequillo are inextricably linked in the history of the modern American thoroughbred, and the nick between them proved one of the most potent factors in that dramatic post-war improvement in American stock which owed so much to 'Bull' Hancock's importations. Another generation on, the two families continued to form an effective cross, Round Table, for instance, getting both Targowice and the good filly Rondeau on Bold Ruler's daughter Matriarch, ex Lyceum, by Bull Lea. *Princequillo was bred by an American, Laudy Lawrence, foaled in England and reared in Ireland, before being shipped across the Atlantic as a yearling. His sire was Prince Rose, bred in England but sold to Belgium as a foal for 260 guineas. There he was 'naturalised' – allowed to race at level weights against Belgian-breds provided the owner undertook never to export him – and he proved one of the best European racers of his generation, winning 1,647,350 Belgian francs and 483,000 of the French variety in 16 wins from 20 starts. *Princequillo's dam, *Cosquilla, a daughter of Papyrus, was bred in England but raced in France, where she won the Prix de Chantilly, Fille de l'Air and a number of other good races. On the track *Princequillo displayed marked improvement as he grew older. His first run, as a two-year-old, was in a claiming race under lease to Anthony Pelleteri, who lost him to trainer Horatio Luro, acting for Prince Dimitri Djordjaze's Boone Hall stable. Although, as a juvenile, *Princequillo earned only $3,575, he blossomed to such effect that, in nine wins from 23 starts at three and four, he won $92,975. He broke the track record when winning the Saratoga Cup, matched it when taking the Questionnaire Handicap and also scored in the Jockey Club Gold Cup, the Saratoga Handicap and the Merchants' and Citizens' Handicap. He entered stud in 1945 at Ellerslie, in the joint names of Prince Djordjaze and A. B. Hancock senior, was moved to Claiborne after the 1946 season and later syndicated. He died in Kentucky on July 18, 1964, aged 24. From 20 crops *Princequillo had 478 foals, 402 starters, 324 winners and 60 stakes winners. His progeny have won $13,349,169 in America, and his sons have taken some nice races abroad, including the

Irish Derby, won by Tambourine II in 1962, the first year 'Sweeps' was added to the title. As a broodmare sire, too, of course, *Princequillo has made a considerable mark.

Claiborne, at the time of 'Bull' Hancock's death, had been extended to 4,570 acres, the 1,600 acres of Xalapa Farm and the 1,067-acres Marchmont Farm having been absorbed in 1965 and 1967 respectively. Some of the Xalapa land is currently leased to Seth's elder brother, Arthur B. III, who struck out on his own as a breeder in 1971 at Stone Farm, which used to be a mere 100-acre spread within the Claiborne demesne, but which now encompasses almost 15 times that area. 'Bull', President of the Thoroughbred Club of America and the American Breeders' Association, Vice President of the Keeneland Association and a member of Keeneland's three-man Board of Trustees, included, among his patrons at the time of his death, Jockey Club President Ogden Phipps, Raymond Guest, Mrs Richard Dupont, F. W. Hooper, the Lazy F Ranch, Roger Wilson, John M. Schiff, J. M. Roebling, Michael Phipps, Mrs James Mills and the Mill River Stud. With such distinguished support, Claiborne has long been able to rely on keeping many of America's best-producing mares on the premises, and as many as 300 may be boarded there in the season, in addition to those owned by Claiborne. The select group of stallions, though, is the most fitting memorial to 'Bull' Hancock. Of the 25 now standing there, 20 are survivors from the 'Bull' Hancock era:

Round Table, world's leading living sire of stakes winners, had sired by the end of 1976, the winners of $12,006,451. His progeny includes Apalachee, Targowice, Drumtop, He's a Smoothie, Baldric, Royal Glint, Knightly Manner, Advocator, Beau Brummel, King's Bishop, Canal and Cellini.

Ack Ack, 1966 (Battle Joined – Fast Turn, by *Turn-to), winner of 19 races from 27 starts and a career total of $636,641, was Horse of the Year at five years old and Champion Handicap Horse. Sire of Youth, Thermal Energy and Greg The Great, Ack Ack represents the great Domino male line, tracing back to him through Armageddon, Alsab, Good Goods, Neddie, Colin and Commando.

Bagdad, 1956 (Double Jay – *Bazura, by Blue Peter) is another tracing in tail-male to Domino. His grandsire was Balladier by Black Toney, by Commando's son Peter Pan. Bagdad, who ran 34 times, and won $353,422, finishing first nine times, has sired the winners of $7,533,753.

Bold Reason, 1968 (Hail to Reason – Lalun, by *Djeddah). This half-brother to Never Bend entered stud in 1972, after winning $304,082 on the track.

Left to right from the top: *Bagdad, Buckpasser, Damascus and Forli.*

Buckpasser, 1963 (Tom Fool – Busanda, by War Admiral), winner of $1,462,014 on the track, has been disappointing at stud, but has sired Numbered Account, La Prevoyante, L'Enjoleur, Pass The Glass, Beau Buck and Swingtime. His son Northcliffe was three-year-old champion and Canadian Horse of the Year in 1976.

Damascus, 1964 (Sword Dancer – Kerala, by *My Babu), a Preakness winner whose track earnings totalled $1,176,781, with 21 victories from 32 starts, has sired Diabolo, Honorable Miss, Gold and Myrrh and Lover John.

Drone, 1966 (Sir Gaylord – Cap and Bells, by Tom Fool) raced only as a three-year-old, winning the four rather modest races he contested for $12,825. Flip Sal and Craft Drone are among the best of his get thus far.

Fiddle Isle, 1965 (Bagdad – Nascania, by *Nasrullah) raced four seasons and picked up $443,095.

*Forli, 1963 (Aristophanes – Trevisa, by Advocate), undefeated in his native country, where he won millions of pesos, earned $26,650 in the United States. In addition to the gelded Forego, American Horse of the Year in 1974, 1975 and 1976, he has got Intrepid Hero and Forceten, as well as a number of runners better known on the other side of the Atlantic, including Thatch, Home Guard and Dapper, who ran second in the Irish 2,000 Guineas and is one of the best horses bred by A. B. Hancock III so far.

*Hawaii, 1964 (Utrillo II – Ethane, by Mehrali), probably the smartest horse to come out of South Africa, won 66,236 Rand and $279,280. The best of his get to date are Triple Crown, Out To Lunch, Sun and Snow, and the A. B. Hancock III-bred two-year-old of 1976, Lullaby.

Hoist The Flag, 1968 (Tom Rolfe – Wavy Navy, by War Admiral), champion as a two-year-old and winner of $78,145 from five wins in six races, sired Against All Flags, Glory Glory, Hay Patcher, Colors Waving, Tepozetco and Respect The Flag in his first crop, foaled in 1973.

Jacinto, 1962 (Bold Ruler – *Cascade II, by Precipitation) won five times at two and three years old, earning $85,900, and has sired a total of 16 stakes winners, including Silver Mallet, Bold Liz, Buzkashi, Thirty One Jewels and Harbor Springs.

*Le Fabuleux, 1961 (Wild Risk – Angular, by Verso), best three-year-old of his generation in France, won, among a number of good races, the Prix du Jockey Club and the Prix Lupin, and stood six seasons at stud in France before coming to Kentucky in 1972.

Nijinsky II, 1967 (Northern Dancer – Flaming Page, Bull Page), first English Triple Crown winner since Bahram, and winner of £246,132, finished second to Sassafras in the Prix de l'Arc de Triomphe. His best-known sons in Europe so far are Silky, Green Dancer and African Dancer,

Nijinsky.

while the best of his American get have been Copernica and Summertime Promise.

⋆Pago Pago, 1960 (Matrice – Pompilia, by Abbots Fell) won £17,095 as a two-year-old in his native Australia. He is sire of Canadian Horse of the Year Jumpin Joseph, while his other stakes winners include Aloha Road, Able Jan, Go Go Roger and Stacey d'Ette.

Reviewer, 1966 (Bold Ruler – Broadway, by Hasty Road) was sire of the great filly Ruffian, out of Shenanigans, by Native Dancer, lost in the match with Foolish Pleasure at Belmont Park on July 6, 1975, after winning all ten of her races, worth $313,428. His Claiborne-bred daughter Revidere out of Quillesian, by ⋆Princequillo, was voted three-year-old Filly of the Year in 1976. On the track Reviewer won nine races, from 13 starts, and $247,223.

Sir Gaylord, 1959 (⋆Turn-to – Somethingroyal, by ⋆Princequillo), who returned to Claiborne for the 1977 season after four years at the Haras du Quesnay, is sire of Sir Ivor, Habitat and Sahib. He won $237,404 on the track.

Sir Ivor, 1965 (Sir Gaylord – Attica, by Mr Trouble), winner of the English Derby and 2,000 Guineas, second to Vaguely Noble in the Prix de

l'Arc de Triomphe and victor in the Washington D.C. International, stood two seasons in Ireland before returning to the United States. He won £116,819 in England, 876,100 francs in France and $90,000 in America. He is sire of Optimistic Gal, Land Girl, Malinowski, Cavo Doro and Ivanjica, who went one better than her sire in the Prix de l'Arc de Triomphe in 1976.

Tell, 1966 (Round Table – Nas-Mahal, by *Nasrullah) won nine of his eighteen races, and $229,668. A son from his first crop, Run Tell Run, ran well as a juvenile in England and as a three-year-old in America. Tell is also sire of Rock of Ages.

Far left: *Reviewer*. Left: *Sir Gaylord*. Below left: *Sir Ivor*. Top: *Secretariat*.

Tom Rolfe, 1962 (*Ribot – Pocahontas, by Roman) has proved a consistent getter of good runners, the most celebrated of his offspring being Washington D.C. International winner Run The Gantlet, Hoist The Flag, London Company and Droll Role.

The most significant addition to the roster in Seth's time is, of course, Secretariat, whose racetrack winnings of $1,316,808 put him seventh in the list of all-time leading money winners, two behind Buckpasser. The 1972 Kentucky Derby and Belmont winner and earner of $1,111,497, Riva Ridge (First Landing – Iberia, by *Heliopolis) also stands at Claiborne now, as does Judger, 1971 (Damascus – Face the Facts by *Court Martial), winner of $240,271 (13 starts, four wins). The most recent acquisitions are Avatar (Graustark – Brown Berry, by Mount Marcy), winner of the 1975 Belmont and Santa Anita Derby, and Navajo, 1970 (*Grey Dawn II – Doublene, by Double Jay), who won the Essex Handicap in 1976 and finished an arduous career with total winnings of $351,532, without ever looking quite the stuff that Claiborne stallions are made of. Claiborne lost one of its most distinguished stallions in 1976 with the death of *Herbager (Vandale – Flagette, by Escamillo), Prix du Jockey Club winner of 1959, whose influence has been strongly felt in Europe recently through his grandsons Star Appeal, Bruni and Matahawk.

The Eclipse Awards for 1976 confirmed Claiborne's position in the top rank of American racehorse breeders. Apart from Revidere, the Claiborne-foaled Forego and the Champion Grass Horse, Youth, the farm takes the credit for standing the sires of both two-year-old champions, since Sensational is a daughter of Hoist The Flag, out of Meritus, by Bold Ruler, while Seattle Slew is by the deceased Bold Reasoning (Boldnesian – Reason to Earn, by Hail to Reason) out of My Charmer, by Poker. Sensational was

Top left: *Nasrullah*.
Top: *Riva Ridge*. Above: *Shenanigans (now dead) with her Damascus filly*.

also foaled on the farm, as was the 1976 champion jumper Straight and True, by Never Bend out of Polly Girl, by Prince Bio.

After the death of 'Bull', Claiborne withdrew, almost entirely, from racing. A. B. Hancock senior had always concentrated on breeding for the market, but 'Bull' won around $4\frac{1}{2}$ million on the racetrack from 1945 until his death. Until 1963 he was Vice President of the Breeders' Sales Company and a prominent consignor to Keeneland auctions, but he then found that it was 'virtually impossible to race part of our yearlings and have a buyer's acceptance for the remainder'. In his later years, 'Bull' Hancock made it his policy to sell a half interest in the entire yearling crop. Claiborne is racing again now, the latest scheme being to sell all the colts and run the fillies.

Altogether Seth Hancock's inheritance is an awesome one. Champions galore – including Kelso, Nashua, Cicada, Never Bend, First Landing, Doubledogdare, Dedicate, Bald Eagle, Misty Morn and Neji – have been foaled at Claiborne, while Nelson Bunker Hunt's 1976 Epsom Derby winner Empery (Vaguely Noble – Pamplona II, by Postin) is among the more recent stars who first saw the light of day there.

Along the road, Bold Forbes took up stud duties at Stone Farm in 1977. Syndicated for $4,160,000, and standing at $25,000 a live foal, this most genuine of classic winners, who earned $523,035 from 18 races, with 13 victories, one second and four thirds seems to have all the credentials to make a successful stallion in America. His acquisition certainly represents

Below: *Bold Forbes*. Right: *Cougar II*.

a step up for Arthur Hancock, whose priciest stallion hitherto has been
*Cougar II, champion turf horse as a six-year-old in 1972 and winner of
$1,151,476 in America in addition to the 139,100 escudos he picked up as a
two- and three-year-old in his native Chile. He stands at $10,000, and is a
son of Tale of Two Cities (by the English St Leger winner of 1944, Tehran)
out of *Cindy Lou II, by Madara. *Cougar II entered stud at Stone Farm in
1974, the same year as three other young stallions, Cabin, Head of the River
and Soudard. Cabin, foaled in 1968, performed fairly well on the track,
winning six of his 31 races and earning $71,620, although not as well as
might have been hoped from his pedigree:

Bagdad	Double Jay	Balladier	Black Toney Blue Warbler
		Broomshot	Whisk Broom II Centre Shot
	*Bazura	Blue Peter	Fairway Fancy Free
		Bura	*Bahram Becti
Rose Bower	*Princequillo	Prince Rose	Rose Prince Indolence
		*Cosquilla	Papyrus Quick Thought
	Lea Lane	*Nasrullah	Nearco Mumtaz Begum
		Lea Lark	Bull Lea Colosseum

He stands at $750.

Head of the River, winner of the 1972 Everglades and a career total of $109,128, is by Crewman, out of First Feather, by First Landing, and therefore a half-brother to Run The Gantlet, while the Belgian Triple Crown winner of 1971, Soudard, is a son of Nord-Sud, out of Tehran's daughter Soumida. The Stone Farm stallion list is completed by two debutants of 1977 – Herculean (Bold Ruler – Fool's Play, by Tom Fool), winner of $52,302, and Queen City Lad, who started 23 times in four racing seasons and earned $119,615, a son of Olden Times out of Queen City Miss, by Royal Union. Arthur Hancock has about 40 mares of his own at Stone Farm, and boards around 60. Since his decision to work outside the Claiborne establishment, the solid development and expansion of Stone Farm have made it more and more a force to be reckoned with, even if there is still a hint of diffidence in Hancock's catchphrase – 'We're trying to raise you a good horse.'

Arthur Hancock III and Stone Farm.

Calumet Stud Farm

Before Bold Ruler made his mark as a stallion at Claiborne, the greatest American sire of the 20th century was unquestionably Bull Lea, a son of ⋆Bull Dog (by Teddy) out of Ballot's daughter Rose Leaves. He was purchased for $14,000 as a yearling at the Saratoga sales in 1936 by Warren Wright, owner of Calumet Farm, Lexington, which he had bought, as a trotting horse nursery, from Henry J. Schlesinger in 1924. The farm had been called Fairland during Schlesinger's time, but Wright, who had made a fortune manufacturing a baking powder called Calumet, renamed it. There had, in fact, been a farm called Calumet, which is an Indian word meaning 'pipe of peace', when Nancy Lewis Greene wrote her book, but that establishment, owned by the Hon Henry L. Martin was in Woodford County 'about two miles from Midway on the Versailles-Midway Pike', whereas the horse farm is in Fayette on the Versailles Road, just along from Keeneland Racecourse. Until 1931, Calumet continued to concentrate on standardbreds, but it was with the transition to thoroughbreds, and, in particular, the acquisition of Bull Lea, that the Calumet success story began. From 1941 to 1961 Calumet ranked as America's leading racing stable 12 times, and Bull Lea was champion sire in 1947, 1948, 1952 and 1953. He was also leading broodmare sire from 1958 to 1961 inclusive. In the Kentucky Derby, Calumet has scored a record eight victories with Whirlaway, Pensive (Hyperion – ⋆Penicuik II, by Buchan), who won in 1944, the 1948 Triple Crown winner Citation, a son of Hyperion's daughter ⋆Hydroplane, Ponder (Pensive – Miss Rushin, by ⋆Blenheim II), in 1949, Hill Gail, out of Jane Gail, in 1952, Iron Liege (Bull Lea – Iron Maiden, by War Admiral) in 1957, Tim Tam (Tom Fool – Two Lea, by Bull Lea) in 1958 and Forward Pass (On-and-On – Princess Turia, by ⋆Helioscope) in 1968. For the last of these victories to be confirmed, protracted litigation was necessary, Peter Fuller's Dancer's Image (Native Dancer – Noors Image, by ⋆Noor) having crossed the line first. He was disqualified when phenylbutazone was found in a urine sample, but it was not until April 1972 that the legal processes were complete. Dancer's Image, sire of Saritamer, Lianga and Godswalk, stood at the Killeen Castle Stud, Dunsany, County Meath, Ireland, until 1976, when he was moved to the Haras du Quesnay. 'The theory that racing class in mares produces racing class has been one of the major points of Calumet's "plan",' a booklet produced by the farm observes, although not,

Above: *Tim Tam*. Below: *Forward Pass*.

of course, without noting that 'many of our fine stakes winners have come from unraced mares.' It has been written of Warren Wright, who died on New Year's Eve, 1950, that he couldn't tell his own horses apart on the farm, which is hard to believe of a man who put enough into breeding to lead the American list, in point of money won, in 1941 ($528,211), 1944 ($990,612), 1947 ($1,807,432), 1948 ($1,559,850), 1949 ($1,515,181) and 1950 ($1,090,286). After his death, Calumet, run by his widow, who became Mrs Gene Markey, continued to head the list every year up to and including 1957 with totals of $1,198,107, $2,060,590, $1,573,803, $1,139,609, $999,737, $1,528,727 and $1,469,473. The farm was top again in 1961 with $1,078,894 won. *The Thoroughbred Record* obituary of Warren Wright noted: 'It has been muttered with more than an incidental element of truth, that the Calumet organization was the first to succeed in applying assembly-line tactics to the production of thoroughbred stock.' Or, as Margaret B. Glass, Calumet secretary, has it in the farm brochure, the system 'may be likened to a factory, which produces as far as possible the best-bred horses from hand-picked sires and broodmares, ever seeking to "improve the breed".' The scale of the Calumet operation now is much reduced from the days of the farm's greatest glory. There are currently about 30 mares there, and many of the training barns stand empty. Yearlings are broken on Calumet's own six-furlong track, and although some of the foals used to be privately sold, they are nowadays all retained with a view to racing. Calumet stands six stallions – Best Turn (*Turn-to – Sweet Clementine, by Swaps), foaled in 1966 and winner on the track of $270,339; Forward Pass, who came within an ace of winning the Triple Crown by running second to Stage Door Johnny in the Belmont, and whose career earnings totalled $580,631; Gleaming (*Herbager – A Gleam, by *Blenheim II), who retired from the track as a five-year-old in 1973 with winnings of $469,245; Raise A Cup (Raise A Native – Spring Sunshine, by Nashua), who ran only as a two-year-old, in 1973, when he won four of his six races and $53,793; Reverse (*Turn-to – Miss Grundy, by Bull Lea), sire of Queen's Turn, Revlynne, Obverse, Miss Rebound (champion handicap mare in Canada) and Lujuria (champion two-year-old filly in Mexico); and Tim Tam, sire of Tosmah, Timmy Lad, Sunstruck and Big Tim, and winner of $467,475, who was another unlucky horse not to win the Triple Crown – his only classic defeat was when he ran second, with a broken sesamoid, to *Cavan in the Belmont.

In Calumet's equine cemetery lie 40 great horses – pride of place naturally going to Bull Lea – with five more of the stable's best runners who died abroad commemorated by markers. After winning $94,825 on the track for Calumet, Bull Lea sired 376 foals, of which 336 ran, and 277 were winners, 57 of them in stakes races. In modern times no sire has got such a trio of top-class runners in one crop as did Bull Lea with Citation, Bewitch and Coaltown. Citation, reputedly the best seen in America since Man o' War and the first ever million dollar earner, was himself the sire of several good stakes winners, including Fabius, winner of the 1956 Preakness, Get Around,

Left: *Càlumet cemetery.* Right: *Office and stallion barn.* Below: *Calumet*

Guadalcanal, Manteau and Silver Spoon. Bewitch, out of Potheen, by Wildair, champion filly of 1947 and champion handicap mare of 1949, won 20 races and $462,605, and Coaltown, a daughter of Easy Lass, and winner of $415,675, was champion sprinter of 1948 and Horse of the Year in 1949.

Greentree and
C.V. Whitney Stud Farms

The international prominence in thoroughbred racing and breeding of the Whitney family traces to an 1897 Lexington sale. Among the crowd was the highly prosperous businessman and erstwhile politician, William Collins Whitney, who had kept a few standardbreds some years earlier, but was now somewhat out of his depth, as he himself observed: 'The whole thing was new to me, and the various horse names in the pedigree were about as unintelligible to the whole party as anything can be, but we sat there looking as much like veterans as we could.' The next year, with Samuel C. Hildreth as his trainer, he burst incognito on the racing scene, running horses in the colours of his son-in-law Sydney Paget. In 1899 he had a string of 27, of which eight were winners. His best was the colt Jean Beraud (His Highness – Carrie C, by Sensation), who won the Withers and the Belmont in his only two starts that year. Of the 55 Whitney horses, now sporting their owner's

W. C. Whitney. Right: *Count Lehndorff, author of* Horse-Breeding Recollections, *and importer of much influential stock, on behalf of the German government, to Graditz in the late 19th century.*

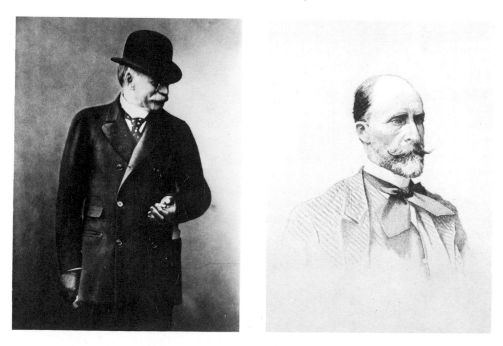

Above: *Volodyoski*. Below: *Upset gives Man O'War his only taste of defeat*.

colours, which earned a total of $92,545 in 1900, 34 started the season in the care of Sam Hildreth. When the best of the two-year-olds, Ballyhoo Bey (Kingston – Ballyhoo, by Duke of Magenta), came out of a race in May with a fever, however, Hildreth was fired and John E. Madden invited to take over. Ballyhoo Bey's next outing, three months later, was in the Futurity at Sheepshead Bay, which he won by $1\frac{1}{2}$ lengths, despite an alleged conspiracy on the part of the other riders to box in Tod Sloan, specially brought back from England for the race and, apparently, handsomely remunerated for his pains. Hildreth, put out in more ways than one, made the mistake, in his cups, of fetching Madden one across the back of the head with a heavy walking stick at the Morris Park Racecourse on October 1 that year. This was an ill-advised method of venting his spleen, of course, and 'The Wizard', springing to his feet and clasping Hildreth by the throat, extracted an apology. That same year Whitney bought La Belle Stud Farm in Lexington, acquired his first stallion, *Meddler (St Gatien – Busybody) and set about building up his broodmare band, which, by 1903, numbered 81, including 32 stakes winners, and, altogether, 59 winners. Total racetrack winnings of these mares was $631,663, Whitney's avowed intention being to practise what Count Lehndorff preached, but he died on February 2, 1904 and left the question of whether good racemares make good broodmares to divert and vex future generations of horsemen. The year before he died, his elder son Harry Payne Whitney had, in his first full racing season, won $170,447 in prize money. H. P. Whitney had a lease on Brookdale Farm, New Jersey, which remained his American breeding and training headquarters until he bought a spread on the Paris Pike, Lexington, from the trustees and executors of the James Ben Ali estate in March 1917 and gradually transferred there. If W. C. Whitney's brief and spectacular racing career had been conducted on an international basis – in 1901 he won more races in England than America, took the Epsom Derby with Volodyoski and scored some notable victories in France – his elder son soon became an even more familiar figure on the European turf, maintaining a stud at Newmarket from where, until the First World War intervened, he annually sent several of his American-bred mares to be covered by French-based stallions. The best of both worlds was in the blood of many imported horses, bred by Whitney in Europe, which appear in top American pedigrees. America's champion sire of 1929, Spearmint's son *Chicle, for example, was imported as a yearling in 1914, going on to win the Champagne Stakes as a two-year-old and the Dwyer Handicap at three. His dam was Lady Hamburg, who won three races for Whitney in America as a two-year-old, a daughter of Hamburg out of *Lady Frivoles by St Simon. Altogether, H. P. Whitney is credited with breeding 192 stakes winners – still an all-time record, although E. P. Taylor was at the end of 1976 on the 189 mark – most of which were foaled on his Kentucky farm. He had bred a number of fine horses before the move, however, including the super-filly Regret (1912, Broomstick – Jersey Lightning, by Hamburg), the only one of her sex to have won the Kentucky Derby.

He also had the distinction of inflicting Man o' War's solitary defeat in the $249,465 Sanford Memorial Stakes at Saratoga in 1919, with Upset, whose pedigree was typical of H. P. Whitney-breds of that era, with a male line to Broomstick, and Domino close up:

Whisk Broom II	Broomstick	Ben Brush *Elf
	Audience	Sir Dixon Sallie McClelland
Pankhurst	*Voter	Friar's Balsam *Mavourneen
	Runaway Girl	Domino *Fair Vision

Shortly after H. P. Whitney died in 1930, his son C. V. on the advice of Jockey Club chairman William Woodward decided to let the great Equipoise (Pennant – Swinging, by Broomstick) take his chance in that year's Pimlico Futurity, which he duly won. Since then 'Sonny' Whitney has proved one of the most successful breeders of all time in his own right, and when his Ski Run won the Louisville Handicap in May 1976 – his 18th stakes winner at Churchill Downs and his 161st overall – it was appropriate that the dam, Spark Plug, should have been by the English Derby winner of 1936,

*Mahmoud, whose time for the race is still a record, the most influential horse to have been at the Whitney Stud in C.V.'s time. *Mahmoud (*Blenheim II – Mah Mahal, by Gainsborough) was bought from the Aga Khan late in 1940 at a time when Equipoise had just died and C. V. Whitney was looking for an outbred stallion. The sire of 68 stakes winners, *Mahmoud died in 1962. Whitney operates today on a somewhat reduced scale, and does not have a stallion on the premises, although he has interests in four, yet he continues to produce good horses. He had four stakes winners in 1976, including Banquet Table, while Avatar, whose maternal grandsire is a son of *Mahmoud, was one of his, too.

   *Mahmoud blood has also been of great significance at the neighbouring Greentree Stud, owned by John Hay Whitney and the heirs of his sister, Mrs Joan Payson, who died on October 4, 1975, mourned not only by the racing world but by followers of the New York Mets baseball team, in which she was a major stockholder, as well. John Hay Whitney, honorary member of the English Jockey Club and one-time Ambassador to the Court of St James's, won two Cheltenham Gold Cups with Easter Hero back in 1929 and 1930, and has remained a well-known figure on the English turf to this day, having, in 1976, won the Cambridgeshire and Cesarewitch Handicaps with Intermission and John Cherry, both by Stage-Door Johnny, to become the first owner to land the Autumn Double since A. K. Macomber in 1925. Whitney, in 1976, was also fourth in both the owners' and breeders' lists in England. *Mahmoud's progeny, generally small and tough, have

Mahmoud led in by the Aga Khan after winning the 1934 Epsom Derby.

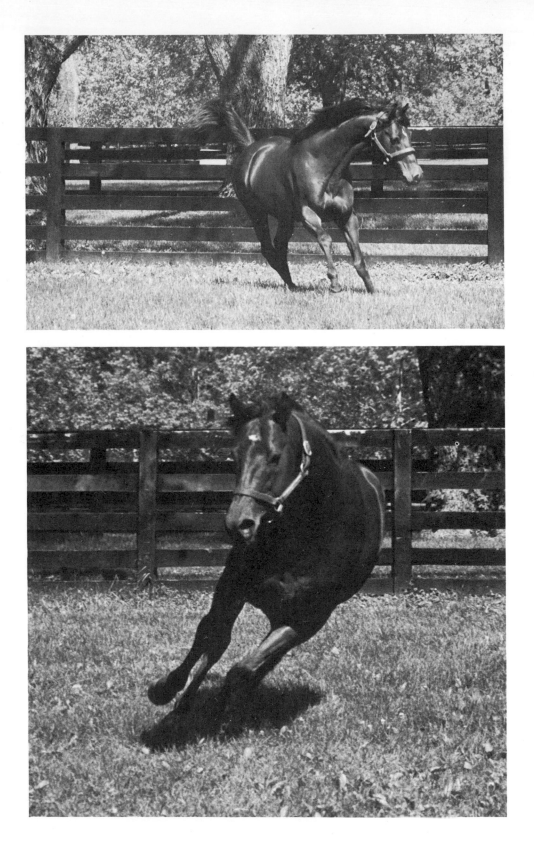

Left: *Stop The Music, and* (below) *Foolish Pleasure*. Above: *Arts and Letters*.

crossed well at Greentree with the Tom Fools, their conformation complementing the ample size associated with that great stallion, who died on the farm, where he was foaled, in 1976, having been retired from stud in 1972, when the sight in his only functioning eye was fading. Horse of the Year in 1953, Tom Fool was a son of Menow out of Goga by *Bull Dog, who won 21 times from 30 starts and earned $570,165 for Greentree. Another Greentree-bred and raced son of Menow, Capot, was voted Horse of the Year in 1949 – in those days there were still two polls, so Coaltown shared the honour – while Damascus's dam was also raised on the farm. More than 20 of the Greentree mares today have Tom Fool blood, while three of the stud's stallions, Stop The Music, who took up his duties in 1976, Hatchet Man and Foolish Pleasure, for both of whom 1977 was the first season, are out of Tom Fool mares. Foolish Pleasure, eleventh in the list of all-time money winners with $1,216,165 from 26 races (16 wins) was bred by Waldemar Farms, but the other two were Greentree-bred and raced, as, until recently, were all the farm's stallions. Now, however, two Paul Mellon-breds, Arts and Letters (*Ribot – All Beautiful, by Battlefield), and Key to the Mint (Graustark – Key Bridge, by *Princequillo) stand at the farm. The home-grown Stage Door Johnny completes the line-up. Arts and Letters, a close second to Majestic Prince in both the Kentucky Derby and the Preakness, won the Belmont, the Jockey Club Gold Cup and several other good races for career earnings of $632,404, Key to the Mint, who entered stud in 1974, picked up $576,015 in three seasons' racing, while Stage Door Johnny (Prince John – Peroxide Blonde, by Ballymoss) won the 1968 Belmont and $223,965. Stop The Music, a son of Hail to Reason out of

Key to the Mint, Bob Green and Tom Fool's grave.

Bebopper, rated second only to Secretariat as a two-year-old, is the winner of 11 good races; his half-brother Hatchet Man, by The Axe II, is the winner of 10. Principal outside stallions Bob Green breeds to are *Hawaii, Tom Rolfe, Graustark, Nijinsky II, Wajima, Delta Judge, The Axe II, Buckpasser, Dynastic, *Gallant Man, Hoist The Flag, Northern Dancer, Gallant Romeo, No Robbery, Big Spruce, Reviewer, Round Table, Tentam, Speak John, Best Turn, In Reality, Sir Ivor and Gleaming. Greentree's 750 acres at the moment accommodates 115 horses, of which 20 are retired and

Graustark at Darby Dan Farm, and Greentree's circular barn.

40 in training. There are 50 broodmares, 10 of which are given a rest each year. Yearlings are broken at Keeneland by John Ward and then shipped to the main stable in South Carolina in November. At two, the Greentree horses are moved on to New York, in charge of John Gaver, an effective, but tough, trainer of the old school, whose demanding regime might just be a bit much for the fillies. Only two Greentree fillies, at any rate, have won stakes races since Bob Green joined in 1958, and, going back to 1930, the figure is a mere six. An analysis of Greentree breeding performance from 1928 to 1958 proved somewhat inconclusive, or, at least, confirmed that, at the farm, as elsewhere, good sires and good mares have proved capable of producing high-class runners even from relatively plebeian matings and that the business is highly unpredictable. Greentree was bought in 1925 by John Hay Whitney's father Payne, brother of Harry Payne Whitney. Payne Whitney's wife, the former Helen Hay, daughter of Abraham Lincoln's secretary John Hay, was the driving force behind the creation of a horse farm at Greentree, in the early days concentrating on steeplechasers. Helen Hay Whitney, who died in 1944, developed an enthusiasm for the flat, however, and won the Kentucky Derby with Twenty Grand in 1931 and Shut Out in 1942.

Helen Hay Whitney.

Darby Dan Stud Farm

Perhaps the latterday successes of the Whitneys, with their fabulous, inherited wealth, have been largely unavoidable. 'Show me a rich man who understands horses – there's no such thing,' opines the half-serious Olin Gentry. Darby Dan Farm occupies part of the old Idle Hour Stock Farm, owned by the legendary Colonel E. R. Bradley, who died on August 15, 1946, and Gentry was manager of that outfit too. By the time Bradley came into the horse business, at the turn of the century, he was a rich man, as he had to be, but a self-made one, and in Gentry's conversation, as he expatiates on mating policies vindicated by stakes victories of decades ago, there are echoes of his dead master's voice, and a tangible link with those free-wheeling days

Olin Gentry and Little Current.

On the presentation stand at Churchill Downs after Burgo King's victory in the 1932 Kentucky Derby are, left to right, jockey Eugene James, Col Matt Winn, E. R. Bradley and Governor Ruby Laffoon. **Right:** *Black Toney.*

when determination and the adventurous spirit saw men rise from poverty and obscurity to proclaim their material triumphs in an unremitting, costly and gentlemanly search for the horse to outrun his contemporaries. Bradley went into racing because his doctor advised that his precarious state of health demanded that he took things easy and spent more time in the fresh air. In 1905, accordingly, he leased the 336-acre Grove Farm on the Old Frankfort Pike, Lexington, and began to breed his own runners. Five years later, he bought and renamed the farm, and gradually expanded his holdings to 1,480 acres. He had, in fact, dabbled in horseracing some time before embarking on this remarkably efficacious therapy, his colours first appearing in a seller at the Harlem track, where a horse called Friar John won him the $300 purse, on July 27, 1898. His first stakes winner was Bad News, thus named on account of the speed with which he travelled, in the autumn of 1903. Thereafter, Bradley always named his horses to begin with the letter 'B'. An abstemious, philanthropic man, Bradley was a born gambler. He left home in Johnstown, Pennsylvania, at the age of 14, in 1874, became a cowboy in Texas, worked as a scout for General Nelson A. Miles during the War with the Apaches and met with great success as a gold prospector in Arizona and New Mexico. Wyatt Earp and Billy the Kid are supposed to have been among his acquaintances during this period, which brought him enough money to invest in Chicago real estate and make a killing during that city's boom. In 1891 he moved to Florida for his health, and in 1898 opened the Beach Club there, an exclusive gambling joint which made him a fortune and remained in business until the Colonel – the title was a courtesy bestowed by the Kentucky State Governor – began liquidating his assets after a 1940 heart attack. The Beach Club was by no means Bradley's first experience of the casino business, since he had had similar interests at Long Branch,

New Jersey, Rockaway, Long Island, and El Paso, Texas. He had also made book at Hot Springs, Memphis and St Louis, attracted to the role of layer after he and his brother had gambled away a small business they had started. Bradley is said to have been reticent about his gambling for most of his life, but, towards the end, he became more forthcoming, as the following exchange during a United States Senate Committee on gambling illustrates:

Huey Long: 'Now tell these distinguished senators just what your real business is.'

Bradley: 'I am a gambler, senator.'

'And what do you gamble on?'

'I gamble on anything, not excepting spitting at a crack.'

Black Toney, Colonel Bradley's foundation sire, was one of four yearlings he brought at auction in 1912, when William A. Prime, having lost a million dollars on the cotton market, was forced to resell the stock he had recently acquired from James R. Keene's Castleton Stud. Three years later Cliff Howard was sent to England and France to buy broodmares. Among those he returned with were Vaila, Padula, Macaroon and Mailbird. Around this time, the young Olin Gentry was riding races in Denver and San Francisco, having spent 1913 and 1914 in Juarez, Mexico, with his brother Lloyd, a first class horseman and subsequently a successful trainer. Gentry, by now too heavy for race riding, joined Bradley in 1922 and had complete control of the horses two years later. The year before he arrived at Idle Hour, Bradley had had the first of his four Kentucky Derby winners with Behave

Yourself (Marathon – Miss Ringlets, by Handball). Unfortunately, the Colonel's money was on his other runner, Black Servant, a son of Black Toney, who may have been distracted by an over-enthusiastic crowd. Behave Yourself, at all events, was never otherwise as good a horse as Black Servant, or another son of Black Toney, Bimelech. The next time Bradley won the Derby, with Bubbling Over (*North Star III – Beaming Beauty, by Sweep) in 1926, he also had the second again, this time Baggenbaggage. Two years earlier a son of Black Toney, Black Gold, out of Useeit by Bonnie Joe, had won the race for Mrs R. M. Hoots.

Bradley was obsessed with inbreeding, and became, principally by mating Blue Larkspur's daughters with Black Toney and his sons, one of its leading exponents in modern times. Blue Larkspur foaled at Idle Hour the year Bubbling Over won the Kentucky Derby, and Horse of the Year at three, himself had, as fourth dam, his sire's grandam.

Black Servant	Black Toney	Peter Pan	Commando *Cinderella
		Belgravia	Ben Brush *Bonnie Gal
	*Padula	Laveno	Bend Or Napoli
		Padua	Thurio Immortelle
Blossom Time	*North Star III	Sunstar	Sundridge Doris
		Angelic	St Angelo Fota
	*Vaila	Fariman	Gallinule Bellinzona
		Padilla	Macheath Padua

Bimelech, a full brother to Black Helen, out of *La Troienne (*Teddy – Helene de Troie) was an important factor in Bradley's inbreeding programme. 'Blue Larkspur had a kind disposition and was a big rugged horse, and Bimelech was temperamental and on the light side, and it worked extremely well with the Blue Larkspur mares or daughters of Blue Larkspur,' says Gentry. Blue Larkspur's daughter Bloodroot (ex *Knockaney Bridge, by Bridge of Earn) produced two first-class race fillies in Be Faithful (14 wins, $189,040) and Bimlette (4 wins, $28,075), who are close up in a number of important pedigrees today – Be Faithful through her daughter Lalun, dam of Never Bend, Bimlette through her son No Robbery. *La Troienne was bought in France on Bradley's behalf in 1930 by Dick Thompson, who also brought back a few other broodmares, including Silver Hue, dam of

Bazaar. *La Troienne, one of the greatest producers this century, was also dam of Baby League, by Bubbling Over, who, mated with War Admiral, produced the super-filly Busher, Horse of the Year in 1945. Among her other offspring were two daughters of Blue Larkspur – Big Event, second dam of The Axe II, and Businesslike, one of the Idle Hour horses acquired by Ogden Phipps after Bradley's death, when she was in foal to War Admiral. The result was Busanda.

Mating Blue Larkspur to Black Toney mares proved a good idea at Idle Hour, too, and the good filly, Buginarug, for instance, was thus produced (ex Breakfast Bell). Mated with *Sickle, she got Bless Me. Black Helen's daughter Be Like Mom, by *Sickle, moreover, having pulled up on her only two visits to the racetrack, was bred to Blue Larkspur, producing But Why Not, a top racemare champion filly of 1947 and winner of the Arlington Classic. Bradley's third Kentucky Derby winner, a son of his second, was Burgoo King, who took the race and the Preakness as well, in 1932. His dam was Minawand (Lonawand – *Mintless), who could not run far enough to win a race, but could work three-eights in 0:34. Bradley, reasoning that no horse could hold full speed longer than that anyway, bought her, but she was at first such a disappointing producer that he decided to get rid of her. Horace King took her, but only on condition that they breed on shares. The last of Bradley's Kentucky Derby winners was Broker's Tip, a son of Black Toney and a half-brother to Roberto's third dam. Roberto, now a Darby Dan stallion, is another classic winner with a sprinter (Rarelea) close up in his pedigree, while, inbred 4 × 4 to Nearco and to Blue Larkspur, and show-

Roberto.

ing several other duplications at the fifth remove, he is, altogether, a horse to gladden the Gentry heart:

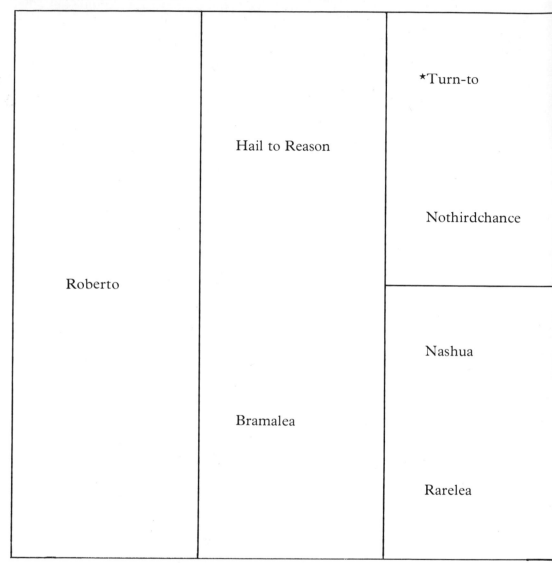

Roberto	Hail to Reason	*Turn-to
		Nothirdchance
	Bramalea	Nashua
		Rarelea

When Roberto followed his English Derby win of 1972 by giving Brigadier Gerard his only taste of defeat in the Benson and Hedges, jubilation at Darby Dan was the greater, since *Ribot, whose unbeaten record thus remained unequalled, had stood 13 years at the farm. Indeed, his death had occurred only on April 27 that year. The original leasing agreement on *Ribot was for five years, but, on its expiry, the great stallion's temperament made it impossible to ship him home. 'Ribot was as nutty as a fruit cake,' Gentry says. 'He would stand on his hind legs and hug the trees, or chew the rafters in his stall. He was always a nut. You know, he would straddle a fence and just hang there. He was a nightmare to handle – he almost killed me

once.' Ribot's best son in America, Graustark (out of Flower Bowl, by
*Alibhai), who broke down nine days before the 1966 Kentucky Derby, for

*Royal Charger	Nearco	Pharos Nogara
	Sun Princess	Solario Mumtaz Begum
*Source Sucree	Admiral Drake	Craig an Eran Plucky Liège
	Lavendale	Pharos Sweet Lavender
Blue Swords	Blossom Time	Black Servant Blue Larkspur
	Flaming Swords	Man o' War Exalted
Galla Colors	*Sir Gallahad III	*Teddy Plucky Liège
	Rouge et Noir	St Germans Baton Rouge
*Nasrullah	Nearco	Pharos Nogara
	Mumtaz Begum	*Blenheim II Mumtaz Mahal
Segula	Johnstown	Jamestown La France
	*Sekhmet	Sardanapale Prosopopee
Bull Lea	*Bull Dog	*Teddy Plucky Liège
	Rose Leaves	Ballot *Colonial
Bleebok	Blue Larkspur	Black Servant Blossom Time
	*Forteresse	Sardanapale Guerriere II

which he was favourite, also stands at Darby Dan now.

The old Idle Hour spread has been a rich source of Kentucky Derby winners, Danada Farm having won the race once with Lucky Debonair, in 1965,
Galbreath twice with Chateaugay and Proud Clarion. Chateaugay (Swaps –
Banquet Bell, Polynesian), who won the race in 1963, is now dead, most of
the good sons and daughters who survive him, Gentry points out, being
inbred to Hyperion. Chateaugay's sire, by Hyperion's son *Khaled, out of
Beau Père's daughter Iron Reward, was Horse of the Year in 1956 and earned
in 19 wins from 25 starts, $848,900. He raced for Rex C. Ellsworth, who,
Humphrey S. Finney recalls, would ride him on errands, hitching him to

S

a rail like a cowboy pony. Before he was syndicated and moved over to Spendthrift in 1967 he was jointly owned by Galbreath and his wife, and stood at Darby Dan. Little Current (Sea Bird – Luiana, by *My Babu) won the 1974 Preakness and Belmont, and a total of $354,704, before retiring to stud at Darby Dan. True Knight, a son of Chateaugay out of Stealaway by Hyperion's grandson Olympia, winner on the track of $739,673, Good Counsel (Hail to Reason – Polylady, by Polynesian) and Graustark's full brother, His Majesty, complete the line-up of Darby Dan stallions.

Galbreath, who also stood Sea Bird on lease for five years in Kentucky, started in racehorse breeding with 110 acres near Galloway, Ohio, in 1930. That farm, also called Darby Dan, now covers 4,090 acres, and the lesser lights are shipped up there every year after the 27–30 best foals have been picked out to remain in Kentucky, where Lou Rondinello is the farm's trainer. Galbreath is something of an anglophile ('Just consider Hyperion's sons Alibhai, Heliopolis and Khaled. Can you count the number of outstanding racehorses and sires they have produced over here?') and in 1972 he gave the Queen's Daisy Chain (Darius – Casual) and Amicable (Doutelle – Amy Leigh) seasons to Graustark and, substituting for *Ribot, the original choice, Never Bend. Benevolence (Never Bend – Amicable) and Ground Work (Graustark – Daisy Chain) were foaled in 1973, and entered training with Ian Balding and Dick Hern respectively, but both were sold at auction in 1977. Benevolence, who seemed decidedly ungenuine, fetched 2,100 guineas at the Ascot August Sales, while Groundwork, winner of a maiden race at Newcastle in June that year, was sold at Newmarket in December for 11,000 guineas. Gregarious (Graustark – Amicable), a three-year-old of 1977, remained in training with Hern, winning the Glasgow Stakes at the York May Meeting while Daisy Chain, for whom the planned 1973 mating was changed, had the Hail to Reason colt Chain of Reasoning with Hern.

Provided there are no incompatibilities – say, of conformation or disposition – Gentry, who has raised more good horses than almost anyone alive today, believes in breeding an 'inbred mare to a stallion inbred to another great line of horses.' The mare, he argues, must be more important than the stallion – some 75 per cent being down to her – since all factors over and above the genetic make-up of a foal depend on her size, physiology and disposition.

Developments in
International Breeding

As a rule of thumb, the quality of a country's horseracing is inversely proportional to the involvement of breeders in its administration, since their short-term commercial interests tend to require the banning of foreign horses from bread-and-butter events. Indeed, the Germans and the Italians are even allowed, idiotically, to restrict Pattern Races to their own horses, but it was the French who were getting all the international abuse in 1977, when the Société d'Encouragement, at the request of the National Breeders' Association, closed certain of their races to horses bred outside the Common Market. Some commentators, predicting an exodus of American horses, interpreted the interdiction as an admission that French horses are inferior to those from across the Atlantic and the proposition, generally regarded as axiomatic, that protectionist policies are self-defeating and bad for the breed was much repeated.

It is, of course, only right that the French should be given a wigging from time to time, and the principle of open competition is no doubt a worthy one, but it does seem a little far fetched to fear a genetic regression just because the aristocrats of European racing decide to exclude alien mediocrities. Horses bred outside the EEC are now prohibited from:

  (i) provincial races worth less than 80,000 francs;
  (ii) all two and three year old races on the suburban tracks of Fontaine-bleau, Rambouillet and Compiègne, when they stage 'provincial' meetings;
  (iii) Parisian races worth less than 35,000 francs to the winner, plus an extra 22 events now introduced on the capital's courses.

There aren't, in any case, many races in Paris worth less than 35,000 francs – all maidens and most handicaps carry more – so good horses are not going to be much affected, except in so far as they may be denied a modest pipe-opener. Almost one in six of the horses running in France every year are selected foreign-breds – the country produces about 4,000 foals every year as against 10,000 in Great Britain and Ireland and 29,000 in the United States – and the French racing establishment, having succeeded in abstracting a great deal of the punter's money for its own uses, is disinclined to see it carried off by second-raters from overseas. Any deleterious effects on the

Left:
Ribot (right) *and Hyperion when both were at Lord Derby's stud in Newmarket.*

275

French breed caused by this understandable self-interest will probably be offset by the increased incentive premiums announced at the time of the ban. The owners of French-bred horses finishing in the first four now receive a bonus equivalent to 50 per cent of the prize money at Longchamp, Chantilly and Deauville. In addition, wherever the race is run, breeders get a 15 per cent premium in ordinary races, 25 per cent in group events. From 1978, an owner with five or more horses in training bred outside the EEC will be obliged to include French horses in his string too.

The only countries in the Northern Hemisphere not operating any kind of ban of foreign competition in 1977 were England, Ireland, Canada and the United States. In Italy, horses imported after December 31 of the year following their birth do not qualify for races worth 5,000,000 lira or less for a period of 12 months from the date of importation. The Germans have, since 1975, restricted flat races worth DM 7,000 or less in first prize money to home-breds, and refused to register imported mares more than 12 years old, or any mare not herself a winner or the daughter or granddaughter of a winner. Fillies imported as foals or yearlings can no longer be registered as German-bred, a condition which already applied to colts. Introducing the new regulations, the Direktorium für Vollblutzucht und Rennen explained that some measures had to be adopted to protect German breeders following fiscal reforms enacted in August 1974, which removed the concession whereby people keeping two mares or more could set off DM 5,000 per thoroughbred against income tax every year. This 13-year-old allowance was available only where a taxpayer's breeding activities were treated as a hobby, and 58 per cent of German breeders are one-mare men anyway, but its abolition was taken sufficiently seriously for incentive premiums to be raised to 15 per cent as well. The German racehorse industry, which might be said to have had its origins in the importation of Dick Andrews as a stallion in 1817, may not yet have grown to a really significant size, but, by 1975, there were 1991 thoroughbred mares in the country, as compared with 520 twenty years earlier.

Even the Japanese have open racing these days, although their transition to this enlightened policy may have gone largely unnoticed in Europe and America. Ever since the establishment of the Japan Racing Association in 1954, their representatives have swarmed round occidental bloodstock auctions, with England and France their principal sources of stallions until they switched their attention to the United States in 1972. Probably the most influential sire ever in Japan was Hindostan (Bois Roussel – Sonibai, by Solario), imported in 1955, while the most successful in recent years have been Never Beat (Never Say Die – Bride Elect, by Big Game), China Rock (Rockefella – May Wong, by Rustom Pasha) and Tesco Boy (Princely Gift – Suncourt, by Hyperion), whose progeny won 818,645,000 Yen, 704,923,600 Yen and 687,763,200 Yen in 1975 respectively. Notable Japan Racing Association importations of earlier years included Galcador, in 1959, and Iron Liege, in 1967.

There were 277 thoroughbred stallions in Japan in 1970, of which 138 were imported, whereas, of the 461 standing there in 1975, 253 had been purchased abroad. In 1975 there were 4,014 thoroughbred runners, as well as 235 described as 'Arabs', to contest 3,049 races spread over 288 racing days at 36 meetings. That year also 427 thoroughbred stallions covered 12,653 thoroughbred mares and got 7,800 foals. Since the thoroughbred trade with Japan is all one way, and there is only the occasional, unplaced, runner in the Washington D.C. International, no yardstick exists to draw any conclusions about the quality of the stock they are producing. That they have brought to the business the virtues of thoroughness and dedication can hardly be doubted, however, to judge from the extent and, occasionally, the shrewdness of their purchases, and from the size and complexity of their turf administration.

Horseracing in Japan is of no great antiquity, and seems to have begun with the English in Yokohama around 1862. The Nippon Race Club was founded at the Negishi Racecourse in 1880, and, on May 10 the next year, Emperor Meiji paid the first of many visits. Chinese breeds were used exclusively for racing until the first importations from Australia in 1895. After 1902 this trade was restricted to fillies, and it was discontinued altogether in 1927, three years after pedigree registration had been introduced. Thereafter the importation of English stallions was officially encouraged, and, in 1936, the Japan Racing Society was formed, absorbing the Nippon Race Club. Japanese versions of the English classics were founded just before the Second World War, with the Tokyo Yuushun (Derby), the Yuushun Himba (Oaks) and the Kikuka Show (St Leger) being run in 1938, the Ouka Shou (1,000 Guineas) and the Satsuki Shou (2,000 Guineas) the following year.

Following the death of Matrice in 1974, imported stallions had the Antipodean scene to themselves, with Oncidium, by Alcide, Showdown, by Infatuation, and Pakistan II, by Palestine, prominent in both Australia and New Zealand. Australia, in 1975, had 1,201 thoroughbred stallions, of which 377 covered 15 mares or more. The same year, in South Africa, Julie Andrews was voted Broodmare of the Year following the victories of her sons, Principal Boy, by *Free Ride, Colonel Pickering and the two-year-old Costermonger, both by *Wilwyn. Principal Boy won the Transvaal Handicap at Turffontein and the Rothmans July Handicap at Greyville, Colonel Pickering the Dingaans.

Indications of a continuing world-wide reliance on the original sources of thoroughbred stock are hardly surprising, and more noteworthy, perhaps, are the successes of some of the South American countries, in particular Argentina, where home-bred stallions have done remarkably well. The genius of the Argentinian horseman is, of course, a byword, and no American and European racegoer will need reminding that Angel Penna sometimes seems to have introduced a divine inspiration to the trainer's art.

The possibility of any country developing a thoroughbred industry

Above: *Blushing Groom (H. Samani) at Epsom on Derby day 1977, when he ran third to The Minstrel and Hot Grove. He takes up stud duties in 1978 at Gainesway Farm, Lexington, Kentucky, where the large and impressive stallion list includes the 1977 debutants Youth (above right) and Empery (below). Although John Gaines did not establish his thoroughbred nursery until 1961, Gainesway has become a major international force, assisted by an association with Nelson Bunker Hunt, whose most significant purchase was Vaguely Noble for 136,000 guineas after his Observer Gold Cup win of 1967. Not only does Vaguely Noble himself hold court at Gainesway, but he is also sire of his fellow stallions Ace of Aces, Empery, Mississipian and Noble Decree.*

comparable with the ancient breeding centres of America, France and the British Isles is too remote to be considered at the moment, however, and it is still the position of Europe *vis-à-vis* the United States which raises the most vital questions. Since the Americans have wealth, ambition and a fiscal system which encourages investment, they are, for the foreseeable future, going to retain their lien on the world's best bloodstock. France, for all the delights of its well-endowed racing, does not have a particularly impressive stallion population – as one would expect in a country where immediate financial gain has always been preferred to the conservation of promising

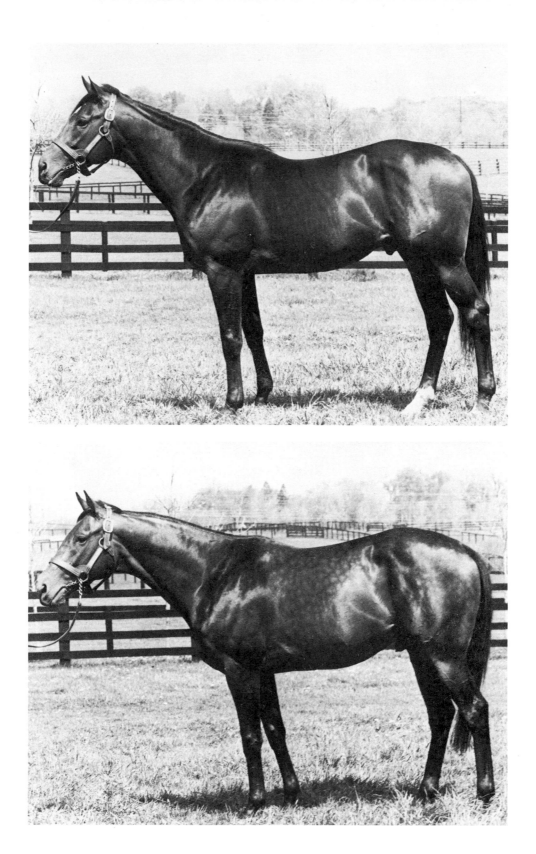

stock – and there never was any possibility that enough money would be found to keep Blushing Groom in the country. There were even suggestions in France during 1977 that the export of home-bred horses with high stud potential should be prohibited, which would be rather like cutting off one's own nose to spite somebody else's face.

If the French need more, not fewer, incentives to breed good horses, what of England? Its breeders, in 1977, were hoping for some relief via breeders' prizes, although Phil Bull's submission to the Royal Commission on Gambling attacked the principle of them with some cogency, and much ferocity. A Joint Racing Board decision on the matter was expected in mid 1977. English breeders continue to suffer a unique handicap in so far as their bloodstock is subject to Value Added Tax, while the percentage of the money levied on betting being channelled into the sport remains woefully low in comparison with the other major racing countries. English prize money, in any case, is hardly likely to approach American levels, and it is difficult to foresee anything but a loss of the best breeding stock and a slump in the export trade as quality deteriorates.

Still, this is not English racing's first crisis and Blushing Groom is not exactly the first great racehorse Europe has lost to the Americans. Some argue that the evolution of the thoroughbred owed much to the geological and climatic factors of the British Isles, and that the Americans will always need to return to the fount. History seems to bear this out, and of the most successful sires in America at the moment, most belong to sire lines introduced there relatively recently. A notable exception, third on the 1976 list, is Exclusive Native, a descendant of Sickle, who is pretty well American on the dam's side too.

Whatever justification there may be for doom-laden talk about the British thoroughbred industry, it lacks the appeal of novelty, fails to convince the public that the turf as we know it is about to go under, and seems merely a local manifestation of the rich man's factitious grief. Protestations of poverty, after all, are the thoroughbred breeder's stock-in-trade, and cries of anguish reverberate round the châteaux of Normandy and the white mansions of Kentucky too.

If there are those who doubt whether horse breeders really are desperately skint, there are others who could contemplate with equanimity a reduction in Britain's thoroughbred population, although it would presumably assist the process of centralisation. What is more important, though, is the effect this would have on the production of quality stock. Some breeders feel that logic suggests a constant relationship between the number of foalings and the number of good horses bred, but others, with experience of ruthless culling, suggest the opposite may even be the case.

Although transatlantic movements of breeding stock are by no means one way, many English breeders would like to see more American horses which distinguish themselves on European tracks remain there at stud, not least because the perception that speed is the racehorse's greatest asset has resulted in great differences in racing styles on either side of the Atlantic. Not unnaturally, the feeling persists in England that their racing is the most absorbing, their trainers and jockeys the best, and there can be no doubt that their riding tactics have revealed in American-bred horses greater reserves of stamina than pedigree students have expected, or even, perhaps, looked for, in the United States. It may be that, partly because of American influence, winning cup races is no longer quite decent, but the English are more likely to remember that horses need speed to win good races over any distance and to avoid breeding out all qualities save those favoured in an unsubtle dash.

People engaged in the breeding, training and riding of horses are forever telling the punter that his sport is really an industry, as, indeed, he knows it must be, when, year in, year out, he sees all the good three-year-old colts syndicated by their prudent owners and packed off to stud in the hope that they will sire other horses too good for all but the briefest racecourse careers. Yet, not so long ago, Paul Mellon and John Hislop showed that it is still possible for sporting owners of great horses to achieve on the track a glory which will live in the racing man's memory long after he has forgotten the dreary succession of half-tried colts dispatched, on accountant's orders, to the stud. The day the grey men convince the public that racing is an industry pure and simple, is the day that it will die. And then there will be some hard-up breeders.

Picture Credits

Index of Horses

General Index

Whitney, Harry Payne 211, *212*, 257–259,.260, 266
Whitney, Helen (née Hay) 266, *266*
Whitney, John Hay 51, 174, 261, 266
Whitney, Payne *200*, 266
Whitney, W. C. 211, 256, *256*
Whitney Purse, Keeneland 149
Whitney Stakes 37
Widener, George D. 199, 200
Widener, Joseph E. 151, 155, 199–200, *201*, 203–204
Widener, P. A. B., III 154, 200, 204, 225
Widener, Mrs P. A. B., II 70, 154
Wildenstein, Daniel 103, 133, 138
Willerby Plate, Beverley 46
William IV 17
William Hill Dewhurst Stakes, Newmarket 53
William Hill Gold Cup, Redcar, 64, 69, 103
William Hill Silver Vase Handicap, Newmarket 49
Williamstown Stud 128
Wilson, Roger 242
Wilson, Judge Samuel 172
Windsor Castle Stakes, Ascot 65
Wings of Man Stakes 230
Winn, Colonel Matt *268*
Winter, Fred 91
Winter, Theodore H. 181

Withers 256
Withington, Fred 199
Wokingham Stakes, Ascot 49
Wolferton Stud 19, 23, *27*, 28
Woodburn Farm 177–190, 191, 195
Woodditton Stud 36, 59, 61
Woodland Stud 35, 81
Wood Memorial 51
Woodward, William 225, 238
Woolavington, Lord 122
Woolverton, Lady *47*
Wormeley, Ralph, IV 164, 167
Wragg, Harry 54, *120*
Wright, Warren 253, 255
Wyvill, Isabel 16

Xalapa Farm 242

York, Duke of 17
Yorkshire Cup 58, 68
York September Meeting 91
Yorkshire Oaks 22, 24, 61, 114, 115, 129
Yorkshire Stakes, Doncaster 49
Youngsters' Stakes, Curragh 118
Yvre-l'Eveque 154

Zeitelhack, Waldemar 29, 40
Zeland Stakes 35–36
Zetland Nursery 47
Zimmerman, Bernard 141
Zukunfts-Rennen, Baden-Baden 86